T0302226

A Magnificent Journey to Excellence

A Magnificent Journey to Excellence

Sixteen Years of Six Sigma at Cummins Inc.

By George K. Strodtbeck III and
Mohan V. Tatikonda, PhD

Routledge
Taylor & Francis Group
A PRODUCTIVITY PRESS BOOK

First edition published in 2020
by Routledge/Productivity Press
52 Vanderbilt Avenue, 11th Floor New York, NY 10017
2 Park Square, Milton Park, Abingdon, Oxon OX14 4RN, UK

Routledge/Productivity Press is an imprint of Taylor & Francis Group, an Informa business

No claim to original U.S. Government works

Printed on acid-free paper

International Standard Book Number-13: 978-0-367-34573-0 (Hardback)

International Standard Book Number-13: 978-0-429-32805-3 (eBook)

Library of Congress Cataloging-in-Publication Data

Names: Strodtbeck, George K., 1954– author. | Tatikonda, Mohan, author.
Title: A magnificent journey to excellence : sixteen years of Six Sigma at Cummins, Inc. / George K. Strodtbeck III, Mohan Tatikonda.
Description: 1 Edition. | New York : Routledge, 2020. | Includes bibliographical references and index.
Identifiers: LCCN 2019035230 (print) | LCCN 2019035231 (ebook) |
ISBN 9780367345730 (hardback) | ISBN 9780429328053 (ebook)
Subjects: LCSH: Organizational change. | Strategic planning. | Six sigma (Quality control standard) | Leadership. | Cummins, Inc.
Classification: LCC HD58.8 .S786 2020 (print) | LCC HD58.8 (ebook) |
DDC 658.4/013—dc23
LC record available at https://lccn.loc.gov/2019035230
LC ebook record available at https://lccn.loc.gov/2019035231

Visit the Taylor & Francis Web site at www.taylorandfrancis.com

This book is dedicated to Tim Solso, Frank McDonald,

Joe Loughrey and Tom Linebarger, whose leadership

made the magnificent journey possible and to the

thousands of people whose work made it real.

This book is dedicated to my mother and father,

Lakshmi U. and Rao J. Tatikonda, whose courage

and dedication to learning continue to inspire me.

Contents

Figures and Tables

Acronyms and Abbreviations

ANOVA	Analysis of Variance
BB	Black Belt
BoD	Board of Directors
BOS	Business Operating System
CACI	Common Approach to Continuous Improvement
C&E Matrix	Cause and Effect Matrix
CDS	Cummins Distribution System
CEO	Chief Executive Officer
CFSS	Customer Focused Six Sigma
CI	Continuous Improvement
CLQ	Customer Led Quality
CLS	Cummins Leadership System
CLT	Cummins Leadership Team
CMS	Cummins Marketing System
COO	Chief Operating Officer
COS	Cummins Operating System
COSO	Committee of Sponsoring Organizations of the Treadway Commission
COT	Cummins Operating Team
Cpk	Capability Index
CPM	Critical Parameter Management
CPMS	Cummins Performance Management System
CPS	Cummins Production System
CTC	Cummins Technical Center
CTS	Cummins Technical System
CTT	Cummins Turbo Technologies
DFSS	Design for Six Sigma
DMAIC	Define, Measure, Analyze, Improve, and Control
DOE	Design of Experiments
EBIT	Earnings Before Interest and Taxes
EBU	Engine Business Unit
ERM	Enterprise Risk Management
FE	Functional Excellence
FMEA	Failure Modes and Effects Analysis

FTA	Fault Tree Analysis
GB	Green Belt
GE	General Electric
HR	Human Resources
IQ	Intelligence quotient
ISO	International Standards Organization
IT	Information Technology
JEP	Jamestown Engine Plant
JIT	Just-In-Time
KJ	A grouping process named for its inventor Jiro Kawakita
KPI	Key Performance Indicators
MBB	Master Black Belt
MBBIT	Master Black Belt in Training
OCS	Officer Candidate School
ODR	Organization Development Review
OE	Operational Excellence
OEM	Original Equipment Manufacturer
MBA	Master of Business Administration
MRG	Management Review Group
MSA	Measurement System Analysis
NBC	National Broadcasting Company
NIST	National Institute of Standards and Technology
NPI	New Product Introduction
NPPD&I	New Product Planning, Design and Introduction
NPS	Net Promoter Score
NSE	New Standards of Excellence
PBIT	Profit Before Interest and Taxes
PDCA	Plan-Do-Check-Act
PPM	Parts Per Million
PPT	Product Preceding Technology
QFD	Quality Function Deployment
ROTC	Reserve Officer Training Corps
RV	Recreational Vehicle
SBTI	Sigma Breakthrough Technologies, Inc.
SFSS	Supplier Focused Six Sigma
SPC	Statistical Process Control
STEM	Science, Technology, Engineering, Math
TBWS	Team Based Work System
TDFSS	Technology Development for Six Sigma

TQA	Total Quality Assurance
TQM	Total Quality Management
TQS	Total Quality System
TRIZ	Theory of Inventive Problem Solving
TS	Technical Specification
UK	United Kingdom
US	United States
VOB	Voice of the Business
VOC	Voice of the Customer
VP	Vice President
VPI	Value Package Introduction
VSM	Value Stream Map

Foreword—Change by Frank McDonald

CHANGE: A word that can strike fear into the heart of every man and woman. It's no wonder we feel that way when the usual verb attached to change is "impose". It suggests an unwillingness and how true that sometimes is. I will start with the big picture. We all know that some change is inevitable.

You will, if fated, get older and, if you do, the consequences are not always great. You may find that however much people value and respect you in your current job, in the future they probably will not.

Your opinion, which people sought out and paid dearly for, will rarely be sought. You might even remember a line Johnny Carson used many years ago at the Oscars. "It is nice to see so many old friends and new faces and new faces on old friends".

You will also likely experience an unwelcome increase in contacts with the medical profession. If you are someone who dealt with problem-solving during your career, then this may be a frustrating experience. The medical profession has made many wonderful improvements, particularly in diagnostics and intervention. I am thinking particularly of scanning, lasers, camera assistance and stenting.

These mostly hardware-related technologies still rely heavily on a good diagnosis by a person. This modern-day "sleuthing," using the improvements in hardware, seems to be a change that the medical profession has yet to match diagnostically. WHY? Because it involves people, including those who graduated from medical school.

Let me give you an example. I woke up one morning and my right eye was swollen shut. As I assumed death was close by, my wife (who thought I was being a little dramatic) called our doctor, who referred me to an eye specialist. After spending the customary 20 minutes filling out insurance papers (another essential change) and family history, the doctor examined me and assured me death was not imminent. The doctor asked me if I could identify what it might be and I recounted the previous day where I spent most of the time getting ready to leave the house for the summer. That took about 15 minutes. I had no family history of swollen eyes.

I was referred to the lab for blood tests. It was then that the battle of the "drillers" and the "frackers" began.

For the less technical among you, drillers are nurses who identify a vein, rub on an alcohol deadener, insert the needle and extract blood. The frackers, on the other hand, after the alcohol rub will insert the needle and then proceed to search for an elusive vein causing great pain to the patient. Under the unwritten rules of medicine, apparently, frackers only get two tries and they're out. If you are really having a bad day, you might get two frackers in a row before they find a driller.

They took eight vials of blood to test for HLA-B27, toxoplasma, CRP, rheumatoid factor, sedimentation rate, FLTA-ABS, blood serology and angiotensin concert. I believe these tests check for cancer, HIV, syphilis and a myriad of other possible causes. Thank goodness all checked out OK, or serious questions would have followed.

After weeks of testing and using different wipes and pills, I was talking to a golf buddy about the ordeal. He told me that when they were moving out for the summer last year, he put some gas-line antifreeze in his gas tank to absorb any moisture that might enter the system while the car was in storage.

He went on to explain that it splattered a little and he unthinkingly wiped the wet back of his hand on his face and his eye swelled up. Well, who'd-a-thought?

The Japanese say that Westerners spend 80% of the problem-solving cycle implementing the "fix," while the Japanese spend 80% of the time *UNDERSTANDING THE PROBLEM*. This is why we, in the US, "fix" the problem multiple times.

Did you ever rush to answer a test question, only to find out you were solving the wrong problem? Or try to fill in the answer to a crossword question that you read wrong—but quickly?

I was really glad to know that the problem with my eye turned out so well on so many fronts. But we never really solved the problem. Because of the technology, we had the ability to "shotgun" the fix before we really understood the problem.

Now that we have the inevitability of change out of the way, let's talk about "imposing" change on an organization. Coincidentally, the change in this case is all about "sleuthing". I will do this by telling the story of implementing Six Sigma at Cummins Inc.

Organizations have gobs of successful leaders who have mastered the art of surviving corporate changes. Unfortunately, however, we also have more than gobs of newly created leaders who are like our Samoyed (it's a dog, trust me), who must pee on every bush to mark his territory. I am not suggesting the leadership technique is exactly the same, but the concept is.

These are the folks who believe in "legacies" that require dismantling whatever went before or perhaps genuinely believe they know a better way. Many approaches including Six Sigma programs fell into the latter case, but many also fell into the former. Some wanted to be seen doing something new. Others saw it as a real solution to a real problem.

To "impose" any program that is strictly for show and not for the legitimate reason of making fundamental improvement will fail. I will not linger on the many, many of those we have all lived through. Instead, I would like to briefly talk about the implementation of Six Sigma at Cummins Inc.

Personally, I was pushed into it. Threats from the CEO are powerful things! I don't regret a minute of the journey—well, maybe a minute.

Let me start by saying that if you are tasked with the job of introducing a major change to an organization or your position requires you to make major changes, you'd better be prepared to meet resistance. To some degree resistance is very healthy, or we would make too many bad changes.

I am in no way an expert on human behavior. But there are two well-accepted insights into our behavior that I believe are important to thoroughly understand if you are going to successfully make a major change. Although from radically different fields, understanding these insights will greatly help with the task.

Firstly, in the field of investing it is believed that human behavior drives the market even more than computer programs. It is usually described as the influence of greed and fear. One of these is a deadly sin. The other, I must admit, I think is just common sense when dealing with my hard-earned money.

Secondly, we have Maslow's hierarchy of needs. Maslow outlines the order of importance of the elements that are required to meet our needs depending on our situation.

So now we have the McDonald Hierarchy of Needs and Greeds:

1. Assuming the use of a program leader to facilitate the change.
2. The leader of the organization MUST be seen as the leader of the effort. This means more than photo ops. It means being constantly, visibly involved.

3. The program leader must be one who has a record of achievement in the organization and a good knowledge and understanding of the people and culture.
4. The organization leader understands and believes that the success of the program is vital to the success of the organization.

When the new Chairman and CEO of Cummins decided to implement Six Sigma to improve the lagging financial performance of the company, I was assigned the role of Vice President of Quality with a focus on implementing Six Sigma across the corporation. I had two qualifications for the role:

1. I had spent my entire career in a line role dodging corporate initiatives.
2. I had a reasonably good track record of successfully running operations.

I had watched many corporate efforts like Baldrige, Cost Improvement, Total Cost of Ownership and so forth at GE and Cummins fail to achieve any meaningful result.

I wrote down the reasons why these programs failed, in my opinion, and how some people had managed to avoid committing to many of them. It struck me that to be successful there was an essential need to understand "what was in it" for each person who was required to make the change a success.

At the highest levels in the company—for example, where the elbows can be the sharpest—there are two requirements: looking good and your "competition" not looking better because of your efforts. If the program leader is a peer, this can be a problem on both counts if the program is successful. It is essential to resolve this up front, as most programs fail through high-profile but professional neglect near the top—in other words, looking good but doing nothing.

There are three answers to this:

1. Publish process and performance results.
2. Give great praise to SOME, whether they deserved it or not.
3. Have a post-program plan for the leader regardless of the outcome.

We did these three things.

As you go down the chain of command, it is essential to know who the informal leaders are in the business. Again, there is a need to understand their needs on the McDonald Hierarchy:

- Recognition.
- Exposure to their boss or the CEO or both.
- Broad acknowledgment of their effort.
- Financial incentives.
- Shirts.
- Certificates.

An understanding of the behavior drivers for each level of the organization is essential. They will vary by individual because you are also dealing with the fact that, normally, one-third of the group will welcome the change, one-third will be against it and the final one-third will wait to see whether the change is real or just another of those "programs-of-the-month." As Casey Stengel said, "The secret to management is keeping the half who hate you away from the half that is undecided."

We introduced extensive training sessions for the Six Sigma Black and Green Belts and included the CEO. In addition, the CEO opened every training session.

We gave certificates of completion.

We gave expensive shirts with unique logos to the Belts.

We created an incentive programs for leaders and Black Belts.

We posted results for every business, department, unit and team in the company.

We had program and project reviews with the CEO and staff.

We had a Chairman's Award for best projects,

We changed promotional policies to include participation in Six Sigma.

We widely publicized successes.

We UNDER-COMMUNICATED in the beginning almost on a need-to-know basis so there was no bragging about what we were going to do UNTIL WE DID IT.

By under-communicating we tapped into the most powerful tool in any organization: the rumor mill. Word spread like wildfire. It was not always exactly accurate, but it did get people's attention.

EVERY function was expected to contribute. The participation of the support functions was a very pleasant surprise. The program unleashed young people to show what they could do and applied a disciplined approach to management of the work in every department.

Did it all work?

The numbers and the CEO said "yes" and, although some paid a heavy price, the result was the beginning of a highly successful period for Cummins.

For those still looking for the secret to sleuthing that I alluded to, read and understand the DMAIC steps of Six Sigma: it's all there!!

Frank McDonald
Cummins Vice President—Quality (Retired)

About the Authors

 **George K. Strodtbeck III** is currently a vice president with SBTI, a leading consulting firm focused on the development and leadership of continuous improvement methodologies and change management systems.

George retired as the Executive Director of Quality at Cummins Inc. in May 2015. His change leadership responsibilities included:

- *World-wide implementation and continuous improvement of Six Sigma beginning July 1999.* Six Sigma is a world-wide effort at Cummins. By January 2015, the company had trained 21,000+ Belts, completed more than 45,000 projects, and eliminated more than $5.5 billion in costs.
- *The Cummins Business Operating System Leadership and Practice.* The Business Operating System is focused on cross-functional integration and continuous improvement of the flows and processes of the company.

Also included in George's portfolio of responsibilities were:

- Measurement Excellence and Lab Operations
- Global Product Safety
- Quality Standards Integration (ISO/TS)
- Quality Functional Excellence
- New Product Development Processes
- Supplier Quality Functional Excellence.

George graduated from West Point in 1976. He then served in the US Army at various sites around the world until 1986, earning an MS in International Relations in 1984.

Following his Army service, George joined Pepsi in 1986 serving as a fleet maintenance and distribution area manager until 1992.

At Cummins from 1992 to 2015 as a member of Corporate Quality, George led several change initiatives including the operational leadership of the 1997 Baldrige application and site visit, a 16-year Six Sigma deployment, and the deployment of the Cummins Operating System.

As a consultant with SBTI since 2015, George has applied the lessons learned from his wide-ranging career helping several companies in their quest to develop continuous improvement cultures.

George has written a book titled *Making Change in Complex Organizations*, published in April 2016 by the American Society for Quality (ASQ).

George is married with four children and lives in Indianapolis.

 **Mohan V. Tatikonda, PhD** is Professor of Operations and Supply Chain Management at the Kelley School of Business, Indiana University, executive of the Indiana Clinical and Translational Sciences Institute, and Life Sciences Research Fellow. He previously served on the faculty of the Kenan-Flagler School of Business at the University of North Carolina (Chapel Hill). He received a B.S. in electrical engineering, M.S. in systems engineering and M.B.A. from the University of Wisconsin at Madison. He received his Ph.D. in Operations Management from the Boston University Questrom School of Management.

Mohan's research addresses improvement, innovation and entrepreneurship in novel, complex and global technological settings, and has been published in *Management Science, Journal of Operations Management, Production & Operations Management, IEEE Transactions on Engineering Management, Industrial & Corporate Change, R&D Management* and elsewhere. His research awards include Best Paper of the Year in the *Journal of Operations Management* and Best Dissertation from the *Production and Operations Management Society*. His teaching awards include the Eli Lilly Award for MBA Teaching Excellence (awarded by students to the top MBA faculty member) and the Schuyler F. Otteson Award for Undergraduate Teaching Excellence.

Mohan's media commentary on international trade, global value chains and health care innovation has appeared in the *New York Times, The Atlantic, USA Today, Bloomberg, The Washington Post, The Independent, Marketplace* (NPR) and numerous other media outlets across the globe. He is an advisor to start-up firms and incubators, and has consulted for The World Bank, SAP, Pepsi, FedEx and Rolls-Royce.

Mohan and his family reside in Indianapolis, Indiana.

1

Introduction and Purpose

Looking back on it now, it is hard to believe how much work the people of Cummins did to make Six Sigma successful. It involved thousands of people working together to transform a company. Cummins became a very different company than it was in 1999, and Six Sigma played a significant role. This book will discuss the details of the transformation during the period 1999 to the end of 2014.

It is important to say right at the beginning that Cummins did not set out to become a great Six Sigma company. Instead, becoming a company that continuously improves products and services for customers was the goal from day one. Six Sigma was the common language that we would use to achieve this goal. The simplicity of the goal and its focus on the company's customers made Six Sigma applicable for any improvement or problem. Six Sigma was not a narrow set of tools and processes used only when the right kind of data was available. It became a flexible common language used by any group of people working together for the benefit of customers and the company. The development of this capability is what this book is about.

Cummins Inc. is a global power systems and components company that began life in 1919. The company has a long and interesting history. That history has been documented in two recent books: *The Engine That Could* by Jeffrey L. Cruikshank and David B. Scilia and *Red, Black and Global* by Susan Hanafee. These books do a good job of providing a sweeping narrative across nearly nine decades. The purpose of this book is to describe one piece of that history that took place starting in the early 2000s.

Organizations change constantly. These changes come in many forms. Some changes are customer requirements. Some are internally generated due to some new technology or product. Sometimes the change comes from the arrival of new leadership. Some change is well thought out and planned and sometimes less so. Sometimes change is forced upon the organization by competition. Whatever the reason, change is a matter of survival. The organization will grow and thrive or decay and die based on how well it adjusts to and incorporates changes. The focus of this book is a culture change that took place in a large corporation. The bulk of the book is based on personal experience, participation in and observation, covering 16 years from 1999 to the end of 2014. The book includes a series of interviews that personalizes the Six Sigma journey. While the Six Sigma deployment at Cummins is the main subject, the basic change framework can be broadly applied.

From 1999 through 2014, Cummins Inc. underwent a startling transformation. The company went from struggling to make a profit to an annual return on profits of 12% to 14% before taxes every year. I was privileged to both be an observer and play a role in this transformation.

The easiest way to see this transformation is through results. Between 1999 and 2014 the company saw an incredible rise as reflected below (from Cummins Annual Reports).

There was no one thing that made the transformation possible, but the decision to deploy Six Sigma in 1999 was an important piece. This book is an attempt to capture this one aspect of that story so that the lessons learned are available to others.

I (George Strodtbeck) joined Cummins in 1992 after ten years in the US Army and six years with a large consumer products company. My assignment was to develop and deliver a continuous improvement training program. The training program was called the Common Approach to Continuous Improvement (CACI). It was part of a larger effort called the Cummins Production System (CPS). The Cummins Production System's purpose was improvement of the manufacturing and assembly plants. The CACI training package was developed and a training plan implemented. Lots of people were trained in the approach. Projects were done. The CEO and key senior leaders supported it and participated. But it just didn't take. While success could be seen in some places, the reality was the company didn't change. Many people just went through the motions and then

Year	Revenue $M	Net Earnings $M	%	Net Cash $M	Engines Shipped	Dividend/Share	Employees
1999	$ 6,639	$ 160	2.41%	$ 74	426,100	$ 1.12	28,500
2014	$ 19,221	$ 1,651	8.59%	$ 2,266	608,100	$ 2.81	54,600

FIGURE 1.1 Cummins financial performance 1999 and 2014.

moved on. The training binders took their place alongside other change efforts that failed to transform the company. Something was missing. That "something" is what is described for you in this book. We will discuss in detail the key elements that made Six Sigma so successful.

The book consists of six main parts:

1. *The purpose and introduction* (you are here).
2. *The pre-history.* From 1979 to 1999 Cummins launched several efforts to improve quality of both performance and its products. Each effort left behind elements which set the stage for the success of Six Sigma.
3. *Maturity of Six Sigma (S-Curves).* Over 16 years Six Sigma saw significant change. Understanding those changes as maturity over time applies to more than Six Sigma. The maturity structure is a guide for use making other broad organizational changes. There are seven distinct S-Curves discussed individually.
4. *Interviews.* Thousands of people participated in the success of Six Sigma. The interviews capture the voices of the key program leaders and others who represent the many people across the company who participated in different ways.
5. *Cross curve analysis.* These chapters discuss actions taken to prepare for the next stage of maturity between the S-Curves.
6. *Conclusions.* A final discussion of recommendations for successful change is made as the book draws to a close.

Periodically, we introduce the reader to individuals who had an important impact on the deployment of Six Sigma at Cummins. The intention is to provide a broad cross-section of voices that will address different members of an organizational hierarchy. The compilation of interviews form a quasi-benchmarking visit giving the reader insight into what made Six Sigma work. It will also be fun to read what people thought and felt about what Cummins was doing.

Lastly, this is a tribute to the people who really made Six Sigma work over the 16 years documented by this book.

You will hear from:

- Tim Solso—CEO (2000–2011)
- Frank McDonald—Vice President Quality (2000–2003)

- Joe Loughrey—President Engine Business and President and COO Cummins (2000–2011)
- Dana Vogt—Black Belt and Master Black Belt (2000–2004), Quality Leader
- Ginger Lirette—Green Belt, Black Belt (2000–2003)
- Michelle Dunlap—Master Black Belt (2000–2005), Quality Champion
- Megan Henry—Black Belt & Master Black Belt (2003–2007), Six Sigma Director, Quality Improvement Director
- Tom Linebarger—PowerGen Business President, Cummins CEO (2012+)
- Julie Liu—Black Belt, Quality Champion
- Holly Duarte—Black Belt

The first story you will read in the next chapter is from Tim Solso, without whom this book would have never been written. There are important lessons to be learned, so enjoy.

As the book has come together, we think the most important parts are the interviews conducted with people who were part of the process. From CEOs to Black Belts, each interview brings a unique personal perspective of the Six Sigma deployment and what it meant to each individual. These interviews comprise a unique look into the workings of a massive, global, companywide change effort. Compiling these interviews made the book worth writing and, we believe, will make it worth reading.

2

Interview With Tim Solso, Cummins CEO 2000–2011

WHY DID CUMMINS PURSUE SIX SIGMA?

I had been with the company 29 years when I became CEO in 2000. Before that, I had been leader of the Engine Business from 1988 to 1995 and then COO from 1995 to 2000. During my time as COO, Cummins had mediocre financial results. The company was negatively affected by industry cyclicality and always seemed to be solving the same problems over and over. We had not shown the ability to drive sustainable improvement.

I wrote a paper in 1999 called "The 7 Points of Profitability." This paper established priorities on what we needed to do differently. Two of those points were to reduce warranty costs and improve overall product quality. This improvement was important because our corporate cost of quality was 3%–4% of revenue. The Engine Business, which made up between 60% to 70% of the total Cummins business, had a cost of quality well over 5% of revenue. Cummins was earning before interest and taxes (EBIT) between 1% to 5% in a good year. So, the cost of quality was equal to or more than the amount of EBIT we were making.

About that time, I became aware of Six Sigma by reading about Motorola and General Electric (GE). I had talked with the CEOs of a large customer and a major supplier. The supplier was about 18 months into deployment. The customer was just getting started. I spent the day with the head of quality at the customer to understand in more detail what they were doing and the results they were seeing. Frank McDonald, the new Vice President of Quality, and I then spent the day with the leader of one of GE's business units. After these visits, I was convinced that Six Sigma could help us effectively improve warranty costs and the cost of quality—two of my priorities. However, I didn't have a real vision for what this could become; I was just trying to make the company more profitable.

WHAT WERE YOUR BIGGEST CHALLENGES DURING THE SIX SIGMA DEPLOYMENT?

Our biggest challenge was change management. Cummins had a history of constantly changing things over the years. No quality change effort lasted more than two years, except for the Baldrige effort which we began in 1997.

Because of this constant change, the organization was skeptical of what could be characterized as "programs of the month." Consequently, the majority of the company had the attitude that this too shall pass. They looked at it and said, "This is not part of my normal work and responsibilities. I already have too much to do. I will just wait for this to end."

Addressing the skepticism was the hardest. I needed buy-in from the leadership group, but this was a mixed bag. Some were curious and thought it was worth a try. But others, like the head of finance and the international business, were very slow to come on board. Finally, I had a couple of conversations with members of my leadership team to make it clear that if they wanted to work at Cummins, they had to get on board and actively support the Six Sigma deployment.

Another challenge was finding the right person to be the leader. I needed somebody who was well respected in the business and had a record of outstanding performance. I recruited Frank McDonald, who was the leader of one of our largest and most successful businesses. Frank was a very successful manufacturing executive who had come to Cummins from GE and had a strong background and understanding in the value of process thinking. Frank was a highly respected operations leader in the company. However, he didn't want a staff job and was very reluctant to take it on. It took a few weeks to convince him, but he finally agreed.

Next we needed to hire the right consultant to help us. The right consultant would be the one who had the right consulting approach. We decided on and signed a contract with SBTI that established from day one that they had two years to make us self-sufficient and self-supportive, which we achieved. This was very important because people in the company needed to feel ownership for Six Sigma. They had to feel that it was a Cummins thing and not an external program.

Another huge challenge was the company's financial performance. From the second half of 2000 to the first half of 2003, we were in the worst recession in company history to that time. That impacted everything we did. We were the most vulnerable that we had ever been as a company. From 2000 to 2002 sales were $15 billion and the company made just $7 million, losing over $100 million in 2001. We had a debt level of 63%, meaning we could not borrow money. Our stock was below investment grade and we could not go to the equity markets. We were burning cash faster than we were generating it and were about to go under. In November 2002, Tom Linebarger (who would later become Cummins CEO) and I went to the capital markets and raised $250 million in junk bonds at 9.25% interest. That cash got us over the hump, and we made it through, but just barely. While all this was happening, our shareholders were upset with us because the stock was way down. One of our major competitors was telling the marketplace that Cummins was not going to survive, and customers should quit buying engines from us. Inside the organization, people were asking why we were doing this Six Sigma stuff in the face of this terrible downturn, and we needed to put fires out. In the face of all these pressures, the fact that Joe Loughrey, Frank McDonald and I stayed with Six Sigma sent a strong message that it was important to our survival.

The approach we took really paid off. I tended to be a bull in a china shop. With the help of Frank and George, we followed a disciplined implementation plan all the way through.

WHEN YOU WERE SPEAKING TO OTHER EXECUTIVES SIX SIGMA WAS STILL NEW. WERE THERE OTHER INITIATIVES OR OPTIONS THAT WERE BEING CONSIDERED AS ALTERNATIVES?

There were all kinds of programs that we had tried: Lean, Just-Do-It, the Cummins Production System. However, none of them was integrated together as a unified system. I felt that we needed one system so we wouldn't get into arguments about which one was the best.

What convinced me about Six Sigma was the use of statistics and its analytical approach. It forced even the experts to go through a process to justify their answers to problems. They couldn't just say, "Based on my experience, this is what the answer is." They had to show why it was the answer. Other approaches use statistics, but Six Sigma was the most comprehensive and integrated.

My focus in the beginning was strictly on manufacturing costs. But the success we saw in manufacturing quickly spread to other parts of the company. I really didn't have a vision beyond improving manufacturing costs. I just wanted to cut product quality costs in half and I saw the greatest potential for that in the manufacturing area.

WITH THE FINANCIAL SITUATION BEING WHAT IT WAS, HOW DID YOU GET THE BOARD OF DIRECTORS ON YOUR SIDE?

I didn't tell the Board initially. It wasn't something that they were going to vote on. I had decided we were going to do it.

After having some initial success, I told the Board what we were doing. They saw what was going on and the improvements we were making and they got excited about it. We started reporting progress to them regularly from then on.

HOW DID IT SURVIVE BEYOND TEN YEARS AT CUMMINS SINCE DOING SOMETHING LIKE THIS IS SO RARE AND DIFFICULT TO DO IN ORGANIZATIONS OF ANY SIZE BUT ESPECIALLY IN A LARGE, GLOBAL COMPANY?

Historically, Cummins had very mediocre financial results and lots of cyclicality. This created frequent organization restructuring layoffs, salary cuts and other drastic actions to cut costs. Even though we have a special value system, we didn't have super morale. People didn't believe that Six Sigma would work because we had no experience or success doing something like this.

It sustained itself because people could see the success as we went along. It worked! We saw improvements in quality, financial results, supplier and customer relations. Investors were happy. We were viewed as a competent company. Success breeds success. Six Sigma didn't just sustain itself; it blossomed.

TO SURVIVE, DOES AN EFFORT LIKE THIS NEED TO GROW AND CHANGE?

I wouldn't use the word "grow". I don't think it is a good idea to want growth for growth's sake in a program like this.

In the early days of our deployment we had set savings targets. These were targets that we wanted people to hit to prove the value of Six Sigma and to offset our consulting costs. We began by mandating an increase in the targets every year. But George encouraged me to change this, so we moved to letting the businesses set their own targets to encourage ownership of the whole process of continuous improvement.

We began to see the application of Six Sigma in a much broader way. Growth of Six Sigma was more spontaneous and natural as it moved into new settings and different applications.

If we had limited it to just manufacturing or engineering, it couldn't become part of the whole company culture in all functions, all regions, wherever Cummins did business. This was culture change, not just implementation of Six Sigma. However, I clearly had no idea that it was culture change when we started it.

Cummins was clearly a much different and better company when I left than it had ever been in terms of business results.

OFTEN SENIOR LEADERS LOSE INTEREST IN A PROGRAM OVER TIME. HOW DID YOU STAY FOCUSED ON SIX SIGMA AND RENEW YOUR ENERGY AND INTEREST OVER TEN YEARS, ESPECIALLY WHEN THERE WERE OTHER THINGS TO TAKE YOUR ATTENTION?

I became CEO later in my career. I understood that less is more. Focus on the two or three things that are most important over a long period of time and you will get better results. Some leaders think that you must change things to keep it interesting. I'll tell you, getting great results and seeing the engagement of people are the things that kept it interesting for me.

One of the great lessons that it took me a long time to learn is that people must hear things at least seven times before they understand it. One of my main jobs, if Six Sigma was going to work, was to repeat the message over and over with every audience I spoke to. This is not glamorous work, but it is necessary if a culture change, like what we were driving, was going to succeed.

It also helped that I was having a good time. Reviewing projects, hearing Belts and their enthusiasm was exciting and gratifying. And, I was seeing this all over the company, in every region of the world.

I was convinced after five or six years that this would make Cummins a better company and that realization held my interest.

WHAT WERE THE CONSTRUCTIVE WAYS THAT THE LEADERSHIP STAFF OF SIX SIGMA COMMUNICATED TO YOU AND YOUR STAFF?

To start with, I met with Frank, and later George, one on one for years after we started Six Sigma. They had direct access to me.

In the early days, we talked about problems, measures, setting goals, Belt selection and other implementation subjects. We worked through many different issues. We often didn't have the answers right off the bat but meeting monthly gave us the time to work through whatever issues we were facing.

After a couple of years, George began giving me a quarterly report. We would go through it focused on key questions; are we progressing, are we doing what we should? I wasn't trying to get down in the weeds. I wanted to gain insight on the general idea of whether or not things were moving.

It helped that we had a wide network of Six Sigma people throughout the company. This helped us to keep leadership at all levels aware of what was going on.

IN SOME ORGANIZATIONS MARKETING OR FINANCE IS RESISTANT TO ADOPTING THINGS LIKE SIX SIGMA. ARE THERE ANY SUGGESTIONS FOR HOW YOU GET RELUCTANT FUNCTIONAL AREAS ENGAGED?

Well, let's be clear, everybody at Cummins wasn't on board from the beginning. There were big chunks of the company that were originally reluctant.

Two things helped a lot. People saw the results from the Engine Business. Joe Loughrey talked about his business' Six Sigma success during staff meetings. This made it easy for me to go to the other parts of the company and say, "get on board or we'll find somebody who will." I told members of my staff to come to the staff meeting and tell us how they were going to make progress. When it became mandatory there was a big second wave of the company that got on board. Even with that, there was one group that continued to drag its feet. They finally had to get on board because everybody else was doing Six Sigma and the success overwhelmed them.

The senior staff had to be on board and waving the flag with me. I told them that Six Sigma isn't optional. The reality is that if the CEO is waving the flag and the other leaders are not, it won't work. I really needed them to be with me.

Additionally, we were careful about saying we were running Six Sigma pilots because that makes it sound like it is optional. At two other companies, I watched them start as pilots. They were not as successful. When we began, I said we are going to start in one part of the company and spread it. We were not testing Six Sigma to see if it was going to work. I think, ultimately, this contributed to the overall success of Six Sigma at Cummins.

WHAT WERE THE BIGGEST SURPRISES, BOTH POSITIVE AND NEGATIVE, ABOUT THE SIX SIGMA DEPLOYMENT?

The biggest surprise was how successful Six Sigma was. I believe Six Sigma saved the company. Financially, we changed from a cyclical company with 5% EBIT to a company that, after Six Sigma, generated 13%–14% EBIT consistently through the business cycles. I attribute this profitability improvement to Six Sigma and the disciplines that came with it. These profits generated approximately a 1,300% return over the ten years I was CEO, which was best in class of industrial companies. As a result of improving company performance, we saw morale go up because it is a lot more fun working in a successful organization.

Another big surprise was that the success in manufacturing spread to other functions. I really didn't expect this. It became much more far-ranging than I anticipated. We started with base DMAIC Six Sigma.

Toward the end of the first year, we added Design for Six Sigma to be used by Engineering in the design of products. We included the supply base, making it a requirement for our key suppliers to participate with us on important Six Sigma projects. We did corporate responsibility projects in our communities. As one example of a corporate responsibility project, we helped a food bank in Indianapolis improve inventory.

We did projects with customers, helping trucking companies, for example, save millions of dollars in fuel costs. We applied Six Sigma in all our staff areas: legal, finance, treasury and shared services.

Six Sigma became a company common language. Walk into any plant, office, or location anywhere in the world, and everybody knows what you are talking about when you ask about Six Sigma.

Another surprise was when a member of the Board said that it was becoming a management development tool, especially for women. We were a very diverse group among our Belts. In fact, there was more diversity among the Belts than there was among the traditional hierarchy of the company. We had a guiding philosophy that the Black Belts were selected from among the best and the brightest. After the Black Belt role, we would make sure that they went to a good follow-on assignment. We had Belts presenting to the Board and senior management.

One example comes to mind. During one visit to Mexico by the Board, a woman Belt presented her project and did a fantastic job. A plant manager change was underway at the same time. This woman wasn't originally on the list for consideration. But because of the visibility gained from her project, she was vetted and became the plant manager. Six Sigma introduced people to senior leadership who, under normal circumstances, might never get noticed. This kind of thing happened all the time.

Six Sigma moved through every element of the company, which is very hard for people to understand. It took ten years to develop, but I had no doubt that it would continue after I left the CEO job; that it would continue to evolve and improve.

This was the only time in my 45-year career that I saw a real culture change effort succeed.

WHEN DID YOU GET THE SENSE THAT THE SCOPE COULD BE MUCH BROADER?

I really started to see the broadening of scope after two or three years. We looked at supplier quality and realized that parts coming from the supply base were a big part of the product quality problem. It was a natural extension to say we couldn't get the quality level we needed without the supplier coming with us. We decided to help them learn Six Sigma. Importantly, we told them that they could keep the savings from the projects. We wanted to see improvements in quality for our customers, not argue over who gets the savings.

We saw the same thing with the customers. We were working hard to become more customer focused. If we could make our customers more successful, we'd be more successful. That was a light that went on! We invited them in. We told them, "We'll do projects that you want us to do and you keep the savings." We developed a standard approach to improving fuel economy. We did a lot more than fuel economy projects, but this was an area of focus.

We began to do a lot of work in our shared services area, where we had combined transactional staff functions (HR, Finance, etc.) to service the whole company. This area was ripe for process improvement. They really embraced it and had some great projects.

Another example was Treasury. We did a refinancing project and saved tens of millions of dollars. We wouldn't have achieved it without the Six Sigma project.

The more success we had, the more creative we became. It really took off after about two or three years.

WHAT WERE THE MOST IMPORTANT THINGS THAT YOU PERSONALLY DID?

I gave the Six Sigma deployment my total and unrelenting personal commitment. Any time I communicated I referred to Six Sigma. When I visited a plant, I would spend time looking at Six Sigma there. It was a standard part of the agenda to review Six Sigma projects with the Belts.

We presented the best of the best projects to the Board. This included attendance by the Board at the Annual Chairman's Award Banquet and project displays awarding the best projects from around the company.

I attended Six Sigma training wherever I traveled and spent an hour talking with the class about Six Sigma. I did this no matter where the training was held.

I went to Green Belt training myself and completed a project so I could tell others that I had done it.

If you ask me what a company must do if they want the success that Cummins had, I will say unequivocally that it will not happen unless the CEO personally commits to it, is personally involved and says to everyone that it is the highest priority. I have seen Six Sigma tried at two other companies where the effort was delegated to the Six Sigma staff and the CEO didn't provide it the consistent support that it takes. These efforts were much less successful.

Recruiting Frank McDonald was another very important thing that I did. His recruitment added instant credibility and had a lot to do with the success that we had.

Prior to Six Sigma, the company was a company of "best efforts" as opposed to a results-driven company. People worked hard, but there was no accountability for results. I wanted to create a culture where people and groups did what they said they were going to do and what they were supposed to do every time. As part of Six Sigma, we measured results and held people accountable for their project commitments, ultimately changing the culture.

I am convinced that making something like this work requires the commitment of the most senior leader. The senior leader must have the senior leadership team going with him or her. The senior leader is responsible to select a person to lead it who has credibility in the organization. Next, make it mandatory that the businesses select the best people as Black Belts to do the projects, not the people who are least busy.

Establishing a strong infrastructure and key measurements is very important to get right. Joe Loughrey commissioned two Black Belts to lead projects on improving Six Sigma in the Engine Business, which changed some of the metrics and the way we went about it.

Finally, you can't underestimate the value of reward and recognition on the success of the program. The more it is pervasive and constant, the more effective it will be. Six Sigma created an environment in which the Belts could say the work that they were doing was important and they were adding value to the company.

3

Six Sigma Pre-history

The story of Cummins Inc. began in 1919 when Clessie Cummins figured out how to do something that nobody else in the world had done: use the diesel engine to power trucks (*The Engine That Could*, pp. 2–3). Over the next 90+ years, Cummins engines powered all manner of equipment across much of the world.

Any organization that can survive this long has many stories to tell. Two books have already covered much of the overall history of Cummins. *The Engine That Could* by Jeffrey L. Cruikshank and David B. Sicilia and *Red, Black and Gold* by Susan Hanafee document much of the social history of the company. This book will not go back over that already well-plowed ground. Rather, we describe the actions taken to deploy Six Sigma successfully with the intention that this provides a template that others can follow in their own organizational change journeys, whether or not they are Six Sigma deployments.

The pre-history is an example of how earlier actions taken influenced and enabled the deployment of Six Sigma. All organizations have a pre-history of things that came before regardless of the organization's age. If undertaking a culture change, it would be helpful to understand what has come before and leverage the good things and avoid the bad things that were done. Understanding the "goods" and the "bads" will give the organization a stronger starting point for successfully making the change.

The pre-history story begins in the late 1970s as Cummins began to focus on quality in an organized way. This early quality journey sets up a set of conditions which were beneficial in a variety of ways to the launch and maturity of Six Sigma over 16 years and forms an important backdrop to the transformation of this global company. The quality programs which came before Six Sigma include:

- Total Quality Assurance (TQA)—introduction of quality tools to the manufacturing shop floor.

- The Achieving Paper and New Standards of Excellence—focused on customers and product flow.
- Total Quality Systems (TQS)—introduced the need for documentation of important processes and procedures.
- Cummins Production System (CPS)—created a common set of disciplines applied to the manufacturing and assembly plants and introduced the idea of functional excellence.
- Common Approach to Continuous Improvement (CACI)—introduced a common process and language for process improvement.
- Baldrige Application—introduced the company to a holistic approach to quality.
- Cummins Operating System (COS)—applied the disciplines of CPS to the entire company.

Each of the efforts listed became part of the company's cultural fabric and contributed to the success of Six Sigma. Generally, their contributions included structure, discipline and activities that Six Sigma would build on during deployment and use to make important improvements for Cummins' customers and business results. A more detailed description of each effort and a few others is described in the Appendices.

For the reader, the application is to take time to understand what came before the currently planned change. What was good and not so good about the previous efforts? What lessons can be applied to the desired change to mitigate problems and barriers before they occur? Frank McDonald's interview does a good job of describing one method of doing this.

4

The Bottom Line

Results

As time passed, Cummins' approach to Six Sigma matured. However, maturity was never guaranteed. As discussed in the previous section, over the years many different change efforts were tried with limited success, if success is based on profitability improvement as a critical success measure for a business. Figure 4.1 shows Net Sales versus profit from 1976 to 2014 and the different operational and quality change efforts (there were others led by other functions) undertaken to improve company performance. During this time revenue trended up consistently while profitability remained unchanged. The correlation coefficient between revenue and profit during this time was 8%, or little to no relationship.

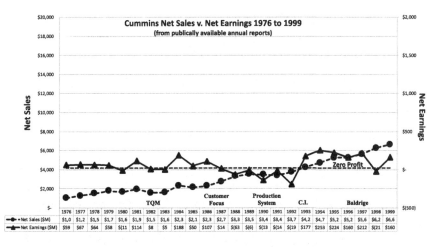

FIGURE 4.1 Cummins net sales and net profit 1976–2014.

One common characteristic among the various programs tried before 2000 is limited understanding of the meaning and necessity of planned program maturity and its impact on success. These programmatic solutions tended to be static and somewhat rigid. The programs were defined tightly and accompanied by an expectation that execution would conform to the defined norms. Grading of success tended to depend on audits of conformance to the norms. Success metrics, if they existed, were generally focused on the activity itself (numbers of people trained, etc.) or on internal operational metric (CPS used inventory turns, productivity, quality defects, safety incidents, and throughput time in a plant) versus impact on customers and key business measures. These early programs would, typically, become stuck at an early stage of maturity (maturity will be described as S-Curves in a later chapter), ultimately decaying and disappearing. There were exceptions (Cummins Production System and TQS), but they were few.

Then a major change took place which would alter the course of the company. Tim Solso was selected to become CEO in 2000. He was a 30-year Cummins veteran who had lived through all the previous change efforts. Tim knew there were needed improvements if the company were to grow and achieve its potential. The key question was how to go about it.

Tim started by developing the Seven Paths to Profitability (described in *Red, Black and Gold* by Susan Hanafee, page 49). These were:

- Reducing the cost of direct and indirect materials by $400 million
- Reducing the cost of warranty from 4% of sales to 2%
- Improving new product introduction
- Improving cash flow by enhancing the return on average net assets and managing receivables and inventory
- Capturing benefits from the company's restructurings
- Capturing sales synergies from a major acquisition in 1997
- Monitoring critical joint ventures

Next, Tim benchmarked with other CEOs to find out what they were doing to improve their companies. One customer and one supplier CEO told him the same thing: try Six Sigma because it works.

Tim knew he needed a strong leader to guide the Six Sigma deployment if it was going to work. He next talked with Frank McDonald about becoming the Vice President of Quality to lead the Six Sigma effort. Frank had spent a very successful career in business operations at GE and Cummins. The strategy in selecting Frank was to provide a strong operations voice within Cummins to verify that it would work and that it was worth devoting scarce time and resources to its deployment.

In a final discussion late in 1998, Tim and Frank went together to visit the leader of one of GE's businesses. The GE leader told Tim and Frank that profitability in his business, which was a commodity components business, had improved dramatically over five years primarily because of Six Sigma. This was all Tim needed to hear. At this point he asked Frank to commit. Frank had never wanted to be on corporate staff but agreed. From this time forward, Tim and Cummins were committed to the deployment of Six Sigma. (Figure 4.2 shows the impact of this decision on company profitability.)

To begin the deployment of Six Sigma at Cummins the company selected a consultant skilled in the processes and tools. Steve Zinkgraf, the founder of this consulting company, SBTI, had been part of the original development of Six Sigma at Motorola and had helped with deployments at Allied Signal and 3M. SBTI's capability was at the head of the pack.

During the initial executive overview training, a three-year target of $200 million was set. There was lively discussion about the feasibility of such a large target. Steve Zinkgraf promised the company leadership that if they followed the Six Sigma process and established the right management systems, he "guaranteed" them that the company would not only hit the target but exceed it. To make a long story short, the company completed projects worth more than ten times its investment in 2000 (the first year) and beat its three-year target by $90 million at the end of 2002. During those first three years:

- The company successfully completed 1,073 projects
- Project savings were valued at $290 million
- Over 1,000 people had been trained as Belts.

By the end of 2014:

- Cummins had successfully completed 45,000+ projects
- Project savings were valued greater than $5.5 billion
- Over 21,000 people had been trained as Belts
- Five thousand projects were active on any given day in the company involving over 15,000 people
- Customers had saved over $1 billion through Customer-Focused Six Sigma projects
- Projects were being completed in the areas of:
  - Strategy execution
  - Customer improvement

- Supplier improvement
- Community improvement
- Enterprise risk
- Supply chain integration and improvement
- All functional areas
- All businesses around the globe.

Even more significant was the impact on profitability. During the years of Six Sigma, from 2000 to 2014, an army of people focused on elimination of waste and variation from the company and its processes. Waste and variation in a company is like taking big piles of money into the street and setting them on fire. Neither waste nor variation adds any value to customers or to the business. They are simply unnecessary costs. By identifying needed improvements, assigning a team to work on them, following a proven process and performing regular reviews, the company completely changed its profitability profile. As Figure 4.2 shows, Cummins changed from a company that struggled to make profit to a cash generator.

Net Sales on the chart was a function of many factors: strong, well-executed strategies, global market growth, improving product quality and emissions cycles that played to one of the company's strengths. These are

The Result - Cummins Net Sales and Net Profit (1976-2014)
From publically available Annual Reports

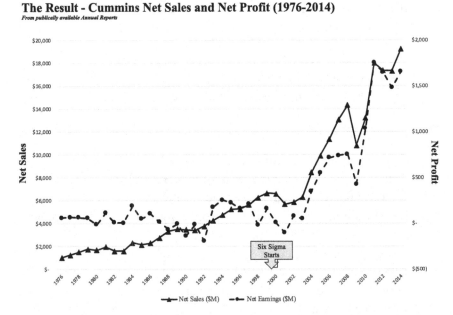

FIGURE 4.2 Cummins revenue vs. profit 1976–2014.

some of the things that worked together to enhance Cummins revenue. Six Sigma contributed to but was not a main factor in Net Sales improvement.

Net Profit, on the other hand, was strongly impacted by the 45,000 projects completed by teams all over the globe. One objective observation that speaks to the truth of this statement is the comparison of revenue to profit before and after the deployment of Six Sigma in the business. From 1976 to 1999, sales trends steadily up while profit remains flat. Statistically, there is little relationship between sales and profit during those years. In other words, it was impossible to predict how much profit the company would make based on its sales.

Following the introduction of Six Sigma, it is obvious from the chart that this relationship dramatically and fundamentally changed. There is a strong correlation between sales and profit giving the company the ability to plan better, invest better and take care of the customer and the shareholder better. Much of this change can be directly attributed to the work of thousands of people over 15 years taking waste and variation out of the company's processes, one Six Sigma project at a time.

Another way to look at the impact of Six Sigma on the company is the value of projects closed each year. Projects were measured by "annualized value," or the one-year value counted in the year the project closed. Figure 4.3 shows that the company could expect 2.5% to 3.0% savings as a percentage of revenue as Six Sigma matured.

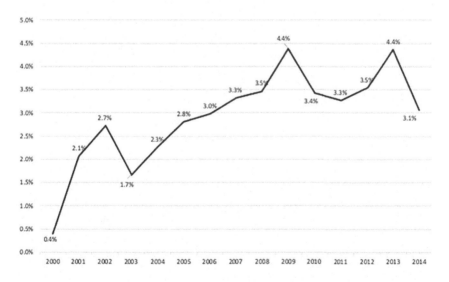

FIGURE 4.3 Six Sigma savings as a percentage of sales.

In fact, the correlation coefficient from 2000 to 2014 improved from 8% (1976–1999) to 95% (2014). This was a dramatic change in the relationship between revenue and profit, improving the capability of the company to forecast profitability and plan for growth given a range of potential revenues.

The company's stock reflected that change as well (see Figure 4.4). Cummins stock grew from $9.56 in January 2000 to $144.17 in December 2014—a 1,400% improvement.

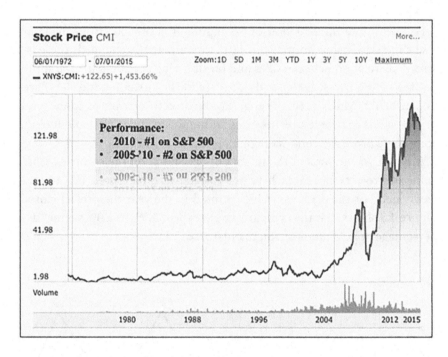

FIGURE 4.4 Cummins stock performance 1972–2015.

5

S-Curves and Kano—Maturity and Sustainability

WHAT ARE THE S-CURVES (MATURITY PHASES) AND TRANSITIONS OF SIX SIGMA?

The purpose of this section is to discuss the phases of Six Sigma maturity and how it can change and grow over time. The best way to describe this maturity and growth is through the use of S-Curves or maturity curves. The term "S-Curves" will be used from this point forward to mean phases of maturity.

First, we need to understand the purpose of S-Curves. S-Curves describe the maturity or growth of a change over time in a way that helps to see both what has occurred in the past and the future plan (see Figure 5.1).

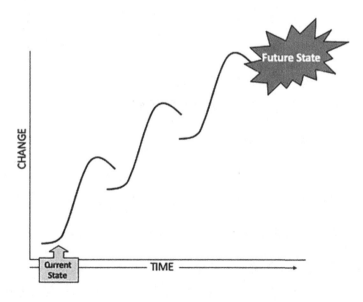

FIGURE 5.1 S-Curves.

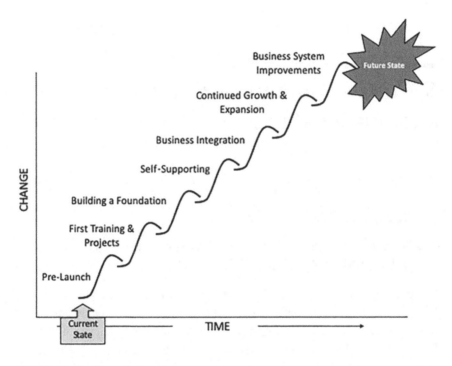

FIGURE 5.2 Six Sigma S-Curves.

The elements of a set of S-Curves are the future state, the current state, phases of maturity, and a timescale. Properly constructed, the set of S-Curves will tell you both where you've been and where you're going.

Let's start this conversation with an example (see Figure 5.2). The reader will see this example again later in this chapter.

Each S-Curve represents a new set of capabilities. The company builds these capabilities by applying Six Sigma to new questions and problems. Each new application leads to the acquisition of new skills and the development of new processes. If this growth does not occur, the change stagnates. Stagnation occurs when the top of an S-Curve is reached with no further progress toward the future state. As movement up the S-Curves progresses, the organization is building on capabilities that are already known and practiced. This is growth in maturity.

To make it simple and practical, let's use an example with which everybody is familiar. Think of a little baby. That baby has all kinds of potential (future state). Assume, for sake of the example, that the baby is destined to become a world-class marathoner. But at ten days old, that baby can't even hold up its head (current state). That baby first has to learn how to roll over, then sit up, then crawl, then walk, then run (sometimes run comes before walk!) and on and on to become world class at the marathon. Each step in the process requires new capabilities. Building on these capabilities, step by step, leads to the realization of the potential at birth. If growth is stopped at any step, world-class marathoner is likely impossible.

Now go back to the example S-Curves above. It is not possible for the company to work on integrated business system improvements that span functions and/or businesses before they have learned the basic tools and processes of Six Sigma. Each step along the maturity journey builds capability for improvements of increasing complexity. A key in this development is the recognition by company executives that the potential for Six Sigma application is very broad.

When S-Curves are used to plan for change, the starting point is always the future state. The future state describes where you want to go or what you want to be in the future. It acts as a stake in the ground for the leadership of an organization to communicate clearly both to itself and to people in the organization about what the future will look like once the changes are implemented. The future state describes expected behaviors. It's meant to help people understand what will be different once the change has taken place. Further, the future state is used to clarify the expectations of leadership for what the organization will become. The future state is used to negotiate and clarify the kinds of changes that leadership will drive. A documented and agreed future state increases the potential that the organization will continue a consistent path even as people change roles over time.

THE POWER OF A WELL-DEVELOPED FUTURE STATE

There's an old saying, the gist of which is: when you don't know where you are going, any road will take you there. Goals guide behavior and activity and give them focus. Lacking goals, both tend to be somewhat random and unfocused. In the same way, S-Curves need a well-crafted future state to provide direction and focus to the work that drives the organization along the S-Curves.

The future state is a description of desired future behaviors resulting from implementation of the change. The initial future state is constructed from research, benchmarking, external consultation and inputs from customers, the Board of Directors, and business leadership. Over time, as the organization matures and learns, the future state is updated. Therefore, the future state is not static. Rather, it reflects the evolution of knowledge and understanding that comes with practicing the skills, processes and tools of the change effort. This review and update is an annual event that precedes the planning process.

The Vision for Six Sigma: To continuously improve products and processes toward perfection.

The Objective of the Six Sigma Program: To make focused improvements which are measurable in Profit Before Income Taxes (PBIT) results.

Based on the vision and objective, we created the first future state for the Six Sigma deployment in December 1999. It was created by a small team whose knowledge of Six Sigma and its potential was, admittedly, minimal. The team did its best with what it knew at the time, focusing on the achievement of the vision and objective of Six Sigma at Cummins. The 1999 Six Sigma future state was a five-year vision that covered several areas. I have included the original future state in the Appendices for your reference.

Defining the future state gave a clear focus to all the work done. The company ultimately achieved most of the future state. In 2004, it was officially updated for the first time. These updates continued annually through 2014.

The 2014 future state goal: The goal of the Cummins Operating System to reduce variation and eliminate waste in critical processes to improve customer and business results is accomplished through the application of Six Sigma processes and tools across the entire supply chain. The future state goal will be achieved through four critical accomplishments:

- Continuous improvement is a major component of everybody's work, resulting in profit before tax of at least 13% annually.
- TDFSS (Technology Development for Six Sigma) enables and supports Product Preceding Technology (PPT). PPT teams deliver robust, tunable technology aligned and delivered via critical parameter trees. The Theory of Inventive Problem-Solving (TRIZ) is actively used for resolving contradictions and exploring new solutions.

- DFSS (Design for Six Sigma) is the methodology and tools that enables and supports Value Package Introduction (VPI) and product development. New products launch at quality levels better than the products replaced. VPI is a well-respected process in the company and is highlighted by leaders within Cummins as an example of a world-class product and process design system. VPI teams and their leadership use Critical Parameter Management (CPM) as a key input for managing programs and resources. DFSS in empowered and expected to execute the improvements and priorities driven by functions.
- Process Six Sigma (DMAIC) is the roadmap and tools for improving processes and solving problems. Six Sigma umbrella projects are used to improve key business processes and flows. Documentation of projects in the Six Sigma databases is important for building organizational knowledge and the implementation of best practices by the functions. Six Sigma is a component of new hire orientation. Targets are set to improve business metrics. Six Sigma is used to achieve the business improvement metrics. Leadership at all levels understands, values and uses the processes and tools of Six Sigma. Cummins is known worldwide by its continuous improvement culture. Six Sigma is a component of leadership development. A BB assignment is a result of an A ranking. Black Belt and Master Black Belt pipelines are continuously managed because these roles are important to management development.

This future state was used to develop the Six Sigma element of the Corporate Quality goal tree. The goal tree was communicated to the Quality Champions of the business units and functions as input to their part of the goal tree cascade.

Following the development of the future state, the current state is created. The current state is based on an assessment of the organization as it exists today relative to the future goal and objective. As with the future state, the current state describes in behavior terms what people in the organization are actually doing in the areas where the change is to occur. It's meant to clearly differentiate where you want to go from where you are.

The difference between the current and future states creates organizational tension between where you are and where you want to be. This tension serves as motivation for achieving the change. It's very important that

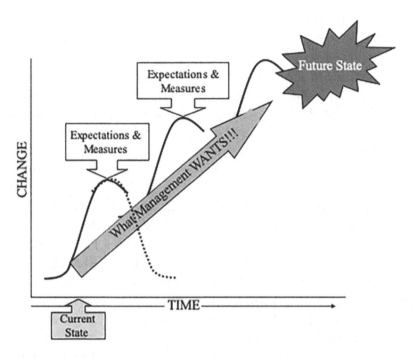

FIGURE 5.3 S-Curves: What management wants!

the future state is demonstrably different from the current state in a way that validates the resources and energy that leadership will expend leading the change. These two documents are broadly communicated as an element of driving buy-in across the organization (see Figure 5.3).

The future state describes a very different organization from today and, typically, management wants to go as fast as possible to reach the future state description. The problem is, especially in large organizations, the number of people whose behavior will change is significant. This can be further complicated by different languages spoken, different time zones, different geographies, different markets, different systems and many other differences that make change very complex (addressed in more detail in *Making Change in Complex Organizations,* ASQ, 2016). So, it's important to give leadership an understanding of how changes take place over time so that their expectations stay in line with the reality of how the change is progressing on the ground. This is the function of S-Curve thinking and planning.

Breaking a change down into S-Curves creates a picture of maturity that happens as a series of system changes over time. Taking this approach also allows for lessons learned to be applied as the change process matures, creating an operational learning organization. What tends to happen in organizations is that following an initiative's launch, there's a feeling of accomplishment. The original goal is achieved. For example, a goal might be that original savings targets are achieved, training is ongoing, and first projects are completed. There is a general sense that the organization is seeing results from making the change. This is just the top of the first S-Curve. And as you notice the S-Curves really are just the left-hand side of a series of bell-shaped curves. Organizations are living entities. Living things need to grow and change. If they don't grow and change, the only alternative is that they decay and die. The same is true of change in an organization. Trying to hold on to the gains at the top of an S-Curve halts growth and the change becomes static leading to a change that will, over time, decay and die, which is the right-hand side of the bell-shaped curve. This is best seen looking at the bookshelves of an organization. One can often find three-ring binders that were used to introduce a change. They are now just collecting dust. In most cases, the binders have not been opened since they were handed out at the initial training event. S-Curves are used to push leadership to think about what comes next as the change effort matures.

Subordinate goals are established at the top of each S-Curve. These subordinate goals serve as milestones on the way to the future state. These subordinate goals include measures. As progress is made up the S's, the measures change. Thus, the organization's scorecards change over time, moving from green to red as the goals change on the way to the future state.

The S-Curves slightly overlap each other. The purpose of the overlap is to represent planning and experimentation that goes on prior to leaping the gap from one S-Curve to the next (this will be discussed as part of each S-Curve section). Also, and this may be a subtle point, the organization goes through a learning process in each S-Curve. These lessons learned enable changes to the subordinate goals as well as the future state as they are reviewed and updated. The result is a more refined future state reflective of what the organization really wants to be and a clear time-based or phased plan to get there.

We can use Cummins as a practical example of the S-Curves (Figure 5.2) in action. After the CEO, Tim Solso, made the decision that Cummins would deploy Six Sigma, some benchmarking was conducted to understand what Six Sigma might look like in the future. The benchmarking resulted in defined requirements for Sponsors, Green Belts, Black Belts and Master Black Belts. Some definition work was done on the types of projects that might be done in the company. There was also an early version of a reward and recognition process. But the company really knew almost nothing about Six Sigma. Cummins was brand-new to the topic. And that's where the first S-Curve began. As the change matured, the future state and individual S-Curves became more well-defined. This maturity sets the foundation for the discussion in this book.

S-CURVES AND THE KANO MODEL

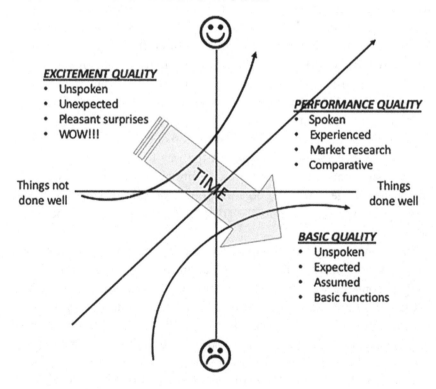

FIGURE 5.4 Kano Model.

The Kano Model is useful for understanding how requirements evolve (see Figure 5.4). The basics of the Kano Model are described below.

Basic Requirements—Basic requirements are expected and unspoken. They are the "ticket of entry" for a product or service. For example, a laptop computer is expected to have a color screen, and it is not something that the typical customer will ask for at this point in the computer's evolution. If done well, the customer doesn't really care because it is an expectation, but if done poorly, it is a major dissatisfier.

Performance Requirements—Performance requirements are comparative. They are things that a customer will ask for because they have seen it before or read about it. It is also something that competitors can do. An example, continuing the computer analogy, is storage, USB connections, hard drive vs. solid state, and battery life. (This is true in 2016 by may not be true by the time you read this!) The more performance delivered to the customer's requirements, the happier they are.

Excitement Requirements—Excitement requirements are like basic requirements, in that they are unspoken. However, unlike basic requirements, excitement requirements are unexpected. They cause the customer to say "WOW!" because it is not something that they have ever experienced before. An example that is already maturing is ubiquitous access to the internet by any wireless device. Fifteen years ago, not many people knew what the internet was. In 2016, it's hard to remember how we did anything without it. Excitement requirements don't have to be done perfectly to make customers happy, and if not done at all don't register with the customer because they are unexpected.

Movement Over Time—Leading to the final major element of the Kano Model: time. Excitement becomes performance, which becomes a basic expected/unspoken capability over time.

Both the S-Curve and Kano models are useful individually for thinking about change. They are even more powerful together.

At the top of each S-Curve, new capability is delivered. This capability starts out as an excitement-type deliverable because it is new. But with time, that deliverable becomes a basic feature of the organization (see Figure 5.5).

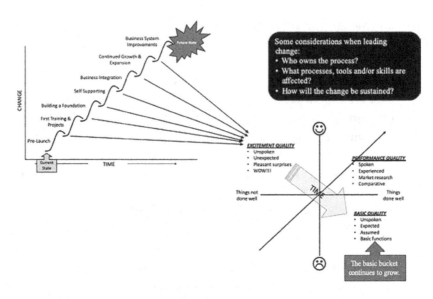

FIGURE 5.5 S-Curves with Kano Model.

Source: Reprinted with permission from American Society for Quality, Quality Press © 2016 ASQ, www.asq.org All rights reserved. No further distribution allowed without permission.

A company produces its services or products through the application of processes, tools or methods, and skills. When there is change, some combination of these are affected. At the excitement level, these tend to be new to the organization. But as time moves along, these become basic expectations within the organization. If the processes/tools/skills are industry-wide, the school systems tend to own developing people with those capabilities. If they are unique to the organization, the organization owns responsibility for training its employees in these basic capabilities. An example of the former is basic computer use. Learning how to use a computer has devolved all the way down to the grade school level. When I was in school, I didn't even see a computer until college, and then it was punch card programming. Using a computer has gone from use only by scientists to a basic requirement for many employees. An example of the latter might be a manufacturing process that differentiates a company's product from the competition. The secrets of the process are closely held but become a basic expectation of the plant and the people working that specific process. If a person can't perform the operation, they can't work in that area.

Each S-Curve follows the same process. With each S-Curve, new excitement level capabilities are introduced with the consequent migration to basic organizational capabilities.

The result is that the *basic bucket of requirements* gets bigger and bigger. The library of processes, the collection of methods and tools and the training of skills requires ownership and management if the people of the company are going to use them. This is especially true over time as people and products come and go. This tends to be the job of the organization's functions.

A couple of examples might help here. The manufacturing function owns the processes, tools and skills used in a plant to produce the products. The finance function owns and trains unique aspects of the company's financial planning processes. The IT function owns the project management processes used to develop new software applications in support of the business. This makes the function the storehouse of the company's knowledge. This storehouse role is a very important one, but one I have found is not well appreciated within many organizations.

Some key questions that must be answered as the change progresses include:

- Who is accountable/responsible for the improvements?
- What processes, methods and/or skills are affected?
- How will the changes be sustained?

The implication is that there are roles and responsibilities that are required if the change is going to be allowed to mature.

A great example of how this works is the US Army (the other military services have a similar structure), shown in a generalized manner in Figure 5.6.

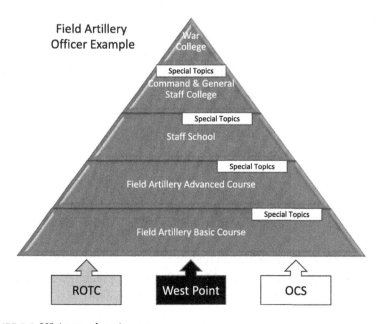

FIGURE 5.6 US Army education system.

Officers enter the Army from a variety of different sources: the Reserve Officer Training Corps (ROTC), West Point, or Officer Candidate School (OCS). Even though these new officers have just graduated from a school, the very first assignment is Branch School (my branch, the Field Artillery, is shown in the example). The Branch is analogous to a function in a business. At the Branch School, the new officer learns the details of small-unit leadership tactics and some higher-level subjects. The officer proceeds from Branch School to a job in a unit. Following time in the small unit role, there is often schooling in a special topic prior to the next job. For example, I (George Strodtbeck) was in the Army, I attended survey officer school prior to holding that role in my next assignment. Then, after that assignment, it was off to the Branch Advanced Course, where company-level leadership and tactics are taught with some higher-level education. This pattern is followed as an officer's career advances.

One of the many benefits of this approach is that military officers are taught the skills of their profession which are then practiced and reinforced during a unit leadership assignment. It also creates a common language which is used across the Branch to foster fast, efficient and clear communications. For example, any former or current artillery officer who happens to read this book will instinctively know what the term "March Order" means and how to do it. During times of intense stress, the value this type of communication clarity cannot be overstated.

The Branch in the US Army is the storehouse of the knowledge of the processes, tools/methods and skills needed by the members of the Branch. This storehouse is continuously updated as new approaches are developed and perfected and old methods discarded as they become outdated.

Businesses may not be able to follow this model exactly. However, if the business expects to survive over the long term, some form of this model that fits the business's needs must be adopted. Absent an organized approach to retaining and training people in the customer critical knowledge of the company, people are left to try to figure it out for themselves, which leads to random actions that may or may not be beneficial to the company's customers.

Using this linkage between S-Curves and the Kano Model as a starting point and Six Sigma as an example, some things to think about include:

- Who owns training and its maintenance?
- Who is responsible for the Master Black Belt pipeline and individual Master Black Belt development and redeployment?

- Who is responsible for Black Belt selection, development and redeployment?
- Who is responsible to ensure hand-off from Six Sigma leader to leader (when the inevitable leadership change occurs) is accomplished effectively with no loss in progress?
- Who owns the post-project control plan audit process?
- Who maintains the library of key repeating documents (C&E Matrices, FMEAs, QFDs, CPM flow-down models, etc.)?
- Who is responsible for best practice identification, evaluation and standardization?
- Who is responsible for evaluating obsolescence of Six Sigma processes, tools and capabilities?
- Who is responsible for project hopper maintenance?
- Who is responsible for maintaining performance measures?
- Who is responsible for assessing organizational capability and maturity?

It is important to remember the relationship between the S-Curves and the Kano Model during the next sections discussing the S-Curve Actions and Cross-Curve Preparations of Six Sigma at Cummins. During the 16 years of deployment, the number of basic requirements grew from S-Curve to S-Curve. We put structures in place to manage this growing list of basic requirements. Keep these basics in mind during the coming discussions of Six Sigma S-Curve maturity.

6

Interview With Frank McDonald— Cummins Vice President of Quality (1999–2002)

WHAT IS YOUR BACKGROUND?

I graduated college in Dublin, Ireland, with a degree in engineering and was employed by General Electric to go work in the US. I joined the GE Manufacturing Management Program, which was three years in duration with two assignments in each of three different locations.

The thing about General Electric at that time was that it was a very disciplined organization in the way they did things. You could do a job in one location that had a very clear set of directions, measurements and methods. You could move into a similar job in a completely different business and the same rules applied. The same measurements applied. The same systems applied. It was a great learning experience in terms of how to manage any manufacturing operation.

I moved from making electronic components in Kentucky to making switchgear in Philadelphia to making locomotives in Erie, Pennsylvania. Because of the training, I was able to move into a job in small appliances in Singapore . . . go figure! I'm being a little facetious here, except for the fact that it's true. People moved around to a lot of different businesses in General Electric. Because there was a set method of doing things, and by having the strict system that they had, it allowed people to interchange businesses easily. I got used to the idea that there was a method of doing things and it was continuously improving.

I spent four years in Singapore working in a startup operation in the early '70s. I moved from Singapore to the Small Appliance business in Australia. I was in Australia working in the GE Housewares and White Goods businesses for about nine years.

Another value of the experience with GE was that I worked in different countries. I met different people. I got used to working with people who didn't think the same way I did. I got used to working in a country where I was a minority, like in Singapore. It opens your eyes to lots of different ways of thinking and working with different kinds of people. That became valuable later on.

That was my early career. My assignment in Australia was shortened. Even though the "rule" at GE was that if you were number one or number two in your industry, you're safe, otherwise you were for sale. That was basically Jack Welch's message. At that time, we were number one in our industry in Australia and worldwide. But the business was sold to Black and Decker and my role as Managing Director disappeared. That caused GE to transfer me from Australia back to the US.

When I moved back to the US, it was a different General Electric. It was also a different world at that time in the '80s, and General Electric was quickly closing down what they called their old traditional manufacturing businesses and getting into more lucrative kinds of businesses like NBC and insurance and financial businesses. These became much more important to the company at that time than the old manufacturing businesses.

I joined the electrical distribution equipment business, which was part of construction equipment. I had 19 plants scattered worldwide. I recognized after about six months that the assignment was going to be how quickly I could close most of them. The emphasis was on cost saving through consolidation. This was quite a change for me, because up to that time I'd been growing businesses, not taking them apart. The whole of General Electric had changed. Its focus had changed. After three years I asked if I could move to a part of the company that was actually growing its manufacturing businesses rather than cutting them back. I was told that, of course, I was free to talk to anybody I wanted in GE. As a result, I found out from my own contacts that basically everybody was cutting back manufacturing operations.

Manufacturing at GE was no longer the thing to be in. If you weren't in the finance business or the insurance business, you were a relic of the past. My number one OEM customer at that time was a company called Onan. Onan manufactured generator sets from very small sets that go into RVs to very large, multi-megawatt units that powered entire villages. They asked if I would join them because they were interested in becoming a global company. At that time, they were purely a North American company and were looking for someone who had some experience outside of the US. Guess where they wanted to go? They wanted to go into Europe, Singapore, and Australia. That suited me very well.

So, I joined Onan in 1988. They were partly owned at that time by Cummins Engine Company, and that's how the connection with Cummins was made. I was head of worldwide operations for Onan. In a period of about four years, we doubled the size of the business and had plans to continue to grow very, very quickly worldwide. By then we had operations in the UK, Singapore, and Australia.

The Cummins interest in Onan grew. They became increasingly interested in taking over all of Onan, which they did. A power generation division was created at Cummins. During this transition, they asked me to both join Cummins in Columbus and to take over what was then a relatively new part of their business: midrange engines. These engines were used in tractors, generators, boats and, of course, Dodge Ram pick-up trucks.

So, I took over the leadership of the midrange engine business in 1992. The midrange engine business at that time was a partnership with the J. I. Case company. The partnership had a major operation in Rocky Mount, North Carolina. The midrange business was less than a billion dollars in sales and had generated losses for a number of years. Over a period of time, we grew the business to a highly profitable $2.5 billion in revenue. In fact, midrange became the most profitable division of Cummins at that time. I led the midrange engine business through 1999, when Tim Solso became the CEO of the company.

The insights, though, that are important to me from the time I worked at General Electric was that everything, as I told you, was disciplined. Everything was organized. Everything was managed so that businesses had a common approach and could be compared, contrasted and improved.

When I went to Onan, it was a well-managed business with a solid team of folks focused on doing things well and profitably. It had been a family-run company for many years. They had a set of systems that worked very well for them. When I went to Cummins, I found a company that was really long on documentation and short on execution. As a supplier of engines to Onan, the parent company's quality and delivery performance was not very highly regarded. This created friction. In fact, at that time, there appeared to be little sense of responsibility for profitability. Compared to GE's focus on financial results, this was a strange world to me.

When I joined the midrange business, we had a few plants scattered around the world. We needed a way of integrating the work that they did and we needed to focus on results.

About that time, Jim Henderson, the COO of Cummins, introduced a system called the Cummins Production System (CPS) as a homegrown approach that copied much of the Toyota Production System. It was part of an overall corporate functional excellence initiative.

The Cummins Production System was not the first effort at Cummins to create a sense of common approach in the plants. However, this one proved to be very successful. It was very fortuitous for me because the deployment of CPS was coincident with me joining the midrange engine business and I got involved in spreading the CPS word.

The Cummins Production System implementation was led by Joe Loughrey. It was a little bit more esoteric than Toyota's version, but it set out clear objectives, clear processes and clear measures. Over the period of time that I was with midrange engines, it became the way that Cummins manufacturing operations worked. It was, up to that time, the most successful program that Cummins had attempted. When we got to discussions about Six Sigma later, it helped that some of the things that enabled acceptance of the Cummins Production System could be applied to the Six Sigma introduction.

HOW DID YOU GET INVOLVED IN SIX SIGMA AND WHAT WERE YOUR EARLY ACTIONS?

When Tim Solso came to me in 1999 to work with him to implement the Six Sigma program across Cummins, I was reluctant. It wasn't a shyness reluctance. I was reluctant because I truly believed that it probably couldn't be done at Cummins. I didn't believe that we could get the whole organization to change because even small change is difficult. And this wasn't just any change but change to a common approach across the company. This kind of change is the most difficult thing in large companies, I believe. Especially, to get a company like Cummins, which had such a lack of execution discipline, to change was going to be a difficult task. So, I tried to avoid being the one that would take it on and fail.

There was a classic failure just before Six Sigma when we tried to introduce the Baldrige approach. It was an approach that should have worked.

As always, the failure was in the implementation. I believe that it was partly because the initiative was led by a newcomer to the company who joined to do that job and didn't really understand the culture and the people of Cummins. Although personally, I am sure he was a very well-qualified individual, the difficulty of making change is what brought it down.

Just to give you an idea why I worked so hard to avoid the job, the day that I was announced as head of Quality, which included the Six Sigma effort, I got a phone call from a very good friend of mine at Cummins, who has now passed away, who reminded me that the previous six Quality leaders of Cummins had all left the company. He just wanted me to be aware of the challenge that I faced—as if I really needed to be reminded!

I had spent my early work life at General Electric watching how the "experienced" guys, seeing a corporate program coming, would find a way to either look like they were doing it or flat out not do it at all. That was just how you operated in a large corporate environment.

The reason for that mentality was based on many bad experiences. The reasoning was as follows: if you went along with the new initiative and the leadership changed or if the leaders changed their minds and that change was no longer the directive, then you had put yourself out on a limb. And more than likely it failed—hence the well-known "program of the month" phenomenon.

This Six Sigma program required that we select the best and brightest people in the company to risk their careers by becoming Black Belts, spending two years with us dedicated to the program. Because if it turned out to be a program of the month, they would have wasted their two years when this or if the next CEO said, "Well, we're not going to do this anymore. We're going to do something else"—just like what happened at General Electric when Jack Welch left and his successor decided Six Sigma wasn't as valuable to the company and basically stopped it.

So, there was no great enthusiasm for me to go into the Six Sigma program. I was quite happy running the midrange engine business. Having the success we were having made it even easier to stay put. However, Tim did say that I had a choice. He said I could either do the Six Sigma job or take early retirement, or at least I remember it to be something like that anyway.

I decided I would use my old learnings and show him that he was wrong, but of course you can't tell a new CEO that. So we agreed we would go to General Electric and talk to people that I knew there. They would tell us the truth about Six Sigma and we could see how it was really working.

I suggested we should see what it was because many of the initiatives in GE were hyped very well publicly and were much more successful in the press than they were in actual implementation. I thought that Six Sigma was probably one of those. After our visit, I figured that I would be able to go back to running the midrange business.

I arranged a meeting with the vice president of the last business that I'd worked in at General Electric. We had actually worked together. I called him and I said, "Listen, my boss wants me to implement Six Sigma. All I'm asking you to do is just tell him the real story. I'm not going to put words in your mouth. You and I know each other from way back. Let us just hear what is really going on."

So Tim and I went to GE in Plainville, Connecticut. The Vice President and his team put on a presentation of their involvement in the implementation of Six Sigma in the Construction Equipment business. They covered the whole DMAIC process, experiences and results. The Vice President had done his homework on Cummins. He knew about the company history and our product lines, and he drew a parallel between his business and Cummins. Both were about 80 to 90 years old. They were old-line businesses that make equipment that had changed incrementally with time, but they were still old-line operations.

They had traditionally run a mid-single-digit net profit in their businesses, but after the implementation of Six Sigma, profitability had moved into the teens!

You can argue about how you measure profitability. But that wasn't the point. This was an apples-to-apples comparison. His method of measuring his historical returns was the same method that showed returns in the mid-teens.

With that simple chart, I was sunk. He determined my fate, because now Tim was absolutely convinced that this was the way to go. I must admit, I was a little mad at "my friend" from GE for a while after that. However, I did call him years later to congratulate him on his retirement as Vice Chairman of GE and to tell him that he was the reason that I got into Six Sigma.

On the plane back to Cummins, Tim was absolutely convinced that this was something that we could and should do. He told me to get on with it. One of the first things I did was make a list of things that I did over the years that I knew would make me look like I was doing this corporate program but wasn't. I needed a program that would address all of those responses and the kinds of concerns that people bring up, legitimately sometimes, that are excuses for why they're not going to change.

I thought if I could go after those things, then maybe we could actually have a shot at making this work. Plus, the advantage I believed I had over previous leaders of Quality that had met a poor end was that I'd been in the business at Cummins for about eight years. I knew the people well. They knew me well. I knew how Cummins worked, so it gave me an advantage that others didn't have. At least that's what I told myself.

Looking at the organizational layers, I tried to answer the question, "What's in this for the Black Belt, the Black Belt's boss, the head of the department, and the business leader?" I did this all the way up through the organization. It was important to figure out what has to be in it for them to make them want to do what we needed them to do.

It was not unlike an FMEA (Failure Modes and Effects Analysis). I did want to know what the failure modes were that impacted previous changes that I participated in and the effects of those. I wanted to understand what I could do to blunt them, change them, or reverse them.

So much of it was about things we had also learned implementing CPS, where there were many roadblocks and people who were uncomfortable making the changes. We did many things to make that easier, both sticks and carrots. Sometimes, it was peer pressure by publishing your results compared against others. In other cases, it was pure flattery of recognition. In other cases, it was financial. It just depended on what the situation required.

One of the things I wanted to know from GE was who they used to support the implementation of Six Sigma. They had worked with a company called SBTI. SBTI had been responsible for supporting the implementation across General Electric. I said, "All right, let's contact those people and insist that we'll hire them on one condition only; the people who worked on the General Electric account would be the people who would work with us." By doing this, we would be assured, at a minimum, that we were following the same trail as General Electric. That was the first move we made to get started. George came on early because he had been working on different aspects of quality for quite a while, and he is disciplined and I am not. I needed somebody who would put some discipline and structure into what we were about to do.

Next, we brought in the Chairman of SBTI to interview with Tim and his staff. He was quite the showman and very charismatic. He put on a great display of the improvements that they'd made not just in General

Electric, but in other places as well. People were impressed because he had real results to brag about, which was good. But you could tell even at that meeting, observing all the leaders of the businesses that were there, that we would get support from some, but others might be a little more difficult. Those who were interested were asking questions and engaging. We knew right away that we had a cross section of people who would embrace it and some who would oppose it. But regardless, Tim was so over the moon about it, nobody was going to say no.

Since the boss was highly engaged, highly involved and highly committed and was brand-new in the job of being the Chairman, the smart money would say that regardless of what one thought, the thing is to say, "Whatever you want to do, boss, we will do." And that's what happened.

At enormous expense, we hired SBTI to do the training and help hold our hands through the early Black Belt and Green Belt projects. I also had a group of people who had worked with me during the implementation of the Cummins Production System in the plants that I used for advice and counsel and to help promote the program. In the very first meeting, one of them, a woman from HR, said, "You know, T-shirts and belt buckles aren't going to work for this program." This proved to be a very important realization.

This was far more complicated than just dealing with plant managers. This effort was corporate-wide, making it that much more difficult. We started on the list of things we knew we'd have to do. First, we needed the best and the brightest, and you only get them, quite honestly, if you take care of them. We did things like pay the Black Belts an annual bonus for being involved in Six Sigma. This "payment" was on top of any normal bonus that they would get for the business that they were in. Basically, it was a flat-out bribe. My friend Adolfo Savelli from Brazil put it another way: it was "pre-performance recognition," not a bribe.

After changing the bonus structure, we cajoled managers into making sure that we only got the people who were recognized as top performers. However, a few people did sneak in that never should have.

We got a commitment from Tim to make an appearance and talk to every single training session for a new group of Belts, which he did faithfully for almost ten years. This was a real demonstration of his commitment.

We talked to business leaders about the measurements that we would use to monitor the overall program, not just the individual projects. Obviously, this included the value of projects implemented, but it went deeper. We monitored the number of projects initiated, the number of projects in process, how long it took to implement the projects, and a number of other metrics that we used to keep track of progress. This also helped us to make sure that there were enough projects coming into the system, that there was sufficient support being given to them to move them along quickly, and that we were getting the financial results that we had hoped to get.

It was a spotty start. As anyone who has run a new program will tell you, the one thing you pray for is an early success, so you can brag about it and show it off. We were quite fortunate in two ways. First, we closed a project that was a huge financial success. The second thing was that the project was outside of the traditional areas that we focused on for improvement. It was in the financial department.

Typically, we focused improvements on engineering and manufacturing. But this was a finance person who came up with an idea for how to redo the entire method by which we were handling international transactions and it resulted in a savings of over $20 million. So right from the beginning we were seeing benefits coming from non-traditional areas of the company.

The other thing that was interesting, because we had enlisted people to become Black Belts from all over the company, we were finding that we were getting people who were outside of manufacturing and engineering. We had people in the Legal department, in Finance and HR who were actually coming up with some great ideas. The program began to self-perpetuate just by virtue of the results that we were achieving in all areas of the company.

Also, there was the attention paid to the top of the house because Tim reviewed the performance results with his leadership team, which effectively put pressure on them to be sure that they were engaged. For them to be engaged, they needed to have meetings with their leadership teams who were involved in the program to get continuous updates on the progress.

DID TIM SOLSO AND HIS STAFF REVIEW PROGRAM-WIDE SIX SIGMA PERFORMANCE RESULTS OR DID THEY REVIEW SOME INDIVIDUAL PROJECTS?

It was an overview of business performance, and within that a review of projects in process. We convinced Tim that he should have Black Belts appear at those meetings to talk about their successful projects, but the main purpose was a review of the overall standing of the program in each of their businesses. The result was the creation of some inter-business rivalry.

Tim and I also completed the training and implemented a project together which helped our understandings and added to the visible commitment that Tim was making.

HOW DID THE PEOPLE FROM THE NON-MANUFACTURING DISCIPLINES LIKE LAW OR TREASURY, INSURANCE AND HR REACT TO BEING INVOLVED IN IMPROVEMENT, MANY FOR THE FIRST TIME?

I don't think they were any different from those that were our usual focus. I'll tell you what I mean. I think in any given population when a change initiative begins, there's a third of the people who relish the idea of a new approach, a new way of doing things, and who are ready to make the change. They just like the idea that maybe we can make this thing better and this could be the way to do it. They are positive about it.

Then, there's a third of the group that will wait to see whether this is really sustainable or it's going to be a temporary thing that shall pass. If they keep their heads down, it will all go away. If it does not go away, they've got a chance to join later.

Then there's a third of the group that love the way it is today, and anything you do to change it feels uncomfortable.

I found that when we went to China, or India, or wherever we went this dynamic existed. The one-third breakdown may not be exactly right, but it's reflective of large groupings of people who say, "Wow! This is a nice idea. Let's give it a try," to those who say, "Oh, no. Not another idea." Interestingly, I found the same thing when I was working directly with a Chinese company in later years, post-Cummins.

In the non-operations departments, we began mining areas that hadn't been mined before. We had disregarded, almost as a culture, that people in the administrative areas could actually return some great financial results. For example, HR had been considered, as in many places, a necessary but purely overhead area. But it dawned on people that all areas influence the profitability of the company, whether it's the law department or the HR department, or whatever. If you improve it, you can have an impact on company profitability. These folks were coming out, the one third if you like, making changes and, I think, surprising their peers.

But don't let it sound like it all went well. This is what happened in the beginning. There was a kind of euphoria getting it started and then it plateaued.

THERE ARE PROS AND CONS TO ENGAGING ALL OF THE DIFFERENT BUSINESS FUNCTIONS INVOLVED AT THE START. IS IT YOUR SENSE THAT THE ONE-THIRD RULE APPLIED THE SAME ACROSS FUNCTIONS?

Absolutely! I think it would have been a shame to do what we had done before and focus Six Sigma just on manufacturing because, quite frankly, the manufacturing areas were the ones that had been worked over many, many times. The rest of them had not.

Do you know what was an interesting thing? The Legal department fascinated me because I was trying to figure out how to measure a law department. What kind of metrics can you use? We're used to quality, cost and delivery measurements in operations, but how do you measure a law department? We didn't know how to do that. It was actually the people in the law department who were interested in making changes and made the suggestion for a project. They used the output of the project to begin measuring the effectiveness of the department. They said, "Look. Here's what we should do. We have a number of lawsuits on our hands that we have to deal with. Some minor, some not so minor. We ought to sit down and 'negotiate' with the head of the business what we think we can settle this case for and how long it will take. Then, we can measure against that." That just made a lot of sense. That was interesting because typically the heads of the businesses either complained about the outcome of cases or did not engage at all. In the past, it was a transaction, and there was a result, but nobody ever asked, "Was that good?" If you understand the thinking of the law department, this was quite radical because they were used to doing what they thought was fair and reasonable, but now they were actually being measured on the accuracy of what they thought they could do.

In many support areas people saw what they did as a set of transactions, not necessarily as a process that could be measured. That was one of the many interesting things that came out of Six Sigma. We didn't go in knowing that this was going to happen, and as I say, the very first big project being a financial department success was definitely not a plan. But that helped people who were interested—the top one third, the ones who want the change—start doing projects and delivering results.

DID YOU HAVE ANY EARLY STRUGGLES? IF SO, WHAT DID YOU DO?

Yes, we did. Later in the first year, we hit a flat spot and were basically wondering if we were going to keep it going. We were finding out that the interest level was waning. "The usual suspects" had found a way of looking like they were involved but really not. We had to figure out how to kick-start the thing. George and I put together two leadership meetings. We got together with the two biggest business leaders separately. We had one meeting in the UK and one in the US with the business leaders and their staffs.

We basically pointed out to them that they were failing based on program measurements for their business. We didn't know what the outcome of the meetings would be, but we were fairly clear that progress in the businesses needed improvement.

It was quite interesting because the meeting we had in the US really did kick-start the efforts. The Engine Business, led by Joe Loughrey, was the largest of the company. He decided right after that meeting to become much more personally involved. He felt that Six Sigma needed a much more structured approach in his business than it had been given in the past. The outcome of the meeting in the UK, the International Business, was not as dramatic. But nevertheless, they did get better.

That was the big breakthrough. I think what happened at that meeting was that Joe took real ownership for the performance and the results of Six Sigma in his business and instituted some follow-up programs for monitoring what was happening. As an additional benefit, we applied much of what he had done to the rest of the company. This gave Six Sigma a second wind.

Tim continued to be heavily involved. In the second year, we instituted a Chairman's Award for the best projects in each business unit. This was a worldwide recognition effort. The business units submitted their best implemented projects to Corporate Quality. George used a common set of criteria to determine the best projects. The Belts and project sponsors were invited to Columbus to be recognized by the Chairman. That was another way of applying pressure between peer groups. Their people were recognized for superior performance and, of course, for some people it was a real honor to come to Columbus, Indiana, especially because Tim presented the awards in the presence of the Board of Directors and all of Cummins senior leadership.

So, there were several things at play simultaneously. There was the award program at the Chairman's level. There was peer group pressure at the Chairman's staff level. There was a process of metrics in place for the department heads. There were financial awards for the Black Belts. There were a few other things, but those were the main things that we found were helping us get rid of my list of potential failure modes that I talked about earlier.

One of the interesting changes to the monthly Chairman's staff meeting was that a part of every session became a Six Sigma business review session that pressured the business leaders in two directions. One was to meet his expectations, but the other was the peer pressure on each of them to perform as the results were being reviewed. Either George or I would be at those meetings to present the details; it was an opportunity to praise people for great performance in front of the boss and maybe give watch-outs to others who needed it. But, generally, George and I agreed that it was always best to over-reward and over-praise than it was to do the other. That tended to get a better result than my typical approach would have been more aggressive than George's.

Reluctantly, we moved from our original "bonus" approach to paying Belts for each successful project completed. Tying financial results to improvements was something we had not done before. The financial results were to be verified by the financial department, not just the guys who did the project. This gave people in finance a stake in the success of the effort right from the beginning.

I've tried to answer the question you asked earlier on the failure modes. Many of the things we did—Tim doing his Chairman's Awards, following up at his staff meetings, publicly acknowledging the success and failures of the program combined with a review the Six Sigma program metrics like how many ideas had been submitted, how many projects we were working on, how long it was taking us to get them done, and the identification of bottlenecks—were done to address those potential failures. And working it down through the system, you get to the point where everybody was touching the program either in a way where the reward is positive, like praise or money, or maybe not so positive when the results were identified as needing improvement. You find yourself working all the way up and down the company.

We also had people in every department in the company who understood how the program is supposed to work. This was something that was helpful in our progress because people knew that they should be helping others who were working on projects. That's because there's a lot of work that goes on in these projects. It's not just the Belt who's leading the project. It's a team effort and there's a lot of people in different departments that are needed to get the projects done. The fact that people corporate-wide understood the program created an understanding of the importance of helping out to get projects implemented.

WAS THE IMPACT OF PEER PRESSURE SOMETHING THAT WAS RECOGNIZED AND PLANNED AT THE TIME, OR SOMETHING YOU REALIZED HAPPENED LOOKING BACK?

Remember, peer pressure in a corporation the size of Cummins is not just about bragging rights. Potentially, this could determine who the next CEO is. There is a normal competition at the levels below the CEO. Peer pressure is also important and comes from the recognition that you have the ability in your business to accomplish the objectives, and not just bragging about the fact that "We achieved this, this and this in Six Sigma," but more "We achieved this and this in Six Sigma and my peer did not." If you follow what I'm getting at.

Peer pressure is about rivals, too. There's an element of peer pressure at this level that's very high pressure. You don't want to be the one who the Chairman is looking at because you are one of his people who is ignoring or not involved or engaged in his pet project. Because we were there showing the business' Six Sigma performance results, the element of peer pressure was pretty high. What I'm really saying is it's not just a minor issue. Peer pressure is quite strong in a corporate structure.

That sense of peer pressure flows down through the organization. If I take it down about two steps, down to the plant managers, they are also being measured against each other. Because you now have a common set of measures across all the plants, you're introducing some peer pressure by making the results transparent. There were a lot of people, when we were implementing the Cummins Production System, who didn't want us to produce a piece of paper that showed all of the plants measured against each other. I remember we had to fight to get it done. The attitude was, "Don't show my plant up against somebody who's really doing better than I am." But the whole purpose should be to identify opportunities for improvement. There's always going to be a top 10% and a bottom 10% when you do that. Continued poor performance is a problem. The same benefit was achieved with Six Sigma when information was available to facilitate sharing completed projects across businesses.

We introduced another element of peer pressure for Belts and Sponsors. We wanted to give the Belts some visible recognition, so we did go back to an old idea but with a new twist; shirts. Not cheap T-shirts like we'd always been giving people. We gave the Belts expensive, long-sleeve white shirts with a unique Six Sigma logo on it. We gave the same shirt to project Sponsors.

We did some other things as well to build peer pressure. The Belts also got a framed certificate to inform the world that they had completed the Six Sigma training. I must have signed 3,000 of those things! They were very nicely done, and people who had completed the training would have them on their desks. I think people appreciated having them.

We added an interesting change to our communications strategy, which Tim was a little uncomfortable with. It was suggested to him that we minimize the amount of corporate-wide communications on this program. We weren't going to tell the company what results we were expecting. We were not going to say in the annual report that we're going to save millions of dollars. We were not going to promise the analysts anything. BUT when you do it, you can tell them you did it. But even more importantly, when you minimize the communications in a corporation like that, but you still give out the information to those who need to have it, rumor serves as the fastest form of communication.

If you don't tell all people what is going on, they're going to find out because they hear about it on the grapevine. The reaction is, "Oh, no! This thing is going on. What is it? How does it work?" It's people's natural curiosity that fires up these rumors across organizations. At Cummins this was working overtime. We were talking to Black Belts and Sponsors. We were talking to their managers. We were talking to the leaders of the businesses. But we weren't saying anything to the company at large or to the analysts or to the wide world that this is what we are going to do. You only found out about Six Sigma by doing the work.

The very first time that Tim actually put it in an annual report was to talk about results. That was really important. Because one of the things on my list was that I was tired of people coming out and telling me in corporate programs, "We are going to save a gazillion dollars and we're going to do this and that." Then the change fizzles, and people think, "Well, that was a waste of time." I would rather communicate success and build on that.

I don't want to leave the impression that we didn't communicate at all. But we communicated heavily only on a need-to-know basis. But, before you knew it, everybody in the company was talking about the program.

This was one of the things on my list that I always hated about corporate programs and was especially true of programs that fizzled, because when they didn't happen, it left a negative feeling with everybody. The one third that supported the initiative felt they wasted their time chasing this rainbow that never materialized and the naysayers felt vindicated.

The failure also undermined the credibility of the entire management team. You can only do "Lucy and the football" so many times before the most credible communication is the rumor mill. I'd seen too many cases of people saying, "I'm going to do this" and then failing.

There was an element of self-preservation, too. I didn't particularly want to raise too many expectations ahead of a program that had all chances to be another failure.

Another thing that helped spread the word was the "bonus". We got swift formal approval from the HR department for that bonus program. We announced that it existed to the Black Belts and nobody challenged it. That one was a risk, but I felt it was one worth taking. Sometimes it's better to seek forgiveness than permission. I also counted on Tim's support and people thinking that I was only doing it because Tim told me to.

WHAT WERE SOME OF YOUR BIGGEST SURPRISES?

One of my biggest surprises was discovering unexpected areas of support and resistance. During the Cummins Production System implementation, the methodology we used to disperse it across the company was to pick individuals to lead specific manufacturing functional excellence areas. This is a group of the traditional manufacturing functions of quality, materials, manufacturing engineering and shop operations. The functional excellence leader chosen for each one of those functions is responsible for functional excellence across every plant in the company, which at that time was about 45 plants.

I was responsible for shop operations and plant manager functional excellence. I visited every plant at Cummins every two years. I would go to a plant and work with them to make sure they understood CPS. I would spend time with them. By the end, I knew every plant manager and every shop operations manager in Cummins. So at least for manufacturing, I knew darn well who was going to be with us and who was going to be a tougher sell.

Also, by being the leader of the midrange engine business, I worked with all the corporate functions, whether it was finance or HR or legal or whatever. Because of that, I had a relationship with every plant in the company and all of the functional leaders.

One of the things that struck me as being a discovery in this whole exercise was dealing with the engineering division of Cummins. Engineering at Cummins is made up of very talented people. They're the people who develop the new products and product applications. When I made the first presentation to the engineering department about Six Sigma, the staggering thing to me was the number of questions specifically about how the projects were chosen.

I mentioned in the talk that we had a financial objective, a time objective, and other parameters of the program. But what they wanted to know was how the project selection process worked. I explained that what we wanted to do was only focus on the important projects and projects that we knew we could accomplish in a reasonable amount of time. We didn't want projects that were overly wide in scope and so forth. I just explained the basic rules of Six Sigma.

What they were all saying in different ways was that they were tired of their managers giving them work to do that they would do for a while, and then the manager would change his or her mind and go in a different direction or introduce a new topic to them that he or she had just thought up over the weekend while they were away or they had just heard of.

More importantly, I was hearing that there was no common direction for what they were trying to achieve and that they were each working almost independently on the directive of their boss.

Now, their bosses were all engineers. They were brilliant people, but for the most part, they had never been instructed in how to manage and steer work. But there's no doubt about it that they truly are smart. Cummins has some of the smartest engineering people you've ever met. The difficulty was that this creates a situation, sometimes, where people just like to do their own thing. The folks down inside the organization feel a sense of being jerked around in this kind of environment.

Another thing that was wrong has to do with the old saying, "What is measured is what gets done." For example, the engineering leader was measured primarily on achieving the annual financial budget. Now, inside that financial budget was a whole series of projects and programs that other departments, particularly manufacturing and marketing, had requested from engineering. As we moved through the year to October and November, in order to achieve their budgets, the engineering guys would stop working on things because it would negatively affect their financial performance. When I would ask why the work wasn't done, the answer often was because they didn't have the money to do it. To me, this translated to being told, "I'm not measured by the achievement of the project; I'm measured by my financial spending."

When a system like that has been in operation for many years and along comes a new program that basically says, "Now we're going to operate on a project basis using Six Sigma, because this thing is great for engineering work when you consider that you have to identify the need, identify the opportunity and so forth." All of a sudden, Six Sigma introduced the concept of a goal tree that focused everyone on projects that contributed to an overall set of business objectives instead of just the financial measurements. Now they had a formal way to set up a project and to measure it that was in alignment with the objectives of the corporation.

COULD ANY OTHER GOOD GENERAL PROJECT AND PORTFOLIO MANAGEMENT SYSTEM HAVE WORKED AS WELL AS SIX SIGMA?

What we're saying here about Six Sigma could be any program that's put in place that has a decent set of metrics, common approaches, and all the rest. What's most important is that you keep doing it year after year after year after year, like the Japanese have done with their production systems, making it better and better and better. Don't keep changing it. I don't care what system you put in place that's just basically a set of metrics and goals and objectives and a methodology—so long as you stay with it over and over again, you will get better. Historically, our problem was that every change of leadership was a change in direction.

Another big surprise that happened in Engineering was not just the fact that it introduced a whole different approach to project management, but it achieved great results, many of which could not be recognized. One particular example made a huge difference to Cummins.

I can't say a lot about it, but we had a "secret" project that provided a solution that was introduced across an entire product line to improve our emissions. The solution reduced the cost per engine significantly over the alternative approach that had been approved. It was an enormous change. The team worked over Christmas and through the new year and came out with a new design to meet the next emission change. It saved both the company and our customers an awful lot of money. However, because it was leading-edge technology and because the competition could copy it if they knew what we were doing, it was never publicized. I think it was one of the key elements of the financial improvement of Cummins. That one project saved an incredible amount of real dollars.

We would never have thought of the solution if it were not for Six Sigma. We wouldn't have even conceived of the possibility of a home run without somebody saying, "Well, you know, here's a real project that if we could do it would just be absolutely enormous." And so, we did it. It was the least recognized project we ever did for obvious reasons that we just didn't want anybody else to know about it. But like I said, I think it was the beginning of the beginning of Cummins becoming a profitable company.

Another surprise centered on the people of Cummins. Over the years, Cummins has hired people from all walks of life and is an absolute believer in diversity and in education. The consequence of that is we had amazingly talented people. I would put the IQ level of the people of Cummins up against any company. Six Sigma unleashed many of these people to show what they could do. Sometimes I was just amazed how good the projects were and how quickly they were being done. I don't know if it's unique to Cummins, but I certainly know we had a great group of people throughout the whole company, particularly at the individual contributor level, in every function and business. They had been chosen for being smart people, and they were being given the chance to demonstrate what they could do. Six Sigma gave these talented people the opportunity to visibly contribute to the company's success.

When we decided to implement Six Sigma, we did not have any idea what it was going to do. We knew the promise it held for the company's financials but not what it was going to do for people. We knew that the people in Cummins were pretty smart. I think the delight was that so many of them were willing to get involved in the program, and as a consequence they achieved some quick results over other things we had tried. I don't know how we would rate it against other companies, but the rate of success of the projects was really very good.

The people who took on the role of the Black Belt, in general, were extremely good people. But it wasn't just at that level. It was throughout the company. It's just smart people being released to do things, and empowered to do it, and feeling that they had the imprimatur of the CEO to do things because it was part of his program. It's an old cliché, but once the CEO is highly engaged and committed to an initiative, it opens up an awful lot of doors to people.

I think we saw this right from the very first group of Black Belts. Because even in the first year or two, we were implementing significant numbers of projects compared to what I expected. I would say it showed up early in the program.

WHAT WERE THE MAJOR IMPACTS ON YOU PERSONALLY?

It's a good question, and it's very hard to really summarize how it impacted me personally. Remember, in 1999 I was quite happy continuing to develop the midrange engine business. So, my comparison is versus running the midrange business. I see Six Sigma as probably one of the high spots of things that I've done. I think it enabled me to apply an awful lot of things that I didn't know I'd learned about people's behaviors, corporate initiatives, and these kinds of programs and do it successfully. It's also special to me because there aren't that many examples of successful corporate initiatives that I've run into.

Another aspect of Six Sigma that makes it special to me is that it was a team effort. We had a small implementation team. People who were really committed to making it work. It was a success in that regard, and it went on to be even a greater success after I left it. It was even more rewarding to see that when I left the program, Six Sigma didn't drop off. The ultimate insult and a reinforcement of the corporate program-of-the-month culture that I had been used to would have been that when the person leading it left—me—the program stopped. In this case, I left and the program just kept going.

I left the Six Sigma role in 2002. I was given the heavy-duty engine business, which had been unprofitable for a very long time at that point.

WHAT ARE YOUR RECOMMENDATIONS FOR A COMPANY THAT'S THINKING ABOUT SIX SIGMA? WHAT ARE THE MOST IMPORTANT THINGS FOR THEM TO DO?

We have talked about it a bit, and in fact, I think we've covered some of it in this conversation already. Clearly, without the engagement of the senior leader, it won't work. I don't know whether it's the CEO in every case. In our case, it was the CEO. But it has to be the leader of the company or the division or whatever. It must be the person who has the power of decision-making, the person who believes it's their program. And not just the person who believes it, but accepts that it's their program to lead and that they demonstrate not only leadership but consistent and constant leadership. It's not about having a big launch and popping all the balloons and then go away to let other people make it happen.

The leader has to be engaged in it all the time. It's got to be a priority. But for it to be a priority, it has to be an initiative that is so significant to the success of the business that you can afford to devote your time and effort to it. In the case of Cummins, we had been losing money, and Tim was determined to turn the profitability of the company around and believed that the Six Sigma initiative was going to give him the profitability improvement that he needed. It's not just the CEO getting involved, but getting involved in a program or an effort that is absolutely consequential to the success of the company. That's rule number one.

Rule number two is having people implement it who know the company. It's important. It can't be the experts or consultants. It can't be people who are going to fly in, drop a report and leave. You've got to have people who know what they're going to face in terms of internal challenges and are willing to put their efforts into doing it because they also believe that it is an extremely consequential effort.

Those are the two main things to do. But I think you can't necessarily replicate experiences; I base it on the variety of experiences I've had with people and companies. I talked about my experience with General Electric. It was just one company, but I was in five different businesses of GE in multiple countries with multiple nationalities and culture. This gave me some appreciation for what makes people tick.

As you remember, I was educated as an engineer. The great thing about an engineering education is that you know a little bit about all sorts of things. I quickly moved into manufacturing where I was able to work with lots of people. The key to Six Sigma was, I think, understanding what motivates people. Understanding what motivates people is one of the things that causes programs to succeed or fail. If you understand those mechanisms, you can think through a structure that helps support the implementation.

I think there was a lot of value having a background working in a diverse set of businesses over time and seeing enough failures in my career to have an understanding of what it looks like and then putting a team in place that's very clever, good at what they do, and are committed to make it work.

We also had our own goals. We didn't just apply the goals to those doing the projects, but we set objectives for the Six Sigma team for how much we wanted to achieve and by when we wanted to achieve it. We set ourselves objectives of achievement, which made sense because if we were going to apply measurements to everyone else, we should have them too. We hit or beat every one of those yearly and quarterly objectives during our implementation.

Another thing that shocked some people, was that we found that some of the Black Belts were very young people, bright but young people. We gave them responsibilities that I'm not sure they would not have gotten any other way and found out that they were highly successful. It drove a lot of careers after Six Sigma. I've seen some of the people who are popping up in senior roles at Cummins and recognize them as kids that started off in Six Sigma. There was a whole series of projects that we entrusted to younger people, so it gave them a much quicker shot at demonstrating their capabilities than they might have otherwise had.

I think another thing that we were mindful of, and that SBTI warned us about, is that during the first six to nine months very little improvement shows up. It's important to stay vigilant so that people don't say, "You see, it failed," because by its nature, it takes time to implement projects. You have to stick with implementing the processes and procedures first while the projects are in process. During the first six or nine months, you've got to be very vigilant about being out there, talking positively to key people at a time when everybody's willing to say, "See, it failed."

WHEN DID YOU GET A SENSE THAT THE PROGRAM HAD SHIFTED FROM RAMP UP OR IMPLEMENTATION INTO MORE OF A STEADY STATE? OR DID IT EVER GIVE THAT FEELING?

It's an interesting question because, I think, that was basically what decided the timing for me to move to heavy-duty. The assignment of heavy-duty was thrust upon me to think about. I felt at that time that Six Sigma was in good hands. It was not necessarily routine, but we had a set of processes that were working, and George was it driving it well. The other thing that mattered was that George is one of those guys who is from corporate and people actually believed that he was there to help. That made the decision for him to take the leadership of Six Sigma over and keep it running easy. It would have been a lot more difficult to move to heavy-duty if I felt that there was nobody capable of continuing to lead it at the same pace that it was running. I felt it was performing well enough that I could go at that time, which was two years after the start.

HOW DID YOU KEEP THE ENTHUSIASM UP DURING THE LAG BETWEEN STARTING SIX SIGMA AND BEGINNING TO SEE RESULTS?

That required an awful lot of talking. We held a lot of meetings and a lot of discussions telling people to keep their enthusiasm going. Of course, we had a lot of training going on at the same time, so we were busy doing the hard work of training while the projects were yet to come to fruition at that stage. But yes, you have to keep everybody enthused enough to begin seeing the first results.

But there is another interesting thing about how this works. I mentioned it earlier and said I would come back to it. After I left Cummins, I did some work with a Chinese company and they reminded me of some of the failures I had seen before. At first, I went to just talk to them, and they said they had implemented Six Sigma. And I said, "That's terrific. Can you walk me through it?" Well, the very first thing they said was that they did it because everybody else was doing it, which of course was the wrong reason. Then they went on to tell me that they had decided they didn't need three weeks' worth of training. That was a waste of time. They were doing the training in three days. And they had trained 50,000 employees. Anyway, I think this is a shortcoming of management globally. Management tends to believe that if it takes three weeks to do it, we can do it in a week. It's like the only value-added criteria many managers seem to apply is, "If you tell me I'm going to need 100,000 to do this job. Great! I'll do it for 80,000." That's their snap decision in many cases, instead of understanding what it takes and understanding what really needs to be done.

It was interesting. That was the classic case of, "I'm doing it because everybody's doing it. We don't have great results, and I've trained thousands and thousands of people, but I didn't waste my time with three weeks of training." And what were the results? They showed me the results and they were pathetic. But all they were doing was touching the base. They weren't committed to it. They didn't really think it was going to have a big, significant impact on their business anyway. And the CEO didn't even understand what it was, so I'm not saying that was because they were Chinese. My guess is a lot of companies around the world, including the US, operate like they know enough to make these sweeping decisions to change this and cut that without listening to the pros who've done it.

And yes, it takes more effort to do three weeks of training than it does three days of training, but if you get the results, it's certainly worth it.

ARE THERE ONE, TWO OR THREE THINGS THAT YOU MIGHT HAVE DONE DIFFERENTLY PRIOR TO THE 2000 START-UP OF SIX SIGMA?

I suppose it's always good to know a little bit about what you're getting into before you actually do it. Having said that, Six Sigma is not exactly a complicated program or process, at least the DMAIC part's not. But again, it would have been nice to know a little bit more about it. When I was given the quality job, it included all aspects of Corporate Quality like quality systems, corporate safety, all those kinds of things. But clearly, Tim wanted me to focus on Six Sigma implementation. It was complicated by the fact that I had no idea what Six Sigma was. It didn't matter. It could have been ABC. As far as I was concerned, any corporate initiative was destined to have problems at Cummins. This is a generic issue rather than specific to Six Sigma. From there it was a matter of, okay, we're in, now what do we do to get this thing rolling?

In retrospect, thinking about the way we did it versus how we could have done it better, the thing I learned about implementation was you really are dealt a hand. You've got to play the hand as you get it, and in this particular case, I made a lot of mistakes in this one. There were people that I read that I thought would support me who didn't. In fact, that made it difficult for personal reasons. And there were people who I thought would be difficult who turned out to be very helpful. But what you learn from that is you're going to get dealt a hand when you start.

A friend of mine used to say something which I believe is important: "It's amazing how much you can get done if you don't care who gets the credit." If you're happy to allow other people to take credit for what you did, it's amazing how much faster things move along. The danger when you're implementing a project like this is that you're the one who's claiming credit saying, "I did this. I did that." I was very conscious about not taking credit for any of the successes of the Six Sigma program. But there are a lot of people who we gave credit to who, quite frankly, we did only to motivate them.

So again, that to me is more of a learning or understanding of people, but if the program leader isn't willing to take a back seat and give all the credit to everyone else, then they become a problem for the program because they model the attitude, "Why would I do this so you can get credit? Why would I do that so you can be promoted over me?" You've got to accept the fact that you are likely not going to go any further in your career. And I did, by the way, go into the role accepting that this was going to be the end of my career. The heavy-duty thing was a separate, unusual, last gasp by the company because they were doing so badly in that business. But I accepted that I was going to be leaving the company the day I finished Six Sigma, so that made it easier for me. I wasn't going to compete with anybody for anything, and I was able to, as I say, allow other people to shine, which they did.

I think this requires having a special relationship with the CEO. Whether it's retirement or promotion or whatever, I think there has to be some agreement before you start because, for me, a promotion would have worked just as well if that was what I was interested in because you know that, regardless of what happens, there's an outcome that's already preordained. It acknowledges that making a change of this sort is incredibly hard and fails more often than it succeeds.

There's a tendency, particularly in the US, to want to shine and show that you're better than your peers and that you achieve more or whatever, and so to tell people that it's important to let other people take the credit is a tough sell. I believe this is an important element of success.

Then the dilemma is how to keep it going. We had a great ride with Six Sigma because Tim was in that role for ten years. The whole notion of consistency and constancy is missing when you start chopping and changing people. Because Six Sigma is such a flexible process, you can wrap it around anything. All that you're doing is saying our initiatives or objectives may change, but you can use the same powerful tools regardless. However, there's a tendency with CEOs to want to stake out their territory in the company so that they can be seen to be successful because of initiatives which they started. There doesn't seem to be a lot of credit given to guys who continue somebody else's initiative. That's a pity.

7

S-Curve 1—Pre-launch

Pre-launch comprised activities needed to plan and manage Cummins' initial Six Sigma program deployment, and included all decisions and actions taken prior to the first training launches held in January 2000. This chapter describes Cummins' activities (also summarized in Table 7.1) in those early days (for more generalized discussion of early deployment, see Stephen A. Zinkgraf's *Six Sigma The First 90 Days*).

TABLE 7.1

Pre-launch S-Curve

• Decision to pursue
• CEO sponsorship (what will the CEO do?)
• Credible senior leadership reporting to CEO
• A clear objective—$$$ within X years
• A clear strategy for implementation
o Belt types and reward and recognition
o Training approach
o Role and size of Corp Six Sigma staff
o Accountabilities (Corp vs Business)
o Expectations and performance review process
• Outside direction/expertise hired—buying consultant's knowledge
• Form a small steering committee
o A communication plan developed
o Establishment of a Six Sigma leadership group representing the businesses
o BB candidate reviews and placement
o Project collection/tracking mechanism established

CEO DECISION TO COMMIT—THE COMPANY AND HIMSELF

CEO Tim Solso made the decision to implement an enterprise-wide Six Sigma program, and to personally commit himself to be its executive sponsor. Solso's sponsorship was active and sustained, lasting over ten years (to his retirement in 2011). Table 7.2 presents some of the general roles and specific activities Solso undertook as program executive sponsor.

PROGRAM SENIOR LEADER

A credible senior business leader, Frank McDonald, was selected by the CEO to serve as the Six Sigma program leader, holding the newly created role and title of corporate Vice President of Quality. McDonald was accountable for the Six Sigma deployment and reported directly to CEO Solso.

McDonald led a critical product business unit (Midrange Engines) at the time and had earned a strong reputation in the company for results. Coming

TABLE 7.2

Executive Sponsor Roles and Activities

- Ongoing engagement with key senior leaders in the company to explain why Six Sigma was important to the long-term future of Cummins.
- Attending the first Green Belt training launch as a Belt trainee with a project to complete.
- Meeting with a Cummins Master Black Belt monthly to learn Six Sigma processes and tools.
- Reviewing early projects to see Six Sigma applications and how Six Sigma generates improvements and cost savings.
- Reserving time on his schedule when visiting company sites around the world to talk with local Black Belts and Master Black Belts how things are going with Six Sigma and to understand whether Six Sigma was really being used and making a difference.
- Reviewing Six Sigma program progress and performance measures, and two successful projects, each month during the Cummins executive leadership meeting. These reviews continued monthly for eight years.
- Reporting on Six Sigma program progress and results in each year's Cummins annual report.
- Reporting to the Board of Directors how Six Sigma was making a difference at Cummins. This included review of select projects.
- Launching the annual Chairman's Quality Award and showcase to recognize the best of the best projects and teams across all of Cummins each year.

from a product business unit rather than a corporate function, McDonald was not typical corporate staff—a key factor in deployment success. McDonald having taken the position signaled, especially to plant managers and other operations leaders, that the Six Sigma initiative was real, worthy of their time and attention, and not just some program-of-the-month.

SELECTED DEPLOYMENT CONSULTANT

Sigma Breakthrough Technologies, Inc. (SBTI), a consultancy with a proven track record and strong references, was selected by Tim Solso to be Cummins' Six Sigma program deployment partner. Solso made this decision based on his discussions with CEOs of similarly large firms and feedback from GE. Selecting SBTI as deployment consultant provided credibility and confidence with Cummins' personnel who, in searching the internet, found SBTI's history of successful engagements with prominent global companies.

SBTI, in the late 1990s, worked with the mayor's office of the city of Fort Wayne, Indiana. A Cummins group visited an SBTI-conducted Six Sigma training session there. This was as a form of interview of the lead SBTI consultant (the SBTI individual serving as the Cummins' account leader) and was important in giving confidence that SBTI could provide support consistent with Cummins' culture and needs.

In early 2000, as part of an annual Cummins Plant Managers Conference, plant managers visited GE's Appliance Park in Louisville, Kentucky. This extensive facility comprised five large manufacturing plants producing diverse "white goods" home appliances including washing machines and dishwashers. Cummins personnel met with GE plant leadership teams, Six Sigma Belts, and shop-floor assembly personnel, reviewed Six Sigma projects, and talked with other leaders at the site. This visit convinced Cummins' plant managers that Six Sigma could work at Cummins.

DETERMINE PROGRAM DEPLOYMENT STRATEGY

Cummins worked with SBTI to develop a deployment strategy for the Six Sigma program. First, SBTI and Cummins agreed contractually that SBTI would be responsible to conduct training for two years and to prepare Cummins' personnel to accept the hand-off of responsibility. At the end of the two-year period, Cummins would assume ownership for all facets of the deployment. This created a significant internal incentive to develop company capability to support the Six Sigma program over the longer term.

Cummins' Six Sigma leadership worked with SBTI consultants to plan training launches, review training materials and understand and clarify Six Sigma terminology. Here it was decided to change "Six Sigma Project Champion," a general term used by SBTI in their training and program materials, to "Six Sigma Project Sponsor," a term and role more familiar to Cummins people. This smallness of the terminological modifications was important. Cummins had purchased the consultant's knowledge, and contrary to industry standard practice, did not try to "Cummins-ize" it. This eliminated multiple cycles of adaptation and review of training material, exercises and tests, and the inevitable other responsibilities which arise when an organization creates its own program language, procedures and training material. This way Cummins could move more quickly and with fewer administrative distractions.

Six Sigma leadership overview training workshops, each three days long, were held with business unit leadership teams (150 personnel in all) in the US and UK. One separate workshop was held for the CEO and his direct staff.

Selection of the first Black Belts began in 1999. Three Black Belt training launches (two in the US and one in the UK) for a cohort of 68 Black Belts began the first week in January 2000. Black Belt candidates were nominated by their business units. Only those with a "1" performance rating (high performers) in the prior two years were accepted into Black Belt candidacy. The Corporate Vice President of Quality, Frank McDonald, reviewed nominee performance records and had final say on acceptances into the first training launch. Business units were told they could not "backfill" the position vacated by a Black Belt candidate with a new hire from outside the company. Leadership of the respective business units had to determine and accommodate reallocation of that person's work without adding to total company headcount.

Next was identification of improvement problems or opportunities that Black Belts would work on (a real-life project) during their training. Training was purposefully project-centric, employing a learning-by-doing approach. A Belt's mandatory ticket of entry to the first training session was a completed project charter. No charter, no training. At that time there was no organization-wide project selection process. Often, projects identified were local area "problems of the moment" identified by respective business leaders rather than those having direct bearing on external customer satisfaction or congruence with company strategy. This early mistake in the project selection process would be corrected later.

STEERING COMMITTEE FOR PROGRAM GOVERNANCE AND FUTURE-STATE VISION DEVELOPMENT

A session was held with a small steering committee, led by Frank McDonald, to define Six Sigma program governance and specify the future state. The Six Sigma program future state was discussed earlier.

This group decided Cummins needed a company unique Six Sigma logo (Figure 7.1). This corporate Six Sigma logo was used in Six Sigma training materials, company communications, recognition items, note pads and other ways. The logo was controlled by the Corporate Quality Six Sigma staff and could be used only in ways approved by that office. This logo branding helped to retain and enhance an aura of specialness and value.

FIGURE 7.1 Cummins Six Sigma logo.

The steering committee also developed the initial Six Sigma program governance, standards, operational definitions and project criteria for Belts. This group stipulated that Belt candidates would only be permitted into training with an approved project charter. They also specified that annual performance evaluations for Master Black Belts and Black Belts were to be based solely on their full-time Six Sigma roles. The term "Belt Cadre" was introduced representing the population of all active Master Black Belts, Black Belts and Green Belts. Operational definitions were defined for all Belt types.

The group determined that Black Belt assignments would be for two years' duration (give or take six months), and not longer. This stipulation was put in place to prevent establishment of permanent, "professional" Black Belts. Rather, the aim was to develop business people having strong problem-solving and improvement skills which they could apply in subsequent business unit positions to make better, data-informed business decisions. This would not be possible if Belts remained too long in the Six Sigma program. The Black Belt assignment was purposefully a means of personnel development, to create better business people (rather than great Six Sigma people). This was a very important decision!

This group recommended that Black Belts would receive a 5% raise upon accepting the Black Belt position and an annual 10% bonus for project completions (later changed to 3% of base salary for each project completed, capped at seven projects per year). This annual bonus was on top of any bonuses they might receive from their respective business unit. The purpose of these incentives was to recognize that the Black Belts were accepting a career risk. The risk was that after a two-year assignment outside of their function, they would have a job to go back to. This was something that the company had never done before, and there was no evidence that we could do it successfully.

Master Black Belts would receive a 10% base salary raise upon completion of the six-month Master Black Belt in Training (MBBIT) period. This base salary increase was to compensate, in part, for loss of Black Belt income (from project completions, which are not attributed to Master Black Belts).

The group decided each active project should receive mandatory Master Black Belt review and coaching at least once per month, both to ensure projects were done correctly and to help Master Black Belts gain experience applying Six Sigma to diverse improvement areas.

The group decided that cost "avoidance" savings would not count toward Six Sigma savings targets. Rather, only bottom-line improvements in earnings before interest and taxes (EBIT) would count. The main reason for this, as discussed in the Tim Solso interview, was that the company needed cash, so we emphasized real bottom-line impact. An additional reason is that avoidance savings are not real and can be anything one wants them to be. This decision helped to reduce game playing and savings fiction.

ASCERTAIN INITIAL PROGRAM SAVINGS TARGET

An initial three-year project savings target of $200 million was set. This target was set by Frank McDonald in consultation with Tim Solso. The target was calculated based on the number of Black Belts the company would have, how many projects they were expected to complete, and the expected annualized value of the completed projects. This seemed outlandish at the time. However, the target was achieved in the first 30 months.

CORPORATE VS. LOCAL SIX SIGMA RESPONSIBILITY

This group made a highly strategic recommendation regarding the Corporate Six Sigma program office staffing (which proved critical to program success and sustainment). A problem observed, in Cummins and other companies, was the growth of large corporate staff groups to lead change efforts, in turn resulting in lack of ownership at the local level. Too often, a "corporate is here to help" cynicism would arise. To counter this possibility, Cummins purposefully decided the Six Sigma corporate staff would remain small, helping ensure Six Sigma program office focus and action on the truly highest priorities. In deciding this, role differences of the corporate Six Sigma office vs. local business units were specified.

The corporate Six Sigma program office would be responsible for consultant coordination and payment, rules and measures, training schedules and material, approval of Black Belt bonuses and upholding the Six Sigma Standards. In contrast, local business units and their leadership would be responsible for all Six Sigma project execution, including project selection, Belt selection, project closure and determination of results. This was decided because it is in the business units where the work of the company is done, and where ultimate accountability for Six Sigma project success should reside. This stipulation also aimed to ensure projects were selected and undertaken to meet specific, real business and customer needs rather than simply a "project for project's sake" or corporate approval.

ORGANIZATION COMMUNICATION STRATEGY

A communications strategy, an important part of the overall deployment strategy, was developed. There was to be no broad organizational roll-out to announce the new Six Sigma initiative. Rather, Cummins people would in time learn about Six Sigma by participating in projects, and from Belts, Project Sponsors, and project team members working on, or having completed, a Six Sigma project.

Cummins purposely adopted this "do and tell" communication approach rather than the more typical "tell and do" approach, where a new initiative is announced with great fanfare. It had been observed that "tell and do" approaches can trigger initial skepticism among company personnel. It could also potentially heighten cynicism and damage to the organizational culture should realized program results not live up to expectations. Cummins did communicate, upon completion of the initial wave of projects, results informing the broader organization what had been done and that more was to come. This communication took different forms. One of the main approaches was the Chairman's quarterly message, in which Tim Solso talked about Six Sigma and introduced different completed projects.

ESTABLISHMENT OF BUSINESS UNIT
"QUALITY CHAMPION" ROLE

A Six Sigma program leadership group representing the business units was established made up of "Quality Champions," a newly created position and role for management of Six Sigma activity in each business unit. Quality Champions were employees of and reported to business unit leadership and had a dotted line relationship to Corporate Quality. Quality Champions were responsible for assuring that local leadership followed established requirements for project chartering, Belt selection for training and specific projects, and performance tracking. Quality Champions also worked with each other to share best practices and provide cross-organization support when needed. As Six Sigma matured, the Quality Champion role expanded to include all aspects of business quality.

BELT RECOGNITION AND REWARDS

Cummins put in place various recognitions and rewards for Belts. These took diverse forms:

- Monetary bonus given to Black Belts for project completion.
- Certificate of recognition, signed by the CEO and the corporate Vice President of Quality, given to Belts upon completion of training ("graduation").
- Embroidered-logo golf shirts given to graduating Belts (with a black bar under the Cummins Six Sigma logo for Black Belts, green bar for Green Belts, no bars for Project Sponsors, and sometime later, two black bars for Master Black Belts).

CREATE ELECTRONIC DATABASE SYSTEM

A basic database system was created to enable project tracking and enhance organizational learning. This database permitted others to reference both completed and current (underway) projects and to identify potential best practices to share. The database made it possible for Master Black Belt and Project Sponsor project reviews to be conducted remotely—a critical requirement in a globally distributed company like Cummins. The database changed over time as new requirements for data and tracking were identified.

Due to the early state of the internet in 1999, Cummins searched for but found no workable off-the-shelf database system products meeting our needs, and so we decided to develop an in-house database system. The original Six Sigma program database captured only DMAIC-type projects. It was built on a Lotus Notes platform and was searchable by current projects ("Active") and completed projects ("History").

The database system supported an editable work area used by Belts working on an active project. The database was organized in D-M-A-I-C sections, and stored any project information, data and documents submitted to it. Team members could add items to the project file. MBBs could refer to the project file during project reviews. The system also prompted during-project charter and contract approval cycles and required end-of-project signoffs (before a project could officially "close").

Eventually, the completed projects portion of the database, or History, was generally open to anyone who had a Cummins Notes account. Belts used it in seeking projects and lessons learned which might help them with a current project.

"Hopper" functionality was later added to the database for collecting, storing and prioritizing ideas for potential projects (nascent project charters) to aid in future project selection and chartering. Any business unit, function or sub-unit, regardless of size, could devise in the database a Hopper specific to their area.

Later, when the Six Sigma program expanded to include Design for Six Sigma (DFSS) and Technology Development for Six Sigma (TDFSS) projects, the database system was expanded to incorporate these new project types, each having their own (non-DMAIC) project-process phases and requirements.

REFLECTIONS ON THE PRE-LAUNCH S-CURVE

The Pre-launch S-Curve concluded in December 1999, with first training launches beginning on-site at Cummins in January 2000 (S-Curve 2, First Projects).

The first group of Project Sponsors received an overview of Six Sigma in November 1999, two months before the first Belt training launch. This overview included a project charter-writing workshop where Project Sponsors completed, and received feedback from the SBTI MBBs on, their first charters.

In December 1999, all Black Belt candidates attended an "M-0 Week" workshop to receive an overview of Six Sigma and their upcoming training. Each Black Belt's project charter was reviewed, and modified as necessary, during this week.

For Six Sigma to be used across the entire company, it was important during Pre-launch itself to broaden understanding of what projects could be done, not solely in manufacturing areas (most common, narrow application of Six Sigma), but also other functions including finance, human resources, marketing and sales, customer and field service, research and development, and purchasing and supply chain. All company products and services derive from interactions among these diverse business functions (as well as their respective underlying and intertwined work processes), thus every single business function, regardless of type, was ripe for improvement.

Pre-launch was critical in starting development of a global language of continuous improvement. In time, the enterprise-wide common language enabled functions, in all business units and geographies, to work together to make improvements and solve difficult business problems.

Following the end of the Pre-launch S-Curve, the first training launches involved Belt candidates from every region of the world, and most key business units and several business functions. Having a broadly inclusive approach to Six Sigma project selection, team composition and carry-through sent a strong message from Cummins' leadership that Six Sigma was indeed a company-wide effort with no exceptions.

Projects conducted in the First Projects S-Curve were more traditional ones, where considerable data was readily available, and reliable data collection systems already established, allowing application of quantitative data analysis and statistical tools common to traditional Six Sigma. Many projects leveraged easily quantified measures of time, throughput, defects and scrap. Table 7.3 lists application areas of projects undertaken by the first waves of training-launch Belt graduates. We will discuss this more in the First Projects S-Curve Chapter.

TABLE 7.3

Typical Project Charters Developed in the Pre-launch S-Curve

Improve . . .	Reduce . . .
- Computer mainframe utilization	- Payroll processing errors
- US vehicle registration accuracy	- Financial close and consolidation cycle-times
- Emissions-testing capability	times
- Plant test-cell throughput	- Design print non-conformances
- Line 15 engine build complete	- Major OEM customer volume-delivery
- Plant bill-of-materials accuracy	lead-times
- Plant engine test and repair processes	- Engine-build cycle-time variances
- Distribution center picking and packing accuracy	- Engine assembly materials shortages
- Aftermarket outbound freight productivity	- Control-panel field failures
- Engine assembly and test cycle times	

8

S-Curve 2—Launch and First Projects

The second S-Curve of the Six Sigma effort began with the first training launches in January 2000. The work of the second S-Curve is focused on execution; examples include conduct of projects, project reviews, project savings. The steps are detailed below.

First, the company began training. At Cummins, this meant two launches in the US and one in the UK consisting of 68 Black Belts with projects.

Governing rules and guidelines were established for how we would conduct day-to-day Six Sigma.

The first of these rules was that training was attended only by those Belts who had a project charter. This meant that people couldn't just sit in on

TABLE 8.1

Launch and First Projects Actions

- Establish and publish governing rules/guidelines, for example
  - o Training only attended by those with projects
  - o Project criteria (be careful!)—examples:
    - $$$ for BBs
    - $$$ for GBs
    - Cycle time target for projects
  - o Position Profiles/Roles and Responsibilities – BB/GB/MBB/Quality Leader
  - o Sponsors held accountable for project failures (not terminations)
  - o Local controllers verify savings
- Develop and train a project selection process for leaders (JIT)
- Define a project chartering process
- Define project close out and control plan audit processes
- Begin first training launch
- Selection of first MBB's – selected for technical and training skills, work with the consultants (decide how long this assignment will be; different from the regular MBB cadre)

training to see what it was all about. This rule instituted a new level of discipline for this type of work.

SBTI recommended that we establish minimum cost savings and timelines for projects. We decided that all projects should be completed within 180 days. A Black Belt project should yield $250,000 in savings and a Green Belt project $100,000. However, this criterion came with unintended consequences. As it played out, it proved the old saying that "what gets measured gets done." Time and again, people behaved based on the target. For example, projects were terminated because they did not meet the savings criteria even though they were important to the business, because people saw the savings criteria as a hard-and-fast rule. Similarly, by establishing 180 days as the time target, some important problems were not addressed using Six Sigma because it was felt it would take too long.

The message here is, be cautious when establishing targets and criteria because they can take on a life of their own and become something that was never intended. The 180-day cycle time for projects is a cautionary tale. The 180-day project cycle time was established initially to recognize the fact that the training itself took five months. We added a month for project completion, resulting in 180 days. This was never intended to be a "target". The target was always to complete projects as fast as required for the business, and we expected Belts to become more efficient with repetition. However, once a perceived target is established, it is difficult to change, and people will work to meet the target. The 180-day time frame became such a target. Some projects weren't launched in the early days of Six Sigma because the leadership couldn't wait that long for a result. Another behavior we observed was that Belts would delay "starting the clock" on a project as long as possible to make sure that they could close their project within the 180-day window. People do crazy things when they believe they are being measured against a target.

In actuality, the time it takes to complete a project is a function of management will and direction. If the project is important, management will allocate the people, time and money necessary to complete quickly. Leadership will also review progress of important projects to make corrections and provide needed support in time to help effectively.

It is better is to see target setting as a driver for desired behavior. For Six Sigma, those organizational behaviors are focusing on customer perceived quality issues, more people doing important improvement work, reducing business operating costs as a percentage of sales, and projects completed as fast as necessary. Representing these measures as trends over time is the best way to communicate them.

Setting targets incorrectly always comes with unintended behavioral consequences. *It is important to proceed with caution!*

Other rules and guidelines that we established included:

- Position profiles were developed describing the roles and responsibilities of the Sponsor, Black Belts, Green Belts, Master Black Belts and Quality Champions.
- The set of Six Sigma standards was published describing all of the governing rules and guidelines (included in the Appendices).
- We created the guideline that if the project failed it was the sponsor's responsibility and if the project was successful the Belt got the credit. This gave the sponsor personal motivation for ensuring project success.
- Lastly, it was a requirement that a finance person sign off on every project closure. This helped to ensure the project savings were credible.

We developed a project selection process and trained leaders across the business. This was an area not well understood prior to our Six Sigma training launches. This became a problem relatively early in the first year because it became increasingly difficult to find good problems to solve with simple brainstorming. Our lack of understanding of the importance of project selection created a brainstorming-based inertia for project selection that was difficult to break once established. Having a clear, well-defined project selection process is an important requirement prior to starting Six Sigma training. This can be introduced to key leadership teams during executive and sponsor training held during the Pre-launch S-Curve.

The project chartering process was defined. The chartering process included:

- Black or Green Belt assigned—more complex projects are assigned to Black Belts. Green Belts work on projects within the boundaries of their assigned work.
- Project scoping—identifying the project boundaries. Often this means the starting and stopping points of the process which is the focus of the improvement.

- Project entitlement—defining the "best it can be" result if the process was operating perfectly.
- Project value—the worth of the project improvement in dollars following improvement.
- Sponsor identification—the project sponsor is accountable for output of the process identified for improvement.
- Team selection—a team of five to seven people is created from people who work in and are most knowledgeable of the process.
- Required approvals—finance representative, the sponsor, the MBB and the process owner are the minimum approvers of the project.
- Identification of the process owner whenever possible—the process owner is responsible for implementing improvements. The sponsor and process owner are often the same person.
- Time-based project schedule—a schedule of completion for each phase, D-M-A-I-C, of the project.

It became clear early during implementation that the charter was management's best guess regarding savings value of the project and even sometimes the definition of the project itself. This meant that during the measure and analyze phases of Six Sigma, changes to the charter would likely occur as more and more was learned about a specific problem or improvement. Therefore, the sponsor and Belt were not committed to the problem definition and savings target until the project charter became a contract following the analyze phase.

Early in the first year of the second S-Curve, the first Master Black Belts were selected. These were people with strong math backgrounds and teaching experience. Their job was to attend all training and document how training was being delivered, how the training flowed, examples used, and how the instructors communicated complex subjects.

S-CURVE 2 EXAMPLE PROJECTS

Each S-Curve introduces new project types. Following each S-Curve discussion, the reader will find some example projects with a short description of each.

S-Curve 2 is the beginning of deployment. Therefore, the projects tend to be more traditional. I have called these projects "scrap on line five" type projects because these projects tend to have lots of data, a clearly definable Y variable, a measurement system, and other characteristics that allow for the use of the statistics of Six Sigma. Additionally, the calculation of savings tends to be relatively straightforward, giving management a clear sense of the payback to the business for the investment of time, money and resources required for a Six Sigma deployment.

What follows are some examples of the projects typical of S-Curve 2 maturity.

Increase production from 13,284 to 14,097 on the filter assembly line— Through the improvements made, setup time was decreased in the pleating operation by 50%. Improvements were also made to the seaming operation, resulting in decreased downtime and increased output. As a result of these improvements Output/LN-Shift increased from a baseline of 13,284 to 14,800.

Reduce scrap on the cylinder head line from 28,000 parts per million (PPM) to 1,500 PPM— This project worked with the foundry to reduce porosity of the injector bores in the head castings. The improvements made resulted in a 95% improvement in scrap for the plant.

Reduce camshaft galling experienced by customers using the product in the field— This project changed the camshaft surface finish to improve lubrication characteristics, eliminating field failures. This project also improved maintenance practices performed by the service centers.

9

Preparing for the Next S-Curve—Cross-Curve Analysis

A Summary

In the following discussion and others following S-Curve descriptions, the reader will find actions taken to prepare for S-Curve transition. The goal in each of these cross-curve analysis sections is to discuss how the company prepared for and encouraged system maturity as the company's understanding of Six Sigma grew.

The difficulty in explaining Six Sigma at Cummins in a book is that maturity is not linear. The company is a system. What this means is that events/changes don't happen in isolation. Change in one part of the system can have effects on other parts of the system. However, people tend to see only what's in their immediate view—those things that are happening directly to them or close to them. This is not dissimilar from trying to write it down. One can only write about one aspect of a change at a time, giving the impression that the events are isolated, stand-alone, and sequential. The purpose of introducing the attached simple system diagram in Figure 9.1 is to address this reality before beginning the discussion of cross S-Curve maturity.

The system is made up of many parts that work together. Each part of the system behaves differently. Additionally, the parts don't move together and are further influenced by the maturity of different organizational business units. The system diagram is very basic. It is intended to serve as an example of the parts and how they work together. For example, the Goals and Objectives of the business determine which Leadership Priorities are set. Those Leadership Priorities are used to guide the Types of Projects Selected and the selection of people who will receive Belt Assignments. Maturity of the system is a function of how these various elements change

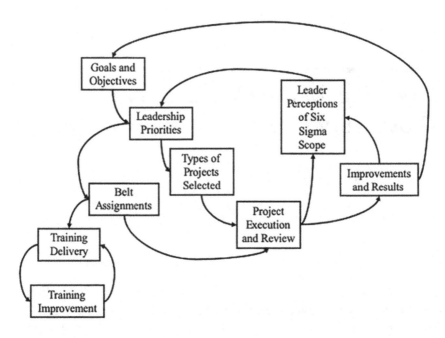

FIGURE 9.1 Six Sigma project system.

and their impacts on each other. If, for example, the goals and objectives no longer include Six Sigma, continuous improvement, or targets for improvement, the priorities of leadership will not include Six Sigma or continuous improvement. Lacking priority, the continuous improvement system will begin to decay, effectiveness will decline and, likely, disappear altogether.

Following a discussion of each S-Curve, we include a section devoted to the work done to experiment and prepare for the next S-Curve of maturity. The intent is to help an organization making change to see the need for system maturity and how that system maturity can be controlled and planned.

10

Interview With Joe Loughrey— Cummins President & COO (2005–2008)

FROM YOUR POINT OF VIEW, WHY DID CUMMINS DECIDE TO PURSUE SIX SIGMA?

To understand the story of Six Sigma at Cummins, you need to understand a little bit about the history of continuous improvement in the company.

It really all starts well before 1999. Tim Solso (Cummins CEO from 2000 to 2011) and I met in 1973 and became friends. One thing led to another and Tim recruited me in to work at Cummins in HR with him. We became very good friends. We both lived in Brown County. We were both attracted to Cummins for similar reasons: the philosophy, the values, the commitment to corporate responsibility, the desire to go global, the quality of the products and the people we met along the way. These were factors that attracted us to the company and were things we talked about during the first four or so years as we drove back and forth to work many days together. We would chat about what we were doing and what we were learning and so, during that time we became close, as did our families.

By 1980, our careers began to go in different directions. My focus became more internal while Tim transferred overseas to run a Cummins company called Holset Engineering, Ltd.

In the mid '70s I was very involved with Komatsu. I went through all the Komatsu courses which included PDCA and their "flag" system.

In 1983 a paper called New Standards of Excellence (NSE) was written at Cummins. I was one of the early session leaders to educate people on the meaning of NSE and the importance of viewing work as cross-functional flows. After that, I was hooked on the idea of creating an internal operating system and even participated in "cause and effect" training given by Dr. Ishikawa himself.

I succeeded Tim at Holset. While at Holset, I started to figure out how to create an operating system and we introduced one after studying many others. It wasn't all that terrific, but it got the ball moving.

When I went to Holset, Tim came back to the US and was in a senior customer and market role.

Along the way, we had conversations about the things we liked about Cummins. We also talked about things that we thought could be better. For example, we saw that Cummins was good at strategic thinking and a willingness to look at the long term and take big market and product risks to pursue its view of the future. But one of the things that had become clear was that Cummins did not always execute well. The company frequently came up with new ideas about how to improve execution. But execution continued to be something we struggled to improve.

The first really good experience we had for improving execution, was introduced in January 1990. We called it the Cummins Production System, or CPS. It was born from a series of conversations among senior operations and manufacturing leaders led by Jim Henderson, the CEO. We learned a lot about how to create focus and an operating system, and about spreading a new way of thinking. CPS had a huge, positive impact on Cummins plants. Over the first five years of CPS deployment, all of the major measures of operational performance improved dramatically.

A part of CPS, one of the ten main practices, was the Common Approach to Continuous Improvement, or CACI. Implementing a continuous improvement approach turned out to be one of the areas where we really struggled during our CPS deployment. It didn't click with people and it just didn't work well.

Next, we introduced the Cummins Technical System, or CTS. The Ten Practices worked well, but again we struggled to implement CACI there too. It was just hard to make it stick. It became clear that of the ten CPS practices, CACI was the weakest.

As we went through the '90s, we tried to get the equivalent of CPS going in other parts of the company, such as Marketing and Distribution. We did this, in part, to help move from a functional structure to an integrated corporation. But it just didn't catch on.

During much of the late '80s and '90s Tim and I met every Monday morning at 6 a.m. over coffee to talk.

At the end of the 1990s, as it began to look like Tim Solso was going to be the next president and CEO, we had more and more conversations about how to improve execution in the company.

In September 1999 I became the president of the combined Engine Business. The company also announced that Tim would become CEO on January 1, 2000. In preparation for the CEO role, Tim planned how to get the company on an even better track. There were a couple of things that he wanted to do. He wanted to build on the good things of the past, like the company's values and strategic thinking, while creating a culture of performance and execution.

As a first step, we needed to rethink the vision, mission and core values to make sure they were aligned with where Tim wanted to take the company. Before he became CEO, we began a huge exercise to get the whole company involved in rethinking our vision, deciding the mission we would pursue, and renewing and revising our core values.

The other major piece was to tackle the performance and execution issue. A central theme for Tim became "performance matters." For it to matter, it meant we had to improve execution at all levels.

In the latter months of 1999, Tim spent a lot of time visiting other companies looking for and getting information about initiatives that might help the company execute better. During a few of these visits he heard about Six Sigma, which we had talked about years before with Motorola. At that time, we didn't think Motorola's literal approach would work at Cummins. He visited with a customer, a supplier and GE to discuss their approach to Six Sigma. He also met with SBTI to understand how they helped companies implement Six Sigma. Tim became convinced that Six Sigma was right for Cummins if we did it more like GE than Motorola. It could be a foundation for creating a drive for performance and improve people's execution skills.

In late 1999, Tim hosted a Six Sigma education session for the senior leadership group. This began the deployment process. By the time Tim became CEO, the leadership team had been trained and had selected our first 68 projects and Black Belts for three training launches in January 2000.

On January 2, 2000, Tim sent a two-page memo to all employees (I still have it) which laid out his agenda at a high level. One of the big themes was that "performance matters" and this is what we will be about. The introduction of Six Sigma for Tim became the primary way that he would drive improvement in execution.

My concern at the time was that Six Sigma in and of itself is not a system, so I wanted to be careful. I knew that it wouldn't be (or replace) an operating system. But our tenth CPS practice was not working well. I thought that, if Six Sigma worked, we could replace CACI with Six Sigma. Beginning with this assumption, I strongly supported Tim's effort to implement Six Sigma while hoping it could replace CACI. So right at the very beginning, I was discussing with Tim about making Six Sigma part of our operating system, which everybody agreed needed improvement.

The whole Six Sigma effort was rooted in acknowledgement that we had done some things very well, but that performance did not always meet our goals and that execution was not a strength. This was very important to Tim getting started as CEO. He made clear that we were going to change while building on some of the fundamental things that were good, like values and strategic thinking. Six Sigma was going to be used to significantly improve our performance and execution capability. It ended up being far better than Tim thought when we got started.

I believe, upon reflection, that without the relationship that Tim and I had, Six Sigma would not have worked. We were complementary people who understood one another, though we didn't agree on everything. Also, we knew what our respective roles would be. It wasn't a snap decision; we generally knew where we were going. I must add, without picking Frank McDonald as the leader and George as "the man," it wouldn't have worked either. But I want to be clear that the relationship that Tim and I had was a really important factor in how Six Sigma implementation worked, because we knew each other well and we talked often along the way about how it was working. We were close and still are. In fact, as retirees, my office is right next to his.

I still carry with me the simple one-page mission, vision and values that came together prior to the launch of Six Sigma. One of the new values that we created was to "deliver superior results consistently".

I want to make sure that you understand one thing clearly. Tim and I came at things from different perspectives. Tim wanted to find something that could best get the organization focused on his goals of driving home that performance matters and improving execution skills. While I agreed with that, my concern was, let's not do this separately from an operating system that we need to build. I wanted to figure out how to bring the two things together. Tim cared less about that in the beginning. I could support the initiative because if it worked, it would replace an important part of the operating system that hadn't worked as well as we needed it to. I felt that our different perspectives complemented each other well.

WHAT DID YOU THINK WERE THE DIFFERENCES BETWEEN THE MOTOROLA AND THE GE APPROACHES? WHAT WERE THE ADAPTATIONS THAT YOU MADE EARLY ON?

Relative to the Cummins culture, Motorola's approach, when we looked at it in the 1980s and again in the 1990s, was literally too statistical and Six Sigma "calculation" oriented. It was literal six sigma. We were less worried about the literal six sigma element and were more concerned about whether we could broadly develop execution skills across the company. Further, the tool set for DMAIC included some of the things that we had learned in our lean and workflow-oriented work in the past.

We saw that the GE approach was less literal and more continuous improvement oriented. That was the part of the original CACI approach that stuck in the company. We saw Six Sigma as more consistent with who Cummins was and what we had learned about how we wanted to make improvements. That gave us a way to teach people about execution more broadly and, I think, it turned out to be a far better leadership tool than we understood in the beginning. By this I mean that Six Sigma not only gave us techniques that helped us understand the impact of variation on why processes didn't work and how to improve them, but it also reinforced leadership skills in the sense that the Belt must work with and engage a whole variety of people who you may not have known, but they sure didn't work for you. You had to use a combination of your understanding of the methodology while being persuasive enough to bring people into the project who had the tribal knowledge and the process understanding to enable the project to work.

It ended up becoming a strong leadership development tool, which I'm not sure would have happened if we had followed the Motorola approach at Cummins.

HOW DID IT BECOME MORE OF A CONTINUOUS IMPROVEMENT PLATFORM FOR THE COMPANY?

One of the things we emphasized, but never really achieved, was the 180-day completion time. We never got better than about 200 days. While that was concerning, we had a lot of projects that did finish in under 180 days. Our focus really was on continuous improvement—decide what's most important now, define a real improvement in the process to get a better result, implement the improvement and then revisit the process when and if it is appropriate to decide what to do next in the same area.

Where we did most of our work initially was in manufacturing and administrative areas. Very few projects were done in the early days in technical areas of the company. There were some projects done in the technical areas, but they tended to be done in the technical administrative support areas. We thought that was the better way to get more people in the company engaged. Ultimately, we did end up taking it into product development.

One of the things that Frank suggested we do after about 100 projects had been completed was to hold a five-day session with key leaders in the Engine Business to revisit DMAIC and the tools using results data from the 100 projects. The last day, we broke into groups. My team discussed how to use what we had learned to improve our performance in the Engine Business. This session was an example of saying "we mean it" to a broader audience than just a few of the most senior leaders in the company. As part of that session, the Engine Business developed a plan to increase our goal to $75 million in benefits the next year. We also launched two Six Sigma projects led by Engine Business Black Belts Dana Vogt and Mark Kelly, who later were among our first group of Master Black Belts. One project addressed improving Six Sigma implementation in the Engine Business. The other project addressed improving individual project execution. My staff made up the team for the two projects and we used the DMAIC methodology. An important outcome of the projects was the introduction of four key measures that we started using across the Engine Business to gauge performance. These measures became the core Six Sigma measures for the whole company.

One of the people in the five-day session was a senior engineer in the Engine Business. He came to me during the session and asked how we could move the Six Sigma methods to the product design side and engage with engineering and influence how we do our work there. SBTI engaged with us and began working Design for Six Sigma (DFSS) into new product introduction. We had started a cross-functional new product introduction process many years before. This became a way to improve the new product introduction process (higher quality and faster at lower cost) and to underpin it with the statistical skills.

Over the years, I've learned a lot personally from the different improvement approaches that we tried at Cummins. One of the things I learned about was the "flag system" used by Komatsu, which ultimately became the model for our goal tree planning tool. The Komatsu flag system was an alignment tool from the top of the company down through the organization. It was a visible way to connect objectives and initiatives together. So I learned from that, from our deployment of New Standards of Excellence and from working with the Fiegenbaums on quality systems. What I learned was that if a new initiative you are trying to implement is going to work, you have to demonstrate in a whole variety of ways that, as a leader, you mean it and that you are going to bring others along with you. I was very focused on making Six Sigma work from its introduction.

I did a lot of little things. For example, I had a session with all the sponsors of the initial Six Sigma projects in the EBU and told them that if the Belt succeeded the Belt would get the credit, but if it didn't work, I would be blaming the sponsor. In that group of sponsors were several company officers. Two of the early projects that were sponsored by officers didn't work. I sent each one of them a letter telling them that I was holding them accountable for the project failure. I put in the record that the project wasn't successful because they weren't a good enough sponsor. I asked them to tell me what they were going to do differently on the next project to be a more effective sponsor and make sure the project is successful. I also asked them to tell me what they had learned from this exercise. The word spread in the Engine Business that Joe meant it when he said we are implementing Six Sigma.

The other thing that I did for several years was review every Belt's first Six Sigma project in a 15-minute meeting with the Belt. I was able to do this in the beginning before there were just too many projects. It was a great learning experience for me but also a way to set an example for others in attendance. So beyond thanking and congratulating the Belt, capturing the lessons learned and sharing best practices, we identified other potential projects in their area and sought suggestions for where else the improvements might apply. One of the great things that George did was create the database that housed all projects. As the number of projects increased, I could no longer review every project. I used the database to see when projects were closing. I would write a short note to the Belt to congratulate them and often comment on the findings as well as suggest to the leader of the area how the project might be further used. Doing this ensured they knew that I knew the project was done and I had read the final report on the project. This was another example of how I demonstrated that I meant it.

In addition, when I was going to visit a plant or other site, I could look up all the projects that had been completed there. I would search the database to find two or three important projects in that plant so that, during the visit, I would go looking for the project control plans. While I was on the formal tour, I would walk up to an operator and ask to see the control plan for the project that I had looked up. Sometimes it was there and being used, sometimes it was there and not used, and sometimes it was not there at all. This became a small way that I could also pass on the message that I meant it when I said that Six Sigma was important, and that part of execution is doing what you said you would do. I would do this both on the shop floor and in offices. This became a regular part of all my visits and reviews.

In the mid-2000s we reorganized and formed Performance Cells. These Performance Cells had their own targets that we would measure using trend and control charts. That's when we began to use the goal tree and reinforce the need to pick projects that were going to help meet the Performance Cell metrics that are on the goal tree. We wanted to drive home the idea that projects were part of everyday work versus something extra. So, for example, the plants are responsible for quality, delivery, inventory turns and lead time. The new question that we started asking during plan time was, how are the Six Sigma projects that you are picking going to improve your key metrics? Another example was that Sales performance cells became responsible for receivables. They were not just responsible for sales. We were asking them how they were going to ensure that we do better on receivables collections.

The bottom line is, we put a lot of effort into making Six Sigma part of what we did every day versus something extra for people to do on the side. We wanted people to do a better job of picking projects that were important and necessary for meeting their business objectives and the plan for the year. Making it part of the planning process was a way that we reinforced the need to better pick projects that helped us meet our objectives and plans for the year. It was a challenge in the beginning.

As more and more people understood what we were after we used the goal trees to create alignment. Performance Cells showed their measures in trend chart form and identified what improvements people were going to pursue. This became the essence of their plan. This led to becoming better at picking Six Sigma projects that made a difference to the business. Ultimately, all of this linked back to one of Tim's main goals of improving performance and execution skills.

I worked hard to demonstrate that I meant it, find ways to get other people to say, "we mean it" and end up connecting it to what we do every day. As we saw more and more success, that led us to move Six Sigma into the business operating system, by making Six Sigma COS Practice 10.

WHAT DECISIONS DID YOU MAKE DURING THE EXECUTIVE SESSION?

One of the things that I learned from the original CPS (Cummins Production System) training in 1990 was that it's important to connect training to real work. This is what happened in the last day of the session. When we started the Six Sigma executive session, we didn't have a clue how we were going to use the last day. During the training, my focus was on connecting the dots for the company; how were we going to drive the connection of Six Sigma to real work and what we were trying to do as a business? So, I began thinking about how I wanted to use the fifth day to make this happen. I was a little disappointed in the quality of the data that we had available from the first 100 projects. It wasn't as good as I had hoped it would be. I came up with idea of using Six Sigma to help us get better as a business and to figure out how to improve the way we manage individual projects. I was responsible for the last day of the executive session, and this helped me figure out how to organize it.

Shortly after the executive session, we were kicking off our corporate strategy process. We were deep into the planning process for the next year. I was also thinking about a potential reorganization in the Engine Business. It was important to know how Six Sigma fit in with all of this.

The executive session was a chance to connect a bunch of dots. How does Six Sigma fit in to how we do work every day; how does it relate to the business restructure and performance cells; how do we get everybody on the same page talking about it in the same way? Going into the session, not everybody on my staff had bought into Six Sigma. But coming out of the executive session and especially after the two Six Sigma projects, everybody was on board ready to lead it and require others to engage, too.

HOW IMPORTANT WERE SIX SIGMA PROJECT HOPPERS?

Something that George also drove was the creation of hoppers. The idea was to collect a whole bunch of potential projects that we might want to do at some point in the future. This meant that there would probably be a bunch of projects in there that weren't high on everybody's list of improvements. But the idea was to get everybody contributing to the hopper and enable business managers to look at the potential projects and think more deeply about the ideas in there and how projects aligned with the improvement objectives that they were supposed to hit in their plans. The hopper was part of the Six Sigma project tracking system, making it easy for people to contribute ideas for other projects and for leaders to review improvement ideas. It was open to the company and gave people real visibility to what others had done and planned to do. If a leader was smart, he/she would be looking at it to find ideas for what to do in their business, asking, "What do I have to do to learn from that and apply it here to get similar results?"

There were lots of projects in the hopper. In the early years of Six Sigma, we were limited in how many projects we could do because there weren't enough trained Belts and sponsors and there were concerns about where the money would come from to pay for it. We had to move people to see that Six Sigma projects were intended to help hit targets and achieve plans, not distract you from your business. This took some time. It was a growing thing. It wasn't simple to go from 5 to 30 to 100 projects. We had to grow into it, but it worked well. In more and more parts of the company in the planning process, leadership teams were creating hoppers and asking themselves where they could go next. Hoppers were being created at many different levels of the company and all kinds of potential project ideas were put in there.

What we had created was a way to collect all the projects and make them available to everyone in the company. Anybody could look at them to find out what ideas were in the hoppers. Leaders across the company could look at successfully completed projects and think about what could apply in their own business.

As the Black Belt group got bigger and as we developed this fabulous group of Master Black Belts, George formalized a process to combine Master Black Belts into teams to work together on really big deals for the company. These groups were getting together to talk about their successes and ideas for the future. This had a synergistic effect on the company.

Key to all of this was that Six Sigma wasn't going away. We built structures and approaches that required people to use them if they were going to become good at it. And, if they wanted to be a good leader at Cummins, they needed to be good at Six Sigma.

Later we began to look at the structure of the company and made some decisions about where we wanted to be in the future regarding Six Sigma knowledge and skill. We identified different management levels and jobs that would require a defined level of Six Sigma capability to hold that job. We looked at a long list of jobs and defined the level of capability that they would need. We were trying to make it a little bit more personal. It took about two years to put it in. At the same time, we wanted to be careful to not turn Six Sigma from a company-wide continuous improvement effort into a "train everybody and his brother" program. This was definitely a concern. Training is necessary but is probably only about 5% of any fundamental sustained improvement process. It's really about connecting what has been learned to the work being done and make the necessary improvements to the work to get better results. There were examples of otherwise qualified candidates who were told that they couldn't be promoted until they had the defined level of Six Sigma capability. We ended up having people with fantastic Six Sigma experience moving up in the company and the fact that they had this was advertised. Dana Vogt was a great example of this. He became the plant manager at Jamestown. He applied what he had learned as a Black Belt and Master Black Belt and also used Six Sigma as the way he ran the plant. That was a very positive thing for the life of Six Sigma.

IF YOU WERE JUST STARTING OUT A SIX SIGMA DEPLOYMENT, WHAT WOULD YOU RECOMMEND TO A LEADERSHIP TEAM TO MAKE IT WORK?

First, the real test at the start is whether or not the top of the house gets it and believes that implementing Six Sigma well can lead to better results for the company. It is better, though not absolutely necessary, that the leader of the whole company gets it and leads it versus the leader of a part of the company. Though, I think it could work the second way depending on relationships.

The top of the house must have a long view. This is not going to be something that's finished by the end of one, two or three years. Although, we saw some really good results in the short term at the individual project level. In terms of impact on the whole organization, you must take the long view and think about it as a building process. I often use the phrase with organizations I'm involved with, that a lot of what execution is all about is "top down, bottom up and communicate constantly." Leadership has to understand what can be done top down and how it is sustained. They need to see where they can build bottom-up initiatives and how they can be spread. Finally, understanding how to make sure that communication is happening to connect top-down work with bottom-up work. This is important because people need convincing that this is going to be around, that the boss is going to hold people's feet to the fire to make progress, and that the boss is going to have patience but be about people getting on with it and get it. Then, you pick the people who get it and do well to play important leadership roles.

Frank McDonald was very important to this whole effort. Frank was from GE and had been engaged in a variety of ways. He was a significant factor on the leadership team for the introduction of the Cummins Production System (CPS). He was a significant factor as a no-nonsense, demanding guy who ended up with an unbelievable partner in George. Finding this core of people who are with it and not afraid to engage and have the attention and involvement of the leader is a critical success factor. Frank and George were very good at getting Tim to do some reinforcing things that Tim may not have done on his own. To put it simply, Tim likely would have said, "This is what I expect, go do it." He would have created the expectation and then delegated to people whose job it was to go do it. The reinforcing things he did with the company leadership team, the awards ceremonies that were created as well as other things that Tim did as the leader of the corporation, were important to show that he meant it and was reinforcing it.

The central core doesn't have to be huge, and it is probably better that it's not because it makes the point that the businesses have to do it. It's not going to be the corporate guy running around finding a whole bunch of Belts and projects that are disconnected from the business. Instead, George focused on how we trained Belts, how we trained Master Black Belts, how we learned from one another and how we reinforced what we were doing. The project work has to happen in the businesses.

The core group and the leadership who believes Six Sigma can make a difference in the top-down piece. Finding places where you may be able to move faster is the bottom-up piece that demonstrates that this stuff works. I think those two pieces worked well at Cummins.

I think we could have done a better job of the "communicate constantly" piece to get leaders in all businesses to move faster than they otherwise would. Having said that, there were some great things going on in communications like the Six Sigma database and the Chairman's Awards and other things that were important elements of the communications that helped make the connection for people that Six Sigma really works and improves the business.

The bottom line on what is needed to make this work is three things. First you need a leader who gets it. Next, a small, strong team that gets it and knows what to do. Then, careful thinking about the top-down strategy, the bottom-up strategy, and the communicate constantly strategy so the top down/bottom up is clearly connected. Then leaders spend a lot of time showing that "I mean it," figuring out how to move people to "we mean it," and finally to "we all mean it." Most organizations suffer at some point from the "program of the month" problem and this is one of the ways to avoid it.

The connection to the top down is being clear about what we need to do as a company and what are we going to do to improve ourselves. That's a big part of the top-down exercise. There were other things like the goal tree that worked bottom up. We started using goal tree in the EBU first, showing that it worked, and it spread to other parts of the company, later becoming more of a corporate tool for communication and alignment across the businesses.

Another important thing that came out of the executive session and the two projects was that people had to come back with their plans for how they were going to use Six Sigma to help them meet their business objectives. I wanted to know things like the list of projects they were going to do and how many Black Belts they would need. In some cases, I didn't accept their initial plan and we changed it. We were still early in the process and people were trying to figure out how they were going to take people out of their jobs to become Black Belts, move people around to fill those roles with no backfill hiring and pay for it all. Then we began pushing on Green Belts too, which had people working on projects while doing their assigned work. There was a lot of initial resistance to that.

There are a couple of other things that are important to success. Paying attention to details, like the quality of the Black Belts in the early launches, is important and something we didn't do so well early on. The early launches had some terrific people who became longtime contributors to the company. But a few of the initial Black Belts were the most available persons at the time in some of the businesses.

Another important action is paying a lot of attention to the connection of the Belt to the project sponsor and the process owner. Sometimes the sponsor and the process owner are the same person, but not always.

Building our own Master Black Belt capability proved critical to our success. Building organizational capability based on our experience of applying Six Sigma to our work became a huge factor in growing Six Sigma in the company. But this really takes time. We required our Master Black Belts to have two years of Black Belt experience before becoming a Master Black Belt. You start by needing two years right from the beginning. Building expertise inside the company was very important to success. We hired very few people from the outside because "Master Black Belt" can mean something completely different from company to company, because there are no globally accepted standards. That becomes a problem in a company and creates conflicts supporting the naysayers. This is one of the reasons that I think patience is necessary to let it work, thinking ahead to know where you are going and having the patience to get there. It also means you have done all the right things along the way to get there. It's a long journey. Even though we had the long view, we had to see results from early projects. That's why thoughtful selection of the right projects, picking the right sponsors for those projects, and picking the right Belts for the projects were important to demonstrating to the organization that the methodology really does work. Then we moved quickly to making sure that the projects that were picked connected to the most important needs of the business so that people see that it really does matter.

WERE THERE ANY NOTABLE TRANSITION POINTS IN THE PROGRAM THAT WERE IMPORTANT?

One "oomph" moment came from the executive session. Because of the two leadership Six Sigma projects, we began to use goal trees to align projects to the needs of the individual businesses and improve how we managed projects. It took Six Sigma from a series of meaningful individual projects to becoming strongly connected to business results within the Engine Business.

Another "oomph" moment turned out to be the deployment of DFSS. That ended up really getting the Technical function engaged in a cross-functional methodology for new product introduction. That was a really big deal.

There were some other things that happened that were really big deals for the company. Customer Focused Six Sigma (CFSS) projects underpinned a strategy we had with OEMs and end users to help them ensure their business success. It became a real plus.

Something happened that we learned from the Cummins Production System. As it spread and people began to see that it could work in technology areas, on new product introduction, in admin areas and in manufacturing we created an organization of people using common methods, tools and terminology. People all over the company were using the same lingo with common understanding of terms and techniques, so that as people moved to different jobs in the company, they were able to go to work right away because a common language was spoken everywhere. In manufacturing they understood how this worked a little better because of the common language that was built within CPS that helped enable us to do things in a common way across the plants. But we saw it happen throughout the company.

When I became president, this was a bit of a turning point as well. I ramped up the pressure on the leaders of the other businesses to more aggressively pursue Six Sigma to improve their businesses. They had no choice. They had to figure out a way to catch up.

This is when the Cummins Operating System (COS) began to emerge as a total company operating system which also helped to drive Six Sigma as a continuous improvement language across the company. This helped to move it from a business unit–only focus and create more engagement with the Corporate functions.

Growth and expansion were more organic and reflective of the rate of progress, asking what we could do next to make this part of what people do every day. Leaders reinforce and require it. I even began imagining that someday there might not be something called a Six Sigma project if we could ever get so far. Everybody in the company would use this methodology and tool set in what people do every day. The tool set—fact-based statistical tools—understanding variation, focusing on continuous improvement as opposed to the never-ending search for the perfect solution, were all part of what made it grow organically.

ANY OTHER THOUGHTS THAT YOU WOULD SHARE WITH LEADERS OF OTHER LARGE ORGANIZATIONS?

A lot of what success is about is attracting very talented people at all levels of the organization and to get those talented people working together in pursuit of shared goals and objectives using common processes and methods. This is something that I learned a long time ago and think a lot about. When I go into an organization I look for this, which tells me whether or not the organization has the foundations of success in place.

A lot of what people are about day to day is finding ways to continuously improve by eliminating waste and reducing variation. We found that Six Sigma could touch both. It is not the only method or always the best method for every individual problem or improvement. But it is really pretty good for most things. It has given me a way to check on whether continuous improvement is really happening.

11

Moving From First Training and Projects S-Curve to the Building a Foundation S-Curve

As the initial training launches began and projects launched, the company began learning how Six Sigma can work. This initial work answers questions like:

- How was Six Sigma different from other programs tried by the company?
- What is a good project?
- What are the roles and responsibilities needed for success? What is expected of each role?
- What actions does leadership take to ensure successful deployment?
- What does this work mean to our customers and to our business?
- Who are the right people to lead the deployment?
- What are the measures of success?
- Is the future state description the correct one?

After the actions of the First Training and Projects S-Curve were underway for a few months, preparations began for the Building a Foundation S-Curve.

First, selection of the first internal Master Black Belts (MBBs). These Master Black Belts are focused on understanding how information and data flow from phase to phase and tool to tool, learning the training material, understanding how to explain complex statistical concepts, looking for opportunities to insert company examples, documenting how the consultant Master Black Belts teach each of the training elements, and documenting and learning how to conduct the different exercises.

Characteristics for these first Master Black Belts include but are not limited to:

- Strong leadership skills
- Strong math skills
- Strong teaching skills
- Strong written and verbal communication skills
- Understanding of the business and its customers
- A process orientation
- Demonstrated adaptability and flexibility.

These first Master Black Belts need to be business people first because they set the tone for what Six Sigma will become in the company. An example will clarify what this means. When I (George Strodtbeck) left the US Army in 1986, I had never worked in business. My first boss gave me this advice that helped tremendously in my transition. He told me I needed to be perceived as a business person who came to the business with unique skills and capabilities from my time in the Army. Further, he told me that I didn't want people to perceive me as an Army person who was trying to do a job in business. People need to know how you will contribute to the business first. They care about where you came from second, if at all. It's the same for these first Master Black Belts. By understanding the business, by being business people first, they see the customers and the business as the priority and Six Sigma as a way to accomplish great things for the customers and the business. No business wants to be a great Six Sigma company. They want to be a great company, providing great products and services to their customers. Six Sigma is a way to achieve that greatness. This perspective is critically important to changing the culture.

The first Master Black Belts began teaming with the consultant Master Black Belts, training the material, and coaching Belts. They would be key to preparing the larger group of internal Master Black Belts with the contractually agreed departure of the consultants after two years.

We held regularly scheduled meetings between the first Master Black Belts and the Corporate leadership to set direction, discuss emerging issues, and generate feedback on the overall progress of deployment and the performance of the consultants.

During this time, we highlighted early project successes and communicated them to the company leadership. This helped them to understand the potential of Six Sigma and whether or not it was really working.

As the Corporate Six Sigma Staff leader, I (George Strodtbeck) reviewed all projects during the first months of deployment to understand the value of Six Sigma and to verify that the deployment norms were being followed.

The CEO, Tim Solso, received individual coaching from one of the first internal Master Black Belts (Michelle Dunlap). These sessions were focused on how DMAIC works as a process, how different non-statistical and statistical Six Sigma tools work together in the flow of a project, basic instruction about Minitab, and reviews of initial completed projects. The goal of these sessions was to help the CEO understand the real value of what he was asking the people of the company to do.

The main function of this work was to assess how Six Sigma was really working in the company, make early corrections to the approach, and continuously communicate with senior leadership so that decisions they were making about the Six Sigma deployment were based on the up-to-date facts on the ground. This proved to be very helpful as time went along.

12

Interview With Michelle Dunlap— Master Black Belt, Quality Champion

WHAT IS YOUR BACKGROUND AS IT RELATES TO SIX SIGMA AND QUALITY?

I started at Cummins initially as a reliability engineer. I have a background in statistics and industrial engineering. Prior to Six Sigma, through our technical center, Cummins offered courses in design of experiments, reliability methods and basic statistics. I was involved in the development and presentation of these courses to our engineers.

When the company started to get really serious about continuous improvement, starting with Six Sigma, this was a pretty natural fit for me in terms of the work that I had been doing prior to the year 2000.

George asked me to get involved with the Six Sigma program very early in 2000, but I wasn't in the first group of Black Belts. I did one Six Sigma project and then rapidly jumped into a Master Black Belt position. So, I was riding the Six Sigma wave very early. I was able to see what went really well and what didn't go so well in our early implementation.

When George first talked to me about getting heavily involved with the Six Sigma program the idea was that I would do one project with Tim Solso, our CEO and Chairman at the time. The project would be something that was important to him. The real benefit of having me do the project with Tim is that I could help him with the project and give him one-on-one instruction on the tools and the process. This gave him a hands-on experience of how the tools and methodologies work.

As you can imagine Tim was quite a busy person, but he attended the training with me, and we met on a weekly basis for almost a year to work on his project. After we finished the project, he asked me to continue coaching sessions with him to explain the tools and to talk through projects I had been involved with as a Master Black Belt.

Tim asked George and the Master Black Belts to bring really good projects to him and his leadership team so that he and they could start to see the breadth and variety of how we were using Six Sigma across the company.

It was a fantastic experience for me to spend so much time with our CEO. I think his personal effort is one of the things that gave him real ownership of Six Sigma. My opinion is that we would not have been as successful using Six Sigma tools and processes to improve our performance if our top leader had not been so engaged and so empowering. Tim drove that ownership down through the levels of the organization. That was the biggest key to our success.

AS ONE OF THE FIRST FOUR MASTER BLACK BELTS, WHAT KINDS OF THINGS DID YOU DO TO PREPARE CUMMINS TO OWN THE SIX SIGMA DEPLOYMENT AFTER THE CONSULTANT DEPARTED?

I went to Green Belt training with Tim in April of 2000. This was both Tim's and my first project. The understanding was that, instead of a normal Black Belt path of two years and five to seven projects, I would do one project and then jump straight into a Master Black Belt role. I would start shadowing the consultant's MBBs, then co-teach with them in preparation to be on my own as an active Cummins Master Black Belt. These first MBB roles were very important because we were planning to be on our own by the end of 2001.

I had 18 months to complete the project with Tim and to learn from SBTI to be prepared to be one of four people who would become the first Master Black Belts for the company.

WHY WERE YOU SELECTED TO BE ONE OF THE FIRST FOUR MASTER BLACK BELTS?

I was working as a statistician. I'd been in new product reliability. I had been part of the team of people who were putting on statistics-related courses prior to the year 2000.

In those very early days, I think we thought that this was more about getting people trained and schooled up on doing projects as opposed to emphasis on the project, which is the important thing now. We may have thought that the training was more important at the time. If you're trying to get yourself ready to be independent of the consultant, then training was kind of a big deal. I'm sure the fact that I'd already done quite a bit of statistics training of others at the company helped me to be an ideal candidate.

WHAT ADVANTAGES DID CUMMINS HAVE BY DEVELOPING ITS OWN INTERNAL MASTER BLACK BELTS INSTEAD OF HIRING FROM THE OUTSIDE?

I will answer the second question first. By preparing our own people, we had to learn the tools, but we didn't have to learn about Cummins. Trying to bring somebody in from the outside, who knows the tools but doesn't know Cummins, would have actually been much harder, I think. The fact that you had four people who had been with Cummins for a while made a big difference.

At the time, I had ten years. Two of the other people, had more than 20 years and the fourth person had at least six or seven years with the company. The four of us had a good understanding of how different parts of the company worked. We'd already built good networks of people at all different levels of the business which we leveraged to help us with difficult processes and projects. I think it's much easier to train the tools than to train somebody on the culture of Cummins.

Going back to the first question, what were the things that we did? From the training perspective, we just spent an awful lot of time with the SBTI consultants. We shadowed them, then co-trained with them, and spent time with them as they were doing project reviews with the Belts. Then, we graduated to doing the project reviews while they were sitting in coaching us. It was really all about making sure that at the end of 2001 the four of us were going to be able to handle training classes on our own, were able to handle Belt reviews, and to make sure that our Belts were able to successfully move through the different phases of the Six Sigma process.

At the time, we had four weeks of Black Belt training. We were trying to scope projects so that they would be done in the 180-day time frame that had been set by the company. We were very focused on making sure that we were going to be able to coach and mentor those Belts, and not let the business down.

Business leadership was counting on us to get these projects done successfully in that 180-day time frame. There was a lot of tactical effort placed on learning the tools, becoming effective coaches, improving our presentation skills, improving our communication skills, etc. There was a lot of that going on.

Secondarily, we were also trying to think about how to apply the Six Sigma process more broadly at Cummins. Where are the improvement opportunities? We had to understand how projects were identified, how projects were selected, how Belts were identified, how Belts were selected, and how sponsors were selected, as well as other process questions. We also had to figure out how to help streamline the overall project process so that Belts were more successful. This was especially true for the two different Belt levels. At Cummins, the main difference between a Black Belt and a Green Belt is full time versus part time. We had to figure out how to scope projects so that Green Belts could be more successful.

We were experiencing all of those things in real time. When something wasn't going very well, we were talking with one another about what we could do to start improving the process of Six Sigma? That meant working with George and others to start making improvements to the selection of Belts, projects and sponsors, as well as the other aspects of Six Sigma at Cummins.

Another thing that we were realizing was the four of us were not going to be able to handle the load forever. We started working with George to identify the next potential Master Black Belts from the pool of Black Belts who started in early 2000. We began by figuring out the characteristics that a Master Black Belt should have going forward to be successful. We used that criteria to select the next pool. Once they were identified, we started to prepare them for the new role. All of that took place as we moved through 2001.

HOW DID MASTER BLACK BELT STAR POINTS START? WHAT ROLE DID THEY PLAY IN THE DEVELOPMENT OF SIX SIGMA?

As we started to gain a critical mass of Master Black Belts, we realized that we were going to need a way for all of us to work better together.

The first four of us were working together well and closely. After the next eight were identified, we started having monthly Master Black Belt calls and sessions. We were all realizing that in the different businesses we supported we were seeing different things about the Six Sigma process that needed to be improved. It was like almost doing Six Sigma on Six Sigma. We spent time improving Belt selection and project selection processes, training improvements, and many other things. For example, we wanted to add our own business examples to the training. We didn't want to use only what SBTI had supplied to us forever.

We wanted to make all of these different improvements. We said, "We've got to divide and conquer." The Star Point concept was developed at Cummins in manufacturing to encourage people to work in teams on the shop floor. We applied the Star Point concept with the MBBs as a way to get us working together on important improvements for the whole group. We had several Star Points. Some examples of Star Points were Training, Six Sigma Database, and Communication, as well as others. The Six Sigma Database Star Point was important because we had started a Six Sigma database to manage the data of the projects and there were improvements that we needed to make right away to make it easier to use. We had a Six Sigma Project Star Point working on how to make improvements in how projects were selected. We had two or three MBBs on each of the Star Points.

As new Master Black Belts began their training, we required that they spend five percent of their time participating in Star Point work. Star Point work was for the betterment of the Six Sigma program as a whole at Cummins, not just something for their own individual businesses.

I think that worked really well. Getting together, even virtually, in these Star Point teams helped us to bring about change effectively and it meant that everything didn't fall on George, who was a one-person team at Corporate, to try and make all of the improvements.

We originally needed Cummins Master Black Belts so that we could take over the training and the Belt mentoring. But it evolved quickly into the Master Black Belt group really becoming the operational leaders of Six Sigma. We were helping the businesses and providing Six Sigma leadership to improve them and Cummins as a whole. We were very engaged leading the businesses to understand how the Six Sigma program could and should work for them and their customers. We stopped being just trainers very early in the process.

WAS FIVE PERCENT RIGHT FOR STAR POINT WORK? HOW DID YOU SEE THE MASTER BLACK BELT STAR POINT CONCEPT CHANGE OVER TIME?

I think the 5% requirement worked out pretty well. I was on the Communications Star Point. There were four or five of us on the team. We were able to divide the work, so it was not overbearing along with the rest of our Master Black Belt responsibilities. At least, in those early days, I think 5% was fine.

To answer the second part of the question, one of the good things about the Star Point structure is that we don't still have the same Star Points 15 years later. This is because we focused on solving a certain set of problems. Once those issues had been addressed, we would take on something new.

I remember as we started getting into Customer Focused Six Sigma (CFSS) projects we said, "We should put a Star Point on this to really figure out how we are going to help the businesses do this effectively." I think if we hadn't identified new Star Points for things like CFSS, or Supplier Focused Six Sigma, or Community Focused Six Sigma, those efforts probably wouldn't have taken off as fast or been as successful. By putting in a focused group of Master Black Belts who could figure out the basics and work with their individual businesses it helped new applications of using Six Sigma get off to a good start.

As things progressed and we felt like we were becoming mature in an area, like Customer Focused Six Sigma, we would disband a Star Point and start a new one in another area of focus. It just allowed us to take on something else that was important to the company. We really used the Star Points as a way of putting fantastically bright process people working on important problems for the company.

YOU HAVE BEEN A QUALITY CHAMPION FOR A WHILE NOW. HOW HAVE YOU SEEN THIS ROLE MATURE AND CHANGE OVER TIME?

In the early days, I think the businesses I supported saw the Quality Champion as the person who owned Six Sigma and its improvement. It didn't mean that the other leaders in the business didn't care or weren't interested in Six Sigma, but I don't know that they felt the same sense of ownership that I did in the beginning. What I have seen evolve is that the leaders of the businesses, and others, started to care a whole lot more and feel personal ownership for continuous improvement of the business.

As the Quality Champion position has evolved, the projects that we put into our hoppers, select from the hoppers, the Belts that we are selecting . . . all of it is just getting so much crisper. We're really focusing on the biggest business problems.

In my Master Black Belt role, I supported everybody who wasn't in the US. That's why I have over a million frequent flyer miles! I can remember that when we were putting together training classes for Six Sigma in various parts of the world, some of the projects were spot on. They were really hitting big business problems. However, some of the projects were just silly. Things like wanting to reduce the amount of copier paper used at a distributor location just weren't critical to the business. The location that wanted to do this only had one copier, by the way. We're talking about a savings of a couple of hundred dollars a year. They chose this project because they knew they needed an approved project to get into training. Their hearts were in the right place. They wanted people to learn these skills, but this kind of project just wasn't worth doing. Our project robustness has certainly gotten a lot better over time.

I think the Master Black Belts are now seen as part of leadership teams around the company. I think the same thing is true for the Quality Champion role. Instead of being seen as the person in charge of the Quality Function and Six Sigma, the Quality Champion is seen as part of the business team bringing specialized strengths and focus. The role is just part of the business team trying to move the business forward.

I've been in the Distribution business for a long time. The Distribution business is responsible for providing parts and services to our customers around the world. In the beginning, I think we had the additional challenge that the Distribution leadership thought that Six Sigma was something that would only work in manufacturing. We had to figure out how Six Sigma could work in Distributor operations. It's been challenging, but it's also been very rewarding, as a Quality Champion, to be able to work with the Distributor business leaders and help them figure it out.

I learned that my first question is not, "What projects do you want to do?" I start the conversation now with, "What are your most frustrating business problems and what are the things that your customers complain about the most?" Now, we think that way. That's how we fill up our project hoppers.

YOU'VE BEEN HEAVILY INVOLVED IN THE CUMMINS OPERATING SYSTEM (COS). FROM YOUR POINT OF VIEW, WHAT ROLE HAS COS PLAYED IN THE SIX SIGMA EFFORT?

I think COS has really evolved quite a bit. The Cummins Operating System is the way that we talk about the business holistically. At Cummins, our businesses are made up of functional leadership and general management. The Cummins Operating System is a way for us to discuss our most critical processes. It gives us a forum to discuss the most critical skills and tools that we need our people to have to do the work of the company. This is "functional excellence," which is one of the key elements of the Cummins Operating System.

The Cummins Operating System is all about making our operations effective by continuously improving for the customer. The Cummins Operating System started with something called the Cummins Production System. That's really where it started. Because of that, I think a lot of our people thought, "Well, having critical processes and tools and capable people, that's just something we do at a manufacturing plant. That's the Cummins Production System." A lot of folks didn't really see that COS could expand to every function and every part of the company.

Thinking about putting the customer first and using our Ten COS Practices to improve processes has taken us from a company that uses gut reactions to drive decision making to, I think, a company that is much more thoughtful in terms of decision making. We work hard to understand what our most critical processes are and how they impact our customers and employees. This gives us improvement opportunities which we turn into Six Sigma projects.

The Cummins Operating System has given us people in every company function who think in a certain way about critical processes, tools and capabilities. Without COS, I think everybody would be doing their own thing at a functional level. We would have a lot of inconsistency, process disconnects, and a lot more variation in how the work of the company is done.

WHAT HAVE BEEN THE CRITICAL SUCCESS FACTORS FOR SIX SIGMA AT CUMMINS?

The most critical success factor was our CEO, Tim Solso. I think he had a huge impact on our success with Six Sigma. As the CEO, Tim said, "We're going to do this, and I'm holding myself and all of you on my leadership team accountable." He demonstrated his personal commitment by doing a project and going through the training. I don't think Tim's impact can be overstated. For eight years or more, he reviewed one or two projects a month. He really stayed engaged and established that same expectation for those working for him. I believe this is why Six Sigma is so successful at Cummins. This kind of effort has to be top down.

You can have some grassroots efforts by people who say, "Hey, this is a really neat tool. I think I'm going to go use it." Or, "Hey, this stuff really works." But, without the top down commitment to fully implement Six Sigma, there's no way that we would have 55,000 people all moving in the same direction globally. There's no way that we would all still be doing Six Sigma projects 15 years later if it hadn't been top down.

I think another critical success factor is the fact that, we kept evolving. The first wave may have focused on manufacturing. Then the second wave focused more on transactional processes. But, we said, "Do you think we could use this in our HR processes? Could we use it in finance? Could we use it in sales?" The answer to every question was, "Let's go try it." We asked, "Can we expand this to our customers more deliberately? How can we expand to suppliers? How can we expand it to engineers?" We just kept asking, "How can we use these tools and methods more pervasively throughout the business?" We didn't let it just become narrowly focused on one function, or one area, of the company. It really could become part of our culture for how we do continuous improvement work.

IF YOU COULD GO BACK, WHAT MIGHT CUMMINS HAVE DONE DIFFERENTLY?

In terms of big lessons learned and things that maybe we would have done differently, I'm not sure we always picked the best people to be Black Belts in the first couple of waves. Don't misunderstand, I think we picked some really great people. But I think we also picked some people who hadn't been successful in anything else and we let them try Six Sigma. To our surprise, they weren't successful here either. That tarnished the image of Six Sigma a little bit when any Black Belt wasn't successful in that role. I also think there were some folks who may have said, "Well, you know, not everybody can do this." This kept some people out of Six Sigma in the early days that could have done a really great job and did later.

The effective use of Six Sigma would have been more pervasive faster if leadership engagement and ownership of all aspects of Six Sigma had occurred earlier.

I think we did some projects that weren't truly the biggest business problems. We probably still did that up until five years ago even. Some of that was because we had a certification requirement that may have driven some of the wrong behavior. I think, also, we had some leadership teams that were not fully engaged. When you're asking, "What are your biggest business problems?" if they're not engaged, they're not telling you.

By working on the biggest business problems, Six Sigma is seen to work, and people say, "Gosh, this was a great tool and we fixed this really big business problem. I want to do more of this."

The other thing I probably would have done differently was how we approached the requirement for Six Sigma certification for different leadership levels in the company. I think the way we defined certification ended up backfiring a bit. I think we should have rethought the whole certification process and long-term goal sooner than we did.

WHAT CRITERIA OR CHARACTERISTICS WOULD YOU RECOMMEND FOR SELECTION OF BLACK BELTS?

Having been a Master Black Belt and having dealt with a lot of Belts over many years, you'll be surprised when I tell you that being really good at statistics or Minitab is not my number one critical success factor for Black Belts. It is much more important to know how to communicate well across time zones, functions and the myriad of other business boundaries and to project manage effectively. Those are the two biggest critical success factors for a Black Belt.

When I was coaching both Black Belts and Green Belts who were falling behind on their projects, the biggest reasons by far were not communicating effectively with their team or their sponsor and/or they were not effectively managing the project.

If team members were not showing up to team meetings, they just canceled them and hoped that next week was better, versus "I've got to figure out a way to keep this project on schedule. I need to think outside the box. How can I get the answers that I need from the team to keep this project moving?" The Belts that figured out how to do this well and were tenacious ended up being the most successful Belts.

Those are the two biggest success factors. There are certainly other things that are important like having familiarity with the process certainly helps quite a lot. Another, in terms of the sustainability of the project work, is having a well-engaged process owner throughout the project. This a very important factor for project success.

WHAT ARE YOUR THOUGHTS, PRO AND CON, ON CERTIFICATION?

The company goal was to drive our key leaders to have the Six Sigma skill set. We wanted them to make decisions based on data and not based on gut feel. We wanted them to think in the Six Sigma way. The thought process was, just being a sponsor isn't necessarily going to give people the depth of experience needed to change the way they behaved. We wanted our folks who moved into senior leadership positions to complete three Green Belt projects at a minimum so that they really learned the processes and the tools.

It is a really great thing to want our senior leaders to be thinking in a continuous improvement way. The problem is, when we created the certification requirement and tied it to the promotion of any person into any role above a certain level, that's where things became difficult to manage. For example, if a person is in aviation and flies a plane, we're going to promote you to senior captain through our certification process. This means that the airplane pilot needs to complete three Green Belt projects to be promoted into the senior captain role. Things like that really happened. People made up silly projects just for certification. For example, let's do a project on reducing the amount of napkin usage on the airplane. Just silly stuff.

That's where I think we could have been a little bit more deliberate. I think early on, we were more deliberate on specific roles that needed both Black Belt certification and Green Belt certification. But we expanded it to all roles above a certain level. If we had left it as a requirement for certain roles, I think it would have been better in hindsight.

Again, the thought was right in that we want all senior leaders to have certain skills. Maybe the senior pilot could have gotten these skills in a different way that didn't require three projects.

13

Interview With Dana Vogt—Black Belt, Master Black Belt, Quality Champion

DESCRIBE YOUR EXPERIENCE AT CUMMINS AND WITH SIX SIGMA?

I've had a very meaningful career at Cummins. I've spent 33 years and I've learned a lot of things along the way.

The first half of my career I spent most of my time in plant manufacturing, in production management and quality roles. The reason that I think this is relevant to the Six Sigma journey is that I have always liked being around a lot of people. I also enjoy technical and engineering work. Basically, I enjoy mechanical things. I like how an engine goes together and how it works technically. I like to know how an engine works. I also like to think about the thousands of hands that have touched the product to put it together and make it run. These things have always fascinated me.

The second thing that has fascinated me throughout my career, and maybe it's easy to see now after 33 years, is solving puzzles. I like to solve problems. It's a natural curiosity I have. I think it's born out of a frustration with things that are sub-optimal, but I'm also inquisitive about how things work. I like the "how" part.

Looking at the first part of my career—let's say the first 20 years—I made reasonable career progress. I was not someone that was destined to be CEO or something like that. As the years passed, I incrementally received more and more responsibility and I was aggressive. But it was not so much that I sought the promotions because I've never really worked to get bigger jobs. I was fortunate to work in areas that needed leadership. And I was comfortable stepping in and working in that environment. So, the plant leadership gave me bigger and bigger jobs.

Finally, in 1996, I first met Rich Freeland. Rich was my plant manager. I was his director of operations. I had a lot of good experiences to reach that role, but Rich was one of the first people that forced me to take a long-term view of my career, not just a short-term view. During a performance review, I explained to him, and I still have the papers here in the filing cabinet, what I thought I needed to do to further develop my career. I wrote things like I need to network more, I need to get broader experiences. I wrote all of the things down that I thought Corporate HR would want to hear since I believed they would be auditing and reviewing this. But Rich really forced me to reduce all of that to real talk and real words.

Rich said, "I asked you what you wanted long-term. What is the pinnacle for you?" I told him that I eventually wanted to have his job; that I'd like to be plant manager. His response to that was one that was telling of his character and his care for his people, because he looked me dead in the eye and said, "That's a great aspiration, but you're not ready yet." But he followed that up by telling me he would help me get ready. I went home and told my wife Lori that I went in feeling pretty good about myself but came out really down because my boss said I'm not ready. That's all I heard him say.

As time went on, Rich gave me more and more responsibilities and broader exposure. For example, at the time, I was the leader in the plant that focused on how many engines we built, how many we were shipping, and what percent were going through engine tests. This was the intra-plant view. So, Rich started exposing me to things outside the plant by involving me in community activities.

There was a community welfare to work program going on that he and Tim Solso were sponsoring. Rich wanted me to get involved and help bring some of the people in the program into Cummins and make them successful. Because I had told him my goals, Rich began giving me experiences that were meant to meet that desire.

I told Rich I wanted to be a plant manager in 1996. In 1998 he said, "Hey, you're having the same experience day after day after day and you're good at it. You're a key member of my staff, but you're not developing new skills. You're not learning new things. You've done every job in the business, but you can't have my job yet. I think you're becoming stagnant. We need to think about doing something different." So, he moved me to a new product introduction (Value Package Introduction [VPI] at Cummins) role at the Cummins Technical Center (CTC), where we were launching a brand new 11-liter product. So I spent a year and a half working on a new product program. As a hardcore plant guy who had always cussed about the technical center, sitting at the technical center looking out the windows at the plant was a bit of a conflict for me. But I got used to it and actually learned a lot in that VPI role. Rich knew that I wasn't a long-term player in VPI but he was, again, working on my development and giving me this experience.

On the Wednesday of Thanksgiving week 1999, Rich called me. I remember that because I was on vacation. I was at my dad's property just south of town and a friend and I were hunting. I got the page—remember this was pre-cell phones and I only had a pager—to call his office. I knew that it had to be important because Rich would never page me while I was on vacation unless it was serious.

My first thought was that somebody had been hurt in the plant or something else bad had happened. At this time, he was still the plant manager. I went to the gas station and put my quarter in the pay phone and called him. By the way, his phone number is still the same today as it was then, so I remember it.

When Rich answered the phone he said, "Thanks for calling. There's a new opportunity that I want you to consider. I think it would be a great opportunity for you. It's called Black Belt." I said, "What the heck is THAT?" I thought it was some kind of exercise thing because when you think of "Black Belt," you think of karate. He said, "You're going to learn a bunch of statistical tools and be a part of new process we are introducing to Cummins. As much as you like to solve problems and as much as you like to fix things, I think you're going to be a natural. I want to sponsor a couple of early projects and I want you to be my Black Belt. This will give you and me an opportunity to work together." Rich also said that I needed to make a decision quickly.

There I was, standing there on the phone in the parking lot of a gas station thinking about what Rich had just asked me to do. Because of my faith in Rich and knowing that he cared about me and my development, without hesitation I said, "Rich, if you think it's a good thing, I think it's a good thing." So he said, "When you come back to work on Monday, Frank McDonald is going to be at the hotel next to the highway at a manufacturing conference. He's going to be talking about Six Sigma. I want you to go listen to him."

If you worked in manufacturing at Cummins, Frank was a person we all respected as being the guy in the company that knew the most about manufacturing. Just having the opportunity to go listen to Frank speak was a big opportunity for me.

I knew within the first ten minutes of the presentation that this is what I wanted to do. The reason that I wanted to do it was not what he said, but because Frank was the real deal. He was somebody I respected a lot because of all the things he had done. If Frank was putting his support behind Six Sigma and endorsing it in such an open way, and if our company Chairman, Tim Solso, was supporting him, then this was something I wanted to be a part of. Six Sigma had instant credibility with me.

My message is that it took someone like Rich to convince me that becoming a Six Sigma Black Belt was the right thing to do, but I was also sold because senior leadership was behind it. I don't know how many times I saw some new programs that turned out to be just the so-called program of the month versus something real. At Cummins, because we had people like Frank McDonald, Rich Freeland and Tim Solso in the game, Six Sigma took on a whole new meaning for me. It wasn't just a program of the month effort and I knew I wanted to be a part of it.

Now, fast-forward to December 1999 at a hotel in Nashville, Indiana. We held what was called a M-0 Launch, which was a time for introduction to what we were going to do. That's where I first met George. I remember it was a room full of people that made up the first two waves of training. One was what we called an Operations Group, and the other was an Administrative Group. There were maybe 50 Black Belts in those first two waves of training. I was in Wave One—the operations wave. I didn't know a lot of people because they were from several spots around the company and I had not worked with them before.

People were introducing themselves and I remember listening to the introductions. There were people in the group with master's degrees and PhDs and other impressive credentials from the impressive schools they had attended.

They finally got around to me. I was older than most of the people there and had a full life of experiences already. I guess in slang terms, I had scars from experiencing loads of problems, both in new products and in current products. At that moment I experienced all the symptoms of the "imposter syndrome." The imposter syndrome is when you think that you've convinced everyone that you're a lot smarter and better than you really are and you feel like an imposter. At that moment I was in full imposter syndrome mode because I felt like, "Oh no, I'm around all these smart people. We're going to be doing this thing together. I'm going to be found out!"

The instructor Master Black Belts started talking about statistics and how we're going to use the tools to design experiments. I thought that somehow or another I'm going to fail. This was going to be the moment in time when I'll be found out. They are going to find out that I'm not as good as what I've said I am.

I knew when we launched into this I was going to have to work hard. I didn't know at the time what that really meant. I began taking the training very seriously from the first day. The first training event was three days for M-0, then four weeks of training spread out over four months.

I didn't miss a minute of class time. This was different than some of my peers, who would show up late and do different things during class, which was a bit concerning and disruptive to me. At the end of each week, we would take a test to see what we had retained that week. We'd turn the test in and it would be graded on the spot by the Master Black Belts from SBTI, who for me were like statistics gods. They were very smart people. They would pass out the quiz at around 3:30. There would be people around me who would have answered the 7 to 10 questions within 15 or 20 minutes. After they turned the quiz in they'd be talking about meeting for a beer. I was sitting there, poring over everything, going through my notes checking and double-checking, making sure I was doing it just right because I wanted to demonstrate that I was retaining the learning. It was really stressful!

There was one other guy, Mark Kelly, who was always in the room with me after hours. We were always the last to leave. Mark became and still is a very close personal friend. He was like a brother in Six Sigma because we had similar work experiences. We even started working together on our projects.

Because I had worked so hard, I found out through that training process that I had, in fact, retained the things that the Master Black Belts taught me. Significantly, I learned that it's not so important that you remember how to use a specific tool as much as it is to understand "why" you're using the tool.

One of the things that George said early on is that Six Sigma is a little bit like a tool box and it's full of different tools. Only, the mechanic knows it's in drawer three and that he needs to pick up that tool because that's the tool you're supposed to use for this job. That's what I engaged in and learned very early; why each of these tools is important and when to use them to solve a problem. I found out by the end of training that regardless of my imposter syndrome, by working harder than everyone else around me, you can, in fact, teach an old dog new tricks. I had absorbed the training and felt good about it.

WE'VE ALL SEEN PROGRAMS THAT HAVE COME AND GONE. WHY DID THIS FEEL DIFFERENT?

What Tim Solso said in the first session resonated with me because he was telling us the reality of why Six Sigma was important for Cummins. You knew when Tim talked, it wasn't scripted. It wasn't for optics. If it was bad, Tim called it bad. If it was good, Tim called it good.

By 1999 Tim had been the COO for a couple of years, and we were used to his candor and his clarity. In that first session, Tim stated his philosophy and the way he wanted the company to work. He said that it doesn't matter where you've gone to school, where you grew up, what experiences that you have had. I think his quote was, "We are moving away from being an organization of promises and best efforts to be an organization that delivers." To have our CEO say that really resonated with me, because as an operations guy, my work was always about delivery!

Tim's seriousness was reinforced with the selection of Frank McDonald as the quality leader, because everybody knew that Frank was a hardcore operations leader. Everybody at Cummins would have assumed that Frank would have been Vice President of Operations or Supply Chain at that time, NOT the Vice President of Quality. The mere fact that they recruited Frank was very impactful. Frank had "mojo". He had credibility with the entire organization. When Frank spoke you knew it was real. In addition, he had always been very candid about some of our shortcomings in the past.

So looking back on it, I think Rich, who had always been my compass telling me where true north was; Tim, who was giving clear direction; and Frank, as the company leader, were the three people who gave Six Sigma credibility for me. And it wasn't just with me; it was with everybody.

What also spoke volumes to me was that Tim came to our Black Belt training sessions multiple times.

The deeper I got into it, the more I realized the entire management team was lined up, because that's where I met Joe Loughrey, the Vice President of the Engine Business. I had never worked with him before, and I got the opportunity to see firsthand his commitment and passion for making this work.

All these reasons contributed to why this felt different compared to everything that had come before.

WHAT DID YOU LEARN ABOUT THE IMPORTANCE OF LEADERSHIP TO A SUCCESSFUL SIX SIGMA DEPLOYMENT?

My intent in telling this story is for other people to read and contemplate how they might organize to install an improvement culture in their company, or business, or their hospital, or wherever they are going to use Six Sigma. I would say that this requires senior leadership involvement. It's not a nice-to-have, it's a have-to-have! They have to be committed from their heart because it's not enough for them to stand up and give a good speech, or for someone from corporate communications to write a nice note on it. Tim, Frank, Joe and Rich were the real deal. They were committed. Their commitment was very visible, from the way they talked about it and their personal involvement in and out of the training.

If you're going to change culture, you have to know that the leader endorses that change and it was very evident to me, as a mid-level employee, knowing what I knew about these leaders, that this was real.

YOU MENTIONED THAT A LOT OF THE OTHER BLACK BELTS SEEMED TO BE A BIT YOUNGER THAN YOU, BUT PERHAPS TECHNICALLY TRAINED AND COMING FROM GOOD SCHOOLS. WERE THERE A FEW OTHERS THAT YOU MIGHT SAY HAD A BIT MORE ORGANIZATION AND LEADERSHIP EXPERIENCE LIKE YOU?

Yes, there were other people with unique experiences that were very valuable. For example, one guy had a lot of field service experience that I didn't. I would lean on him and others for the unique skills that they had. We had other people that were in training to be Master Black Belts. One Master Black Belt in Training (MBBIT) was Michelle Dunlap who I still work with on a daily basis which is refreshing. They all had what I consider to be superior skills or more advanced skills in certain areas.

In general, I would say that the people selected to be the first Black Belts were a good demographic mix, comprised of people that had from 5 years to someone like me that had 20-plus years in the company.

HOW DID YOU KEEP SIX SIGMA
GROUNDED IN THE "REAL WORLD"?

How the tools are taught leaves one of two impressions; either this is an academic, intellectual exercise or there is a real-world reason for why we're doing it. As I went through my Black Belt career and went on to be a Master Black Belt, I tried to bring a unique method to how I would use and teach the tools. I would engage people in thinking about the real world reasons very early on.

Some people for instance, would be all hung up on the statistical theory. We would teach the ANOVA tool and, inevitably, there would be two or three people who would take a very academic view and demand that we show how to hand-calculate ANOVA. I'd show them but, also, try to help them understand that you can stay up late at night learning how to do that, but I'd really reinforce with them that the only time you might need to do ANOVA by hand is if you are ever on a deserted island. If not, and you're working on a project at Cummins, you've got a computer and Minitab. I don't want you to take the extra three hours to do ANOVA by hand. I want you to just plug the data into Minitab and get the answer because the tool is not just there for the tool's sake. The tool is there to give you an answer to help you advance the problem you are trying to solve a step further.

I think how you teach matters, because that's how you're going to reinforce the practical side or the academic side. Far too often I've seen both inside Cummins and outside, the Master Black Belts spend too much time proving how smart they are and how impressive they are with what they know about statistics versus trying to help the students be successful by giving them what they need to know to solve their problem. It's easy to fire up that laptop and demonstrate to you how smart I am. I've seen Master Black Belts caught up in that. This also means that it's very important to select the right people for the Master Black Belt role.

When I was a Master Black Belt, I didn't consider myself to be super smart, but I could use Minitab to analyze data and show the Belts who I coached that I know enough about Six Sigma to help them. But I had decided that instead of focusing on the statistics, I could come at it in a more "street smart" sense and say, "This is easy, there's only five buttons you have to push in order to do a sophisticated ANOVA or design of experiment." I think how you teach it matters. Sharing a real-world approach with your class or with other people who you are coaching is important.

WHAT WERE SOME OF YOUR PERSONAL SIX SIGMA EXPERIENCES?

I think an interesting story happened in 2000. We were working on my first Six Sigma project focused on improving industrial engine assembly cycle time. Cycle time is the amount of time it takes for an industrial engine to flow through the assembly process. The hypothesis was that they took a lot longer than their automotive counterparts. In fact, anyone from the shop floor would tell you that's true. But we proved it with data and then used the project to understand why those engines were getting hung up in the process to eliminate those bottlenecks and improve line flow.

Inadvertently, because 20% of the engines were industrial and 80% were automotive, that first project unlocked how to make ALL of them go faster. It was a huge savings. I think it was $600,000 worth of savings for the project and our target was only $250,000.

I drove myself and the team to get the project done in six months because that's what the original project charter said. I think it was either the first or one of the first two or three projects completed at Cummins.

Sometimes Six Sigma project work puts you on a bit of a forced march to make sure you're accomplishing the task. I think we learned very early on that some people didn't make as much progress as quickly as they should have because they didn't drive the action. I was always very insistent that we achieve the savings spelled out in the project charter and achieve it in the time frame that we were supposed to.

I remember we had a meeting in the first six months. All the Engine Business Belts were called together to present to Joe Loughrey. Joe had taken the time to become familiar with all the projects so he asked good questions.

This was each Belt's first project. My project presentation received very positive feedback for having closed and produced savings in such a short time. I think the thing Joe liked about my presentation more than anything else was my energy. I was honestly excited about my project and the results!

One of the unexpected benefits of Six Sigma is its impact on people's careers. One example can be seen in that first project. One of the team members was a lady by the name of Deandra Arnholt. She's been married since the project and her name is Deandra Henson now. Deandra was a shop floor, hourly employee who I selected for the team because she was a master mechanic for industrial engines. Following my first project, Deandra was on many other projects as a team member. Because of her participation in Six Sigma, she became the very first hourly Green Belt at Cummins. She liked the work, demonstrated understanding, and wanted to go to training. Deandra went on to get her college degree and has since been given increasingly important roles at Cummins.

It was different than the model the company had created. As designed, Six Sigma training was not intended for the hourly employees. But with Deandra as the test case, we quickly made a modification demonstrating that everyone is welcome in Six Sigma. That was the first of many paradigm shifts we went through as an organization.

The second big paradigm shift involved product warranty, which was the focus of my second and third projects. Warranty is paid to customers whenever there is a product failure within the warranty period. This was a significant cost to Cummins in the early 2000s. Warranty projects didn't meet the classic definition of a Six Sigma project because it took a long period of time to see the "Y" variable move. The changes made today may take a year and half or longer to manifest themselves. We wanted to use Six Sigma on warranty problems, but we weren't sure how to do it because it was hard to measure the savings. Our SBTI Master Black Belt allowed Mark Kelly and me, who were the first Belts to engage in this kind of project, to create what we called the "surrogate Y," or the measure that would allow us to see the results more quickly and in real time. We were then able to know whether or not we were going to make a difference on the product's performance in the field. Proving that the surrogate Y was directly connected to the field failures was very important.

The reason I tell this story is because we didn't use Six Sigma to solve only classic Six Sigma sorts of problems. Very early on we said that we needed to aim Six Sigma at the company's biggest problems. At the time, these warranty problems were one of the biggest problems, so that's where we wanted to focus. We found a way to adapt the tools and the process to achieve that.

WHAT WAS IT LIKE BEING A CUMMINS MASTER BLACK BELT?

About a year and a half in, while I was still a Black Belt, George first approached me, and later so did Frank McDonald, and asked me to consider being a Master Black Belt. That old impostor syndrome kicked in and I said, "No, I'm not smart enough. I can't teach these tools. I'm a good practitioner, but I'd never be good at teaching." Frank told me that my real-world experience and street smarts is what they wanted as added diversity to the new Master Black Belt team. The new Master Black Belt team was a good mix of talents.

Both Mark Kelly and I added the street smarts and experience to the first Master Black Belt group. There were some others who had strong math backgrounds that taught us different things about the tools. For instance, Michelle Dunlap, who was also one of the original four Cummins Master Black Belts, was a company-recognized expert in design of experiments. We would leverage her strength and knowledge in that area to help us figure out how to teach and support the DOE tools. We leaned on each other for help and support. I am still good friends with several of that first group of Master Black Belts.

I was fortunate to be one of the first Black Belts and one of the first Master Black Belts. At about the two-year mark, we moved away from the SBTI Master Black Belts and figured out how to support Six Sigma on our own and be independent. It's not that we had to split with SBTI; we did it with their guidance. It was a part of the maturing process that we sustained and maintained Six Sigma by ourselves. SBTI helped look after our system health rather than teaching all the classes and coaching Belts doing projects. They were very helpful because every once in a while we'd have some trouble and we'd call them to ask for help. They had loads of experience and would be able to help us through the rough spots.

I had a really good experience as a Master Black Belt because I always said "yes" whenever George would ask us to do something. I'd just say "yes" without even knowing what it was because I liked all these new things that we were doing. I was very enthused!

One good example of something we were asked to do was the Executive Management Training held in mid-2001. George asked me and three other Black Belts to help lead the session with assistance from the SBTI Master Black Belts.

Joe Loughrey, the Vice President of the Engine Business, and all his main leaders attended with all the other top leaders in the company. They all sat in the same room with me, and I was the teacher. Teaching those tools to the senior leaders gave them a better understanding of how Six Sigma worked. We used Cummins real-world examples to demonstrate the power of the tools.

I remember one specific thing that happened during that session one day during lunch. Normally, as a Master Black Belt, you're always busy preparing for the next part of the lesson plan during lunch. But this time, Joe wanted me to sit with him because he wanted to ask me some questions and dig deeper about what he was learning. It was at this lunch that he started putting things together for how he wanted Six Sigma to impact his business. He was a master at connecting dots. Joe's the one that said, "Hey, let's figure out how to do a Six Sigma project about how to actually accelerate and improve Six Sigma." This sounds simple for me to say now, but it was revolutionary at the time.

The leaders took the executive session seriously and learned quite a bit about Six Sigma because of it. They were good students, and we didn't cut them any slack either. I think that it was a watershed moment because I could see people becoming more positive about what we were doing during the training. As a final confirmation, Joe called on everybody at the end of the session and asked them if they were in or not. It was a watershed moment for senior leaders at Cummins because it wasn't just Tim and Frank and Rich anymore; the whole management team was now aligned.

Because of the executive session, I had the opportunity to work directly with Joe, along with Mark Kelly, on a couple projects that helped shape how we were going to manage Six Sigma in the Engine Business going forward. This gave me a lot of exposure, personally, and gave me an opportunity to help influence the future direction of Six Sigma.

WHAT DID YOU LEARN DURING YOUR TIME AS A MASTER BLACK BELT?

First, I felt honored to be one of the first Master Black Belts. It felt like pioneering because we had to improve all the training material by adding in Cummins examples. We very quickly learned that using Cummins examples made the training more impactful. We reworked much of the training material in a way that made sense for Cummins. We did it all with SBTI's help and approval to make sure we weren't making mistakes. Our goal was to make it our own.

As Cummins people took over full responsibility for deploying Six Sigma, we created what we called Master Black Belt Star Points. The company had decided that the corporate organization would remain very small, but there were many things to manage deploying Six Sigma in a global company. The idea of Star Points came from our use of team-based work systems in the manufacturing plants. The purpose of the Star Points was to make sure that all the things that needed to be managed had a leader from the Master Black Belt team on behalf of the whole group. These leadership roles were delegated to Master Black Belts. Therefore, the Star Point structure made sure that every Master Black Belt had a mission in making Six Sigma work for Cummins. As examples, some Master Black Belts focused on management of the training classes, others focused on the Six Sigma database, and some Master Black Belts focused on the training material. We had several Star Points giving the Master Black Belts a chance to more fully engage and demonstrate leadership capability. The Master Black Belts spent a lot of time together in this work and became a very close group.

One of the most important tasks we had was to select the next wave of Master Black Belts, because the Master Black Belt assignment was only for two years; then we were going back into the business. The guidance that George gave us was to pick somebody who was better than ourselves— somebody who we would want to be our Master Black Belt. To do that, we did something that I still think was revolutionary. We created a process that required that a new Master Black Belt candidate had to be endorsed by a current Master Black Belt. Then the senior Master Black Belt was assigned to be the new Master Black Belt candidate's mentor. We also created the Master Black Belt in Training process (MBBIT) for new Master Black Belt candidates. The Master Black Belt in Training process lasted for six months. The Master Black Belt mentor's job was to help the Master Black Belt candidate create a development plan and monitor progress to make sure there was continuity. Since the Master Black Belt role was a two-year role, we had to quickly replenish ourselves. With a six-month training period, one year into your time as a Master Black Belt you had to select your replacement and personally make sure he or she was capable of taking your place. I think that it was either out of dumb luck or genius that we did that, but it worked really, really well because it gave us real "skin in the game" as Master Black Belts. Becoming a Master Black Belt wasn't just Frank's or George's decision because he liked this person for whatever reasons. This was one of our roles.

Being a Master Black Belt led to a surprising opportunity in June of 2003. The Jamestown plant manager was scheduled to be in Columbus. I knew him and he was another operations guy. He needed a ride to pick up a car to drive back to the airport to catch a flight back to Jamestown, and he asked me if I would take him to the car rental store.

It was a Friday afternoon and I didn't think too much about it. I picked him up and as we were driving around the plant he said, "Dana, I have good news. I received a promotion." And I said, "This is great news, you're a good guy, and I'm really glad to see you being successful." But he followed up with, "And I have great news for you. I'm going to be the business' general manager and you're going to be the new plant manager for Jamestown." I was hit with the impostor syndrome all over again because I thought, "Oh my gosh, they're considering me for this role. Can I do it?" Remember, it was only in 1996 that Rich told me that I wasn't ready to be a plant manager. It's now 2003 and they just asked me to be the plant manager for one of the largest plants in the company. He explained that they had thought about it carefully and thought that I was the right candidate and wanted me to seriously consider and accept the job.

It scared me to death! It ruined my weekend because I had all the emotions one gets when taking on a big job. It took me about three weeks to say yes; one week to decide that I wanted the job and two weeks to get over the fact that I didn't feel I was qualified or the right guy. What sold me on accepting the job was a conversation with Rich Freeland. In his quiet way, he explained his reasoning for why he thought I was the right guy and convinced me that I could do it, that he'd help, and that it was my time.

One of the reasons I was selected was a problem we were having at the Jamestown plant. We had just combined two engine assembly processes into one plant. This was another change that Frank McDonald led as the new leader of the heavy-duty engine business. Some things weren't work as well as required, so they needed somebody who was a process and a data expert to help lead the plant through the improvements. So I said yes and moved my family to Jamestown, New York, which was a big move for me.

When I first walked into the plant, what I found was worrying. The people were working seven days a week, 12 hours a day trying to build 125 engines a day. It was painful to watch. People were mad, upset, and frustrated. They loved the idea that they had work to do because they had gone through a period when they thought the plant might be closed. But now they had too much work to do. It forced them into a work environment that was very difficult because they couldn't produce enough product no matter how many hours they put in.

There were two big moments that had an impact on me. The first was when I went to my first production meeting. The plant staff holds a daily production meeting at 8 a.m. All the team leaders get together and they talk about the day's work. There are about 35 people in the room. I started attending those meetings because it was important for me to hear what was really going on and understand where the bottlenecks were. This was in my first week at the Jamestown plant.

The first person to speak was the assembly line team leader of Zone 2, who managed engine turnover. He was mad because his team had to work again on the upcoming weekend and they hadn't had any days off for some time. He asked me the question, "Hey Dana, if you're from Columbus and have had all this Six Sigma experience and you're supposed to be so smart, why do you think we can't build the amount of engines we need to and get some days off?"

I thought about it for a minute and said, "Do you want the real answer or something that sounds politically correct?" and he said, "I want to know what you really think." I said, "You come to work every day expecting to lose. You all play like losers. You act like losers. Therefore, you lose. What we have to do is figure out how to play like winners. The way we do that is to define a target and drive ourselves to win by achieving the target."

The plant quality leader, who was sitting in the room at the time, calculated that we needed to produce 180 engines in eight hours to meet the demand for the product. So that afternoon, we started a "180 in 8" initiative.

Initially, when I said they played like losers it was hard for the Zone 2 team leader to hear. It really stung at first. But he got on board right away. In fact, he was famous in the plant for making tie-dyed shirts and the very next day, he wore a shirt that was tie-dyed with great big block letters across the front that said "I CAN." He made one for everybody on the assembly line and whipped up enthusiasm for believing they could change in a very positive way.

We started the "180 in 8" drive by chartering Six Sigma projects for improvements in each zone. Because we were using Six Sigma, all our improvements were led by the data. For example, using assembly data we found out that it was relatively easy to identify where the cycle time problems were by team and by zone. Belts were assigned to the projects and people were assigned to the team from each zone. We included the operators on the teams as leaders of the projects because they were the most knowledgeable about the work. We put the operators in charge of the teams. We were working for them. I kicked each of the projects off by giving an introduction to each of the teams. I began by drawing an organization chart that had the assembler at the top with all the engineers, facilities people, plant management and HR working for the assembler.

The teams began each project by writing down the items that were important for improving the process. This was followed by the creation of a C&E matrix to pick the right five or six problems to work on. By combining the will of the people to win with data and Six Sigma tools, we quickly moved up the ramp and began making real improvements.

I remember when we got our first Sunday off. That was followed about three weeks later by taking our first Saturday and Sunday off. This was a huge win! When people went home on that Friday, it felt like when we were high school students on the last day of school before leaving on summer break. People were giddy!

Two days off for them was euphoria. It created a sense of confidence in the plant that by using data and this process, most anything was possible. It created a strong pull in the organization to do more. For instance, after we fixed the assembly line, the block machining line said, "Can you come over and do some projects with us because we don't like working seven days a week either." So the people in the plant began to realize the power of using these improvement tools to actually make their lives better.

This all happened in about four weeks because the results were immediate. There's this false idea out there that a Six Sigma project needs to take six months. No! This is wrong thinking. You can see almost immediate results if you've got the data and the desire to go fast.

I don't know if you've ever watched the movie *Contact* with Jodie Foster? We used to watch it as Master Black Belts. Jodie's received this signal. She keeps tuning, tuning, tuning until she can hear what they're saying. That's just how data behaves in a Six Sigma project. The project just kept tuning, tuning, tuning until we find out what the issues are and we take care of the biggest issues right away.

I have to tell you that it made the manufacturing engineers, the industrial engineers and the facilities people a little mad in the beginning because they were used to being in charge and dictating where and what fixes we were going to make. Now, all of a sudden, the assemblers and the data were leading them. But magically, this approach made a bunch of different things improve. It definitely caused the people in the plant to pay attention and they began to pull it in to help them.

My manager wrote about Six Sigma in my performance review. After listening to me talk in the all-plant meeting, he said to me, "Dana, you understand this Six Sigma stuff so well, you need to be careful how much you're using that terminology because I don't think the people in the plant get it." I listened to what he said, but I didn't agree with him, so I quietly continued doing it. So it was a special compliment when, during his retirement ceremony, he told me that I was right and he was wrong.

By continuing to talk to the people in the plant about Six Sigma, it helped them understand what the power of the process was and it caused them to start pulling—and pulling hard—for doing projects all over the plant.

This meant that the Belts who were working in the Jamestown plant at the time were working in a fertile place. They weren't fighting to get something done; they were being pulled in to all sorts of problem areas to help.

WHAT IMPACT DID FRANK MCDONALD'S BUSINESS GOAL TREE HAVE ON WHAT YOU DECIDED TO DO IN THE PLANT?

The business goal tree focused on driving profitability. It is the thing that tied everything together at Jamestown because it demanded that the business become profitable. The goal tree was cascaded from senior leadership to Jamestown with a mandate to get very focused. It was like a giant C&E matrix. We had to agree on the 10–15 things that we're going to work on to achieve the bigger goals that Frank had for the business.

The company had committed to the investment community that by combining assembly operations to one plant in Jamestown, we were going to produce several million dollars in savings each year. That was the business goal. The goals we set for the plant helped us achieve the bigger business goal. The goal tree, which was born out of the Six Sigma Process, created a refined approach to developing the short list of improvements we were going to work on versus a long, disconnected list. The goal tree has been a very valuable tool for us.

HOW DID THE GOAL TREE PROCESS WORK?

Imagine your boss has 10 or 15 objectives to achieve. You're working down inside this organization and you look at those objectives and you say to yourself, "How can I use my organization and my projects to help achieve those objectives?" The overall business objectives are received at a goal tree cascading event from the business president. In traditional planning, there are a lot of different conflicts, like arrows pointed in different directions, that get in the way of achieving the objectives. Using the goal tree enabled us to line up all the arrows to point in the same direction. This gets everybody working to deliver the objectives. Goal tree is a very powerful tool!

IS GOAL TREE PART OF THE SIX SIGMA PROCESS?

No, the goal tree process is separate from the Six Sigma approach. We learned about goal tree from the SBTI Master Black Belt who introduced the process to Cummins.

We were trying to figure out how to make sure we were selecting projects that would help us meet our company goals. During a meeting, he heard us talking about setting priorities using a voting process. The Master Black Belt shared that using a goal tree would be a more effective way to align our projects with company goals. The goal tree was introduced at the executive training that I talked about earlier and Joe Loughrey grabbed ahold of it as a great way to articulate work priorities for the business and cascade them.

At Cummins, goal tree was born out of Six Sigma, but it was pulling in a best practice from one of the consultant's Master Black Belts. We still use it today. In fact, I recently reviewed the goal tree for both the company Quality function and Cummins.

I can illustrate the impact of the goal tree by going back to the Jamestown experience. We were aiming Six Sigma at our biggest problems. We were not trying to produce Six Sigma results. I think that's the big difference in how we approached Six Sigma and an important point I'd like to make sure I get across. If you create targets and goals for Six Sigma and you need to produce X dollars' worth of savings, people will do exactly what you're asking them to do. They will get X dollars' worth of savings. If you aim Six Sigma at your biggest problems, the result is that you will produce meaningful results for your customers and the savings will be a natural outcome.

Now, you can't run an organization without targets and goals and I'm not advocating that. But how you aim is extremely important. For Jamestown, it became how we worked. It was not led by a department or some vague quality initiative. It was how we were working.

Here's an example of what I mean by "how we were working." Jamestown has a computer room with about 30 PCs in it. It was mainly used as a training room. After we started to show real results from our Six Sigma work there were lots of people, both hourly and exempt, who were in there trying to learn Minitab because they wanted to figure out how to analyze the data they had. It became important to people in the plant that we continue to use a data led process when making decisions. As I said earlier, it made some people angry. There were some people that left because this was a watershed moment for them. When you've always been in charge and what you say goes, and now all of a sudden the data is in charge and it dictates what we do, that was hard for some people to take.

When we aimed at that "180 in 8" goal, it included everything. We streamlined our hiring process because we were growing so fast we had to hire people, and the hiring process that HR was using was lethargic, so we did a Six Sigma project on that.

We used data to set our wages by using Six Sigma tools to do our economic review. We looked at a 60-mile radius of other like manufacturers to find out what they paid and make sure that what we were paying was fair.

We started using Six Sigma to rate our employees at the end of the year. We had 83 management staff at Jamestown. The rating process was always a big emotional fight on who were going to be rated top performers, who would be rated average and who would be rated below average. We used a Six Sigma tool to get very clear on rating criteria and rate each person using the criteria. Doing it this way helped to take the emotion out of it. It didn't take the significance of it away, but it took a lot of the emotion out of it.

We were using Six Sigma for almost everything. The process and the tools just became a normal part of our conversation.

YOU MENTIONED THAT "180 IN 8" WAS, IN REALITY, A SET OF SIX PROJECTS. WAS THIS CUMMINS' FIRST UMBRELLA PROJECT?

Yes, but we didn't call it that. We didn't know enough to call this an umbrella, but, in fact, that's exactly what we were doing. Even though I was called a plant manager, I was still a Master Black Belt. I think that's an important distinction for Cummins. Once you've been a Master Black Belt, it changes the way you think about things. So, once a Master Black Belt, always a Master Black Belt. As the plant manager, one of my roles at Jamestown was to be the umbrella manager. And it, was a BIG umbrella project! The umbrella was all about achieving "180 in 8" because no one team or one section could do it without the people before them and after them. It was a very positive emotional journey.

WHAT IMPACT DID SIX SIGMA HAVE ON YOUR CAREER?

Six Sigma gave me the opportunity to hold several rewarding positions. Following Master Black Belt, I was the plant manager at Jamestown from 2003 to 2007. I continued with some senior supply chain roles in the engine business from 2007 to 2010. Then I went to Cummins Turbo Technologies (CTT) as the quality leader from 2010 to 2013, because they had some significant product quality issues. I continued to use the Six Sigma tools there. When George retired, I became the leader of Quality for the company.

I was recruited to CTT to work as a quality leader because the business leader wanted me to think about quality in a broad way. In a business, there's little "q", which are the typical manufacturing quality functions like, for example, testing, part verification, and bad part segregation. This "little q" is different than the "big Q." Big Q is the orchestration of all the business processes to produce quality products and services for the customer. This is the way quality should be. Quality sits at the top of the Cummins Operating System and influences the whole. Working at CTT gave me an opportunity to employ that methodology as a quality leader. Then in 2013, I progressed on to even more senior roles as supply chain leader and quality leader for the engine business doing both roles together.

I wouldn't recommend this to anyone, because it really was doing two jobs at once. Then in 2015, I came to the quality role for Cummins after George retired.

I will tell you that I'm humbled to have a role like Cummins Quality leader, especially from a Six Sigma perspective. One of the unexpected benefits of Six Sigma was the impact on employee development. Six Sigma helped shape me and sharpen my skills. It helped me develop, give me exposure, see lots of new things, and meet new people. I am absolutely convinced that had I not spent that three and half years in Six Sigma, I would have never been close to officer level at Cummins. I am absolutely convinced of this. I think that the value the company placed on Six Sigma and being a part of it gave me an opportunity that I would not have gotten otherwise.

IS THERE ANYTHING YOU WOULD LIKE TO ADD?

Yes, there are two things I want to make sure is clear. First, before beginning a change like Six Sigma, I believe a company must express very clearly the "why." What is the thing that we want to change by starting Six Sigma? If, for example, I'm running a company, like one of our key suppliers, and I want to become a Six Sigma organization, I must be able to explain to people why are we doing it. What's the business reason? Then, learn from the experiences of others, like Cummins. In Six Sigma terms, what are the key "Xs" that make it work. It's important to express it in this way. Because, as any Belt will tell you Y, or the outcome, is a function of Xs, or inputs. Being able to think about it in this way gives an organization a better chance of success.

The second thing that I want to make sure is clear is that Six Sigma works anywhere. For example, I'm currently doing two Six Sigma projects for the county. One of them with the sheriff's department and one with the County Council helping them put together a more structured and robust budgeting process because it's always a big emotional blowup. I think sharing these tools in services that impact the population at large like healthcare, the county or state government can make a real difference.

I'd like to end with a story that sheds some light what Six Sigma maturity looks like. Last year I was invited to attend a Company Operating Team (COT) meeting. The COT was debating the annual plan. The conversation led into a discussion of how to make up a several million-dollar shortfall to the targets that we had committed to for the following year.

After, some time spent in discussion the COT decided that we needed to come up with a list of projects that focused on the target shortfall. At the end of the conversation, Rich Freeland, who is now the company president and COO, said, "What do we need to do to start these projects and shore up next year's plan because I'm not going to submit a plan that comes up short. We have to meet our commitments." Then he walked around the table and puts his hand on my back and says, "Dana, I know you've just been through a difficult meeting with us and maybe we actually forgot you were in the room, so we were talking pretty candidly. You're a process expert. What would you do to create a process for this because we don't want to lose this list or these projects that we want to do?" I said, "Well, there is something that we can do, but my mind is running ten million miles an hour right now. Why don't you give me a little time to think about it?" That was on a Thursday.

I spent the entire weekend thinking about what to do. I couldn't sleep because I was constantly thinking about how to manage these projects and get the results that the company needed.

That next Monday I met with Rich and shared my proposal. I coined a term for the project list—"Beat the Plan"—because they were projects we needed to do to beat the plan. Because I'm not a member of the COT, Rich fully deputized me to lead the process and come to every COT meeting to report on progress. He also asked me to have a regular meeting with him in between COT meetings to facilitate the "Beat the Plan" projects.

We created one-page charters for each of the projects because we needed clear measurable targets. The charter included who's on the team, a time-line, and all the other stuff you learn in Six Sigma. All I was doing was replicating what I had learned once again.

Rich thought that it was groundbreaking. At first the COT didn't see it as an application of Six Sigma. But Rich finally caught on and said, "You're doing a Six Sigma project with us, aren't you?" And I said, "Yes, and the Y is the plan gap. That's what we need to close to beat the plan." We were managing a portfolio of projects focused on the target of closing that plan gap.

Since that first experiment it's taken on a life of its own and is now a regular part of the COT's processes. In fact, the COT has come up with a set of Wave 2 projects.

My main point is that as a Master Black Belt, as a Six Sigma user, you learn how make order out of chaos by using the Six Sigma tools.

This is how to use Six Sigma to manage the business. It's critically important to realize that Six Sigma is not the goal, improving the business is the goal. If a company takes that approach, using Six Sigma becomes a very natural part of running the business. This is really what Six Sigma teaches you if you stay with it long enough.

14

S-Curve 3—Building a Foundation

The third S-Curve saw Cummins move into the second year of Six Sigma implementation. We began monthly progress reviews with the senior leadership team and with the business Six Sigma leaders. These reviews would cover Six Sigma progress against savings targets, training launch data, training launch effectiveness and best practice examples of Six Sigma projects. These reviews continued monthly for eight years.

In the second year, it was clear that the company wasn't progressing as fast as we thought we could. We decided that we needed a program boost.

TABLE 14.1

Key Actions for S-Curve 3—Building a Foundation

- Monthly progress reviews
  - o Senior leadership team to the CEO
  - o Business Six Sigma leaders to the leader of Six Sigma
- Executive session—reenergizes leadership (12–18 months)
- Conduct Six Sigma projects on Six Sigma to understand how to make it better
- Introduce common measures (examples)
  - o Project launched by month
  - o Time to close
  - o Project value—total and by Belt type
  - o Terminations
  - o Projects closed by month
- Business group reports—using the common measures
- Determine how many MBBs are needed and select the second group of MBBs from the early BB pool (how will they be prepared to be effective?)
- Introduce Six Sigma recognition award given by the CEO
- First annual review of progress with BoD
- Begin planning for DFSS (integrate into phase gate system)—this is important!
  - o What is a project?
  - o What is the role of the Belt?
  - o What is the role of the MBB?

To create that boost, we organized an executive reorientation session to be held in the middle of the second year.

The purpose of this session was to show the leadership of the company completed Six Sigma projects, Six Sigma results measures, and reintroduce them the Six Sigma process and tools. This was an opportunity to demonstrate the value of the process in a tangible, practical way. A key outcome of this executive session was that it reenergized leadership in the engine business led by Joe Loughrey and was key to real progress made over the next few years. The main elements of the executive session included:

- A complete review of DMAIC and the tools used.
- Group exercises using some of the more basic tools to address the question, "How can we improve our Six Sigma deployment?"
- A measures review. These measures at the time were profit before income taxes (PBIT) value to the company and project terminations.
- A review of four Black Belt projects.

Following the executive reorientation session, two projects on Six Sigma were conducted in the engine business. The Black Belts for these projects were Dana Vogt and Mark Kelly. The leaders of the engine business were the team members. The yield of these projects were improvements in how the Six Sigma effort was managed, the measures used and the project process itself. As an example of the improvement of how Six Sigma was managed, the engine business leader began sending letters of recognition upon completion of every Belt's first project. Another example is the adoption of a common set of measures:

- Project dollar value for both Green Belts and Black Belts based on improvements made.
- Time to close a project as measured from project start date to official project closure and approvals sign-off.
- The number of project terminations, which are projects closed early with no Improve and/or Control phases.
- Projects closed by month.

Ten Master Black Belt candidates were selected from the initial Black Belt pool. From July until the end of 2001, we prepared the Cummins MBBs for the departure of the consultant at the end of that year.

The Chairman's Quality Award was initiated during this year. The Chairman's Quality Award recognized the best Six Sigma projects completed across the company for the prior year. As part of the recognition, an elegant crystal trophy was given to the winning Belt and sponsor. A formal sit-down dinner for 150 people, including business leadership and members of the Board of Directors, was held prior to the company's annual meeting. During the annual meeting, a project expo was conducted during which all of the winning projects and Belts were available to explain their projects to the public (see Figure 14.1).

In the third and fourth quarter of the first year, of Six Sigma implementation Cummins began planning for the inaugural training launches of Design for Six Sigma (DFSS). Important considerations made when planning for the DFSS launch included:

- What defines a DFSS project?
- What is the role of the Belt?
- What is the role of the Master Black Belt?

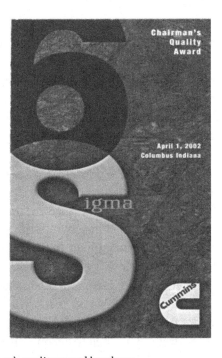

FIGURE 14.1 Chairman's quality award brochure.

Most importantly, we needed to understand how the tools of DFSS integrated into the new product introduction process. This was something we did not do well prior to launching DFSS. We learned over time that this was a mistake and that the organization must be careful to put the emphasis on new products and introducing those new products with no customer experienced defects versus emphasizing DFSS training, DFSS stand-alone projects and tools. The organization's goal is to provide great products and services to their customers. It is not to become great at the application of DFSS tools. Integrating the DFSS tools with the new product introduction process keeps it from seeming like something special or different from the new product introduction work. Some other mistakes made during deployment of DFSS:

> *Deciding to train engineers in the use of the tools.* Once trained, they would begin using them in their work. This didn't happen because there was a lack of clarity about when and how to use different DFSS says tools during the design process. Also, it wasn't clear to the average design engineer that the DFSS tools were better than the tools they were already using.

> *Because DMAIC was begun first and was very successful using a project-centric learning approach, the same technique was applied to DFSS deployment.* This meant that each Belt came to training with a defined project charter. Often, these projects were not part of the engineer's normal work during new product design. The result was that the engineers felt like DFSS was something different from new product design. It was not an integrated part of the process. The better approach was to clearly connect DFSS projects to the deliverables of the phase gates of the new product introduction process. This was done sometime later but the old habits that had been established proved difficult to overcome.

> *The role of the DFSS Master Black Belt was treated the same as that of the DMAIC Master Black Belt.* This means that the DFSS Master Black Belt would only be in the assignment for two years, similar to the DMAIC Master Black Belt. However, a DFSS Belt is typically a trained engineer accustomed to using math and other analysis tools in their work. This means that the DFSS Master Black Belt must have credibility with the project Belt that is being helped. Two years is not enough time for the DFSS Master Black Belt to become an expert in the use of the tools and gain credibility within the engineering community. This

created some unintentional barriers to acceptance of DFSS concepts of variation in product design.

―――――――――

S-CURVE 3 EXAMPLE PROJECTS

In S-Curve 3, many of the projects continue in the pattern of S-Curve 2 projects. At this stage of maturity, non-operations projects become more common. Some examples are shown in this chapter.

Improve the time to close high priority IT help requests from 75% to 90% meeting agreed customer commitments—This project created new tools used by IT technicians resulting in improved time to close to 93% meeting the customer commitment on high priority requests.

Reduce the amount of data required to improve the steady state engine calibration method—This project introduced the use of advanced statistical modeling techniques to reduce the amount of data required while improving accuracy and the time required to develop engine calibrations.

Improve annual market growth by region and product line—This project analyzed each product and region to develop models for use by sales teams to grow annual market penetration.

15

Moving From Building a Foundation to the Self-Supporting S-Curve

The work of the Building a Foundation S-Curve can last for 18 months or more. At 12 to 18 months following the start of deployment, preparation began for the Self-Supporting S-Curve.

We conducted an assessment of the first several waves of Black Belts to determine who would make up, in addition to those originally selected, the initial Master Black Belt cadre supporting the company following the departure of the consultants. Selection was based on the following criteria:

- Recommendation of local leadership.
- Review of the quality of their projects.
- Interviews with each candidate to determine their desire to accept the new position (this was the most important criterion).

We conducted an executive session (see also Chapter 8 on S-Curve 2) with the CEO and direct reports to review Six Sigma, how it is currently working and example projects with the Black Belts who led them.

Following the executive session, two projects focused on the improvement of the Six Sigma processes were launched in the Engine Business. One project focused on improving the Six Sigma system: project selection, common measures, Belt selection and so forth. The other project focused on the individual project process: Master Black Belt reviews, project charters, project trackers, Sponsor responsibilities and so forth. This and other projects like it demonstrated the broader value of Six Sigma for making improvements.

During this time, the first launches of Design for Six Sigma (DFSS) began. The deployment approach used for DMAIC was generally followed for the DFSS start-up because DMAIC was proving to be successful and the thought was to follow the same approach for DFSS to see similar results. This proved to be a mistake because there are several things that are different about the two approaches.

The Process—During a DMAIC project, Define-Measure-Analyze-Improve-Control IS the process. The project follows this process as a set of steps using different improvement tools to drive a change in the process or to eliminate a problem. DFSS is NOT the process for DFSS projects. The company's new product introduction process is the process within which the tools of DFSS are used. In fact, SBTI, our consultant, told us not to launch DFSS before merging it with the company's new product introduction approach. They did not know how to do this for us, and we didn't understand the importance of this step during the early deployment years. The resulting project-centric training proved less successful for DFSS because the basic context was incorrect. We later corrected this first error.

The Audience—The audience for a DMAIC project is anybody in the business. Many of the people involved in the projects have never done continuous improvement work and, therefore, are open to coaching and help from the Master Black Belts. The audience for DFSS projects tends to be engineers who are educated in the use of tools and math. This is their work. They are less inclined to take direction from a Master Black Belt who often has less experience and, therefore, lacks credibility with the person they are assigned to coach.

The Result—For every DMAIC project, the result is a control plan handed off and monitored by a process owner. This common result and the standard process made it easier for Master Black Belts to learn and coach projects because of repetition. For DFSS, each project follows a different path because the results required of the new product introduction (NPI) process are variable depending on the stage of NPI using the DFSS tools. This makes it difficult for the DFSS Master Black Belts to learn how the tools work within the process.

Cycle Time—For a DMAIC project, the cycle time is generally six months or less, especially in the early deployment days. Cycle time differences tend to be based on project complexity and the priority and importance of the project to the business. For DFSS, the cycle time of the NPI process can be years depending on the product and the number of new features and/or technology included. Each project is unique and, therefore, so is the cycle time. *I want to be clear here that DFSS is not the new product introduction process; it is a set of tools used in the defined design processes of the organization.*

Savings—DMAIC projects receive significant positive press in the organization for generating savings in the business. As variation and waste are eliminated from the processes in the company, savings are nearly immediate. For most DFSS projects, savings are of the avoidance variety. The actual spending of money doesn't change, rather spending in the future never occurs. Examples of avoidance are warranty expense, capital acquisitions, premium freight, plant efficiencies, increases in inventory and this list goes on. This is often counted as company money that isn't real and, so gets less attention and credit from leadership.

Before starting DFSS, it is my firm recommendation that the company fully understand and document how the tools of DFSS are to be used in the company's NPI process. Consultants today can be very helpful in this process (see my discussion of consultants in the *Making Change in Complex Organizations* book). Following this, work with the consultant to develop a training approach that recognizes that the tools are only taught as they are needed to accomplish the tasks of NPI.

As opposed to the DMAIC Master Black Belt who typically holds the position for two to three years, DFSS Master Black Belts are treated as positions in the business with their own career path and recognized value. This is important for the DFSS Master Black Belt because the audience must see them as credible coaches. The focus of DFSS is the products and services offered to customers. The DFSS tools only have value to the extent that they improve the quality experienced by the customer meaning the full range of the supply chain from raw materials to customer use and disposal of the company's products and services must be accounted for. Coaching designers to use tools with which they are unfamiliar requires a high level of trust. This trust comes from credibility that is only earned with time.

Moving beyond the Building a Foundation S-Curve into higher levels of organization maturity is a function of the scale and scope of the Six Sigma deployment. The example in Figure 15.1 contains a series of Venn diagrams to demonstrate the relationship between maturity and scale and scope. This next section is devoted to explaining what this means in practical terms.

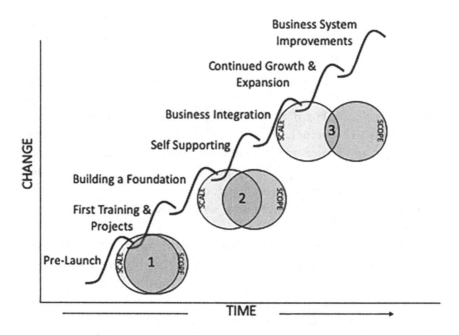

FIGURE 15.1 Scale and scope of Six Sigma maturity.

Scale—the size of the deployment. How many people are trained as Belts? How many functions in the organization are included? How many regions? The more elements of the company included in the deployment the greater the scale. The speed of increasing scale is a function of management decisions about the amount of resources that will be committed to the effort.

Scope—the variety of problems, improvements, and questions addressed using Six Sigma. If reducing scrap on line five is an example of a traditional Six Sigma project, broadening the application of Six Sigma to address transactional, HR, IT, supply chain, finance, supplier, customer, design, product, community and strategy as well as other issues affecting the organization is expanding the scope of the Six Sigma deployment. Increasing scope is the result of actively leading the maturity of the Six Sigma deployment up the S-Curves toward the future state.

In Venn diagram 1, scope and scale are largely overlapped. The reason for this overlap is that everything is new to the organization in the early S-Curves. Scope and scale move together because each new training launch increases the number of people and organizations involved (scale) and each project is something never done before (scope).

With more training launches, the scale broadens. Increasing scale results in a critical mass of people possessing the common language of Six Sigma. The inflection point is reached when there is a critical mass of people with the requisite knowledge and experience so that experimentation with different project types is possible. Therefore, the circles begin to separate. Scale continues to grow, but it is independent from the growth of scope. Different project types are no longer dependent on scale because Six Sigma is no longer new to the organization. This is what is represented in Venn diagrams 2 and 3 in the figure.

The S-Curves and Venn diagrams work together in an important way. If scope does not increase, progress up the S-Curves is impossible because there is a lack of growth and change necessary to the achievement of the future state. Therefore, Six Sigma never reaches escape velocity from basic project types and is pulled back into the strong gravitational pull of statistics. The potential of Six Sigma as a basic framework for all types of improvement is lost and the program stagnates.

16

Interview With Megan Henry— Black Belt, Master Black Belt, Six Sigma Leader

PLEASE TELL US A LITTLE BIT ABOUT YOUR BACKGROUND

I completed my engineering studies at the University of Michigan, heavily influenced by the automotive industry. I can remember sitting in a TQM class. There were no Six Sigma classes at that time, but that's one class that has a connection to Six Sigma that I vividly remember. That was one of my favorite classes.

Then I had two internships that connected me with Six Sigma. The first one was at Allied Signal, where I was a team member. As part of supporting a Six Sigma project, I learned a little bit about the process. My response at the time was, "Oh that seems really cool. I'm glad I can put that on my résumé." I went back to school for another year. My next internship was with GE. The internship was a team project and we were hired as Green Belts. We went through GE's Six Sigma training. They were only training Black Belts at the time. So, it was a unique privilege to go to that training. Our Six Sigma project was focused on welding quality in an Ohio factory. It was a very enjoyable experience.

I went back and finished school. After graduation, I came to work at Cummins. Cummins was my first full-time position after college. I've now been here 19 years. It has gone by very fast. I started in a manufacturing rotational development program. I was lucky enough to make several important personal connections through that program.

I remember the day that Cummins made the announcement that they were going to start a Six Sigma program. I knew that's what I wanted to do. It was like a switch flipped in my mind. I wanted to somehow get connected with that in my career.

One of my rotational roles happened to be with the person who became the Quality Champion responsible for Six Sigma in the business unit I was in. That opened the door to conversations about becoming involved in Six Sigma as part of my early career. It worked out that after I had my first child I came back and started as a Black Belt. I liked that a lot. In fact, the very first day in training I remember thinking that for my next assignment I wanted to be a Master Black Belt. Those are some key moments that I remember.

A couple of the first Cummins Master Black Belts co-trained me along with SBTI. It was Michelle Dunlap and Dana Vogt's first training launch. It was 2001, I remember because one of the SBTI trainers was delayed because of 9/11. That's just one of those weird things that I remember.

In my first Black Belt role, I was assigned to a manufacturing plant. As I did my projects, I had conversations about becoming a Master Black Belt as my next career goal. Being a Master Black Belt gave me great experience. I leveraged the network that I had built in the earlier rotational program to get things done. I felt like I was making a real difference because I could see what I was delivering, and I could measure it in savings. But it was also a great role for a new mom because it gave me a certain amount of flexibility that I needed at that time.

I was a Master Black Belt during the era that the role was strictly time-bound. The rule was two years and out. But I loved being a Master Black Belt for a variety of reasons and I wanted to stay. I negotiated with my manager at the time to make my two-year assignment carry over for three years. Part of it was because I loved the work and part of it was we had a second child, and by being a Master Black Belt I could better manage job stress and my time.

I frequently talk to people who are thinking about career choices about the potential of becoming Belts. I tell them that as a Belt you're absolutely accountable for results, but it's your schedule to control versus the customer, the production line setting your schedule or your boss. It allows you to maintain a balance between growing and developing in your career and time with your family. This was something that I realized during my time as a Belt. It's part of your professional development and I make sure to share that with people.

I was about two and a half years into my Master Black Belt time and really enjoying it. I was stretching myself and looking for ways to add value to the business and to the Six Sigma community by doing extra projects and participating on a Master Black Belt Star Point team. It was about then, in 2007, that the corporate Design for Six Sigma (DFSS) leader role came open. At that time, I didn't know what came after Six Sigma and being a Master Black Belt, because after five or six years I had met my career goals. I was asking myself, "What do I do next?"

I didn't think I was capable of doing the DFSS role, but somebody I respect sent me an email that said maybe you ought to consider it. The encouragement caused me to reflect. I knew I wanted it; I knew I wanted to stay connected to Six Sigma. It was personally fulfilling, and I knew I was having an impact. I've always said that my career priorities are to be a mom and wife first and make sure that my work life added more value than it took out of the business. It is important to me that I make a net positive return to the company I'm working for. That's why I liked Six Sigma.

I was hoping that I wouldn't be kicked out of Six Sigma just because my time was up. I was able to get the corporate DFSS leader role that then grew into the Six Sigma leader role. That's how I transitioned out of project oriented Six Sigma roles.

I spent about four years in that corporate Six Sigma leader position. Then in 2011 it was time to go back into the business. This is important because I was beginning to suspect that if I didn't go back into the business I was going to be in corporate forever, and I didn't want that. I took different roles, but the key is I've always had Six Sigma as part of my responsibilities.

WHAT ROLES DID YOU HAVE AFTER YOU MOVED BACK INTO THE BUSINESS?

My first move after the corporate role was to the Fuel Systems business. I stayed in Fuel Systems for three years. I was the Quality Champion, so the Black Belts and Master Black Belts reported to me. I was extracting continuous improvement needs out of the business and handing them to my team, with different levels of success. The Quality Champion is the person responsible for creating and managing the project hopper for the business unit.

At the time, Six Sigma wasn't as well supported in Fuel Systems as it was in some other businesses. While there, I was able to make a positive impact, and I learned and grew in several ways while I was there. After a couple of years, I realized I wanted something different. The role I'm in now was right after the Fuel Systems Quality Champion role. This new role is in the Components business. I have some Master Black Belt responsibilities, so I've managed to maintain a role in Six Sigma.

The Components business is a grouping of several businesses. I'm a quality manager responsible for Six Sigma, quality system certification, our TS and ISO, and I act as a Master Black Belt. I also lead significant quality improvement projects.

HOW DID THE SIX SIGMA PROCESS EVOLVE?

There are a couple of events that I remember when we introduced new tools. The first one was in 2003 when I was early in the Master Black Belt role and we added process redesign to our project tracker.

We recognized that tools from the DFSS suite were needed in our DMAIC process and teaching. Some of the tools we added were the voice of the customer tools including customer interviewing, KJs, Pugh Concept Selection, and voice analysis. I think that was probably our most successful training evolution step because it was probably the most structured. We took well-established training that was also already accepted in Cummins. We started by training it independently as a stand-alone process for how we would improve IT solution support for Six Sigma projects. We gave it a road map on how it fit in a Six Sigma project that clearly included it in the DMAIC tracker. We did a lot of work to define it and teach people how it fit with overall DMAIC and how to use the tools in a new way. We named it the Process Redesign track. We said when you get through the Analyze phase, if it is clear the current process needs to be redesigned, drop down to the Process Redesign track and do that work. The tracker then leads back to the Improve phase and on to project control and completion. It still gave Belts a very specific path to follow. I still think that's why Six Sigma works so well. You give people a recipe that they can follow to make any improvement. I think we gave people in the company a very good recipe.

Another thing that made it work was that we didn't try to create it. We worked with SBTI. They put the original package together. It started out being separate, but it was just going to be too confusing if we kept this and DMAIC separate, so we folded everything in together.

We took another big evolutionary step by re-looking at the overall training, which resulted in reducing training from four weeks to three weeks. We did it as a Six Sigma project and it became another successful change. We were very intentional and thoughtful about what we were trying to do. We used data from the Six Sigma database. We had the right stakeholders involved in this change from the very beginning, so that we had good supporters and advocates for it.

One change that didn't go so well was the incorporation of TRIZ (Theory of Inventive Problem-Solving) tools into the Six Sigma tool set. We tried to incorporate TRIZ because we recognized that there is a gap that exists in the Improve Phase. For D, M, A and C we have a very specific do this, then this, then this approach for each phase. In the improve phase we have improvements defined and improvement implemented. There really isn't anything that tells you in a stepwise way how to do it. TRIZ had the potential to get at that. We brought in an external consultant to deliver some very interesting training to the Master Black Belts on the roadmap for applying TRIZ to solve problems. It looked promising for inclusion into DMAIC, but we weren't very successful making it work.

One of the reasons is that we didn't do a good job of clearly defining the entry and exit points in the project tracker. We just didn't give Belts a robust enough road map to follow the way we did for the Process Redesign track.

Also, it was several years later into the Six Sigma journey. We had a much larger population of Belts who had already been trained and had been practicing our basic approach. This made it very difficult to introduce people to the additional tool set.

Another barrier was that we weren't addressing a specific problem. Process Redesign was intended to help with IT or really broken processes. TRIZ is about innovation. We would use TRIZ in the Improve phase of DMAIC. But it wasn't clear to people that there was a problem in that part of Six Sigma.

It just never worked as well as other changes that we made. There are still TRIZ tools in the DMAIC tool set. I am probably part of the generation of Master Black Belts that knows them the best because I learned them in a stand-alone way. They became diluted when we added them into the training. Many of the Belts that I've talked to don't even recognize the tools today. I think this was one time we did not do a good job of changing DMAIC. Ultimately, the evidence of success is great projects that help the customer and the business. We could point to success with process redesign. We just didn't have those standout successes with TRIZ that we could advertise and get people to use it.

If you see Six Sigma as the DMAIC process that is enabled with a big basket of tools that are applied situationally based on the data coming from the problem or improvement, then experimenting with TRIZ was important even if it didn't work as well as we had hoped. It's also why the Master Black Belts are so critical to the successful application of Six Sigma. The cadre of Master Black Belts needs an understanding and knowledge about how to use all of the tools so that they are prepared to help Belts apply them. The reality is that few individual Belts will ever experience using all the tools because they won't do enough projects to see the variety of ways they can be applied in the context of a project. But all of the Belts aggregated together will likely use all of the tools at some point. That's why the Master Black Belt role is so critical. I am still working to ensure that we maintain this larger tool set in our Master Black Belt community and that we continue to invest in the Master Black Belts greater than we do in Black Belts regarding tool awareness and development. TRIZ is an example of this investment. We need our Master Black Belts to know about TRIZ because sometimes these tools can be very valuable in a project. For example, TRIZ can be a key catalyst for two projects, not help on the next three projects, but then be needed again. I think it's the Master Black Belt community's responsibility to invest in and know how to use all of the available tools.

Thinking of the role of the Master Black Belts in S-Curve terms, we are constantly seeking to grow our influence in the company over time. If you keep applying the same tools, you're not going to grow your influence. That is absolutely part of it. A Master Black Belt partners differently with each group. The partnership with a very operationally focused group tends to be tactically oriented, while other groups can be more strategic. I remember training a strategy group. The conversations we had and the focus that we had on the tools was very different. For example, we had an hour-long discussion about correlation values during the training and what they would accept in their work as a relationship and what a Master Black Belt would accept in a typical plant project. The lesson is that if you cannot talk the language that your customers are talking, then they're not going to trust you with their biggest problems because they don't believe you understand their issues.

A second example of a less successful effort is how we engaged with Operational Excellence (OE) or the lean team, which is owned by the

Manufacturing function. We could have done a better job partnering with the OE team so that the lean processes and tools fit together better as part of a whole system. This would have reduced some of the conflicts that went on. There were disagreements about whether an improvement needed Six Sigma or OE when it is all continuous improvement. We tried creating road maps that merged OE and Six Sigma, but nothing worked that well. Our goal is to present one face to the Belts who need to apply continuous improvement for the business. It was important to figure out how to merge the two systems so that the question of how to improve would be less confusing for people.

These were examples of how we made changes and evolved. I think we have always had a plan to evolve because if you're not growing, you're dying. George would always talk to the Master Black Belts about that. He would always challenge us to think about what is coming next.

When I took that Six Sigma role, George gave me the challenge to figure out what comes next. So, one of my projects was to determine what the next change would be. Some of the change has been driven by business conditions and some of it has been focused on how to serve the business better as it continues to grow, but it was always a challenge that we had to meet. We used Six Sigma to help us think about that, to logically work our way through to an answer.

I am convinced that something, some approach to continuous improvement, always has to come next. If Six Sigma went away, it doesn't mean the business doesn't need continuous improvement. We need something. The history of the company shows that we knew we needed something, and we kept trying to figure out what's going to serve our company to help us improve. Six Sigma ended up being the thing that has worked for us the best.

HOW DOES SIX SIGMA HELP THOSE WHO MIGHT NOT OTHERWISE HAVE A PLACE AT THE TABLE TO BE RECOGNIZED AND DEVELOPED?

I am so thankful that I had the opportunity to participate in Six Sigma because I think it is the reason for where I am today. I benefited from both skill development and exposure to leaders by both participating in conversations and observing conversations that they had with each other. As a

Master Black Belt, I facilitated workshops where the senior leadership was thinking about what comes next for the company. I facilitated the development of planning goal trees. I was helping company leadership think at a level that I never imagined for myself. For me, observing that has been a huge personal development opportunity. A session only required a couple of hours of my time, but I learned a lot by hearing the questions that they're asking each other and their interactions. That's a great way to invest in a person.

To lead important work and show what I've been responsible for has been a big boost to my career. I led projects sponsored by a business unit leader when I had only five to seven years in industry. That was really great!

There are several people who I have met along my journey who I have suggested consideration of a Six Sigma assignment because I can see real potential in them. I am now working for some of them. They were a Black Belt or a Master Black Belt who would have been comfortable staying in a sourcing manager role or a plant facilities role and topping out at a middle manager level, but they used Six Sigma as a springboard to bigger things. They would have stayed in more traditional career paths because their ability to solve problems and deliver results made them really good in a plant environment, but those same skills can be very useful in a larger role.

When I would talk to Master Black Belts, I would ask them, "How often do you have 90 to 100 other people doing the same role that you are, with different leaders in different locations around the world?" Master Black Belts have the opportunity to talk to other Master Black Belts any day and compare notes and talk about what they are learning and how they are being successful. There is a huge network. The network that I built as a Master Black Belt included meeting 50 new Master Black Belts every six months at its peak, which is just amazing. I continue to run into people who tell me, "Oh, you trained me." I didn't remember training my boss in Fuel Systems, but he remembered. That gave us something in common—a real connection. This was all so critical to my career at Cummins.

There is an informal club of Master Black Belt alumni, because once you're a Master Black Belt, you're always a Master Black Belt. I could call up anybody who's also been a Master Black Belt and ask for support if I need it. I saw a former Master Black Belt at the end of the street the other day. Just because we were Master Black Belts together, we greeted each other and I said, "How's it going? I need some help with this, can you help?" It's like a fraternal bond.

There's a camaraderie that exists like few other experiences in the company. When someone applies for a role, they list their Six Sigma experience and the projects they've done. That's a key part of their resume. The projects that I've been a part of are my legacy with the company.

Recently I was talking with a gentleman from the UK. His Six Sigma project is moving production from one site to the other. He has 42 people in this pyramid of work that he's leading. That's an amazing project. We're trusting a Black Belt who has ten years of experience in the company to lead this very significant production change project because we trust the Six Sigma process and experience.

So yes, Six Sigma experience has been a huge factor in improving career opportunities for people.

IS THERE ANYTHING ELSE THAT YOU WOULD LIKE TO SHARE?

I would like to say one more thing about personal development. In my various roles I have met some people who are really good problem solvers. It's just in their nature, but they don't necessarily want to be out in front leading a large organization. Six Sigma gives these people the opportunity to have a significant impact on the company and its customers without all of the pressure that comes with leadership roles. I believe this has been a major benefit of Six Sigma at Cummins that we really didn't expect.

17

S-Curve 4—Self-Supporting

The fourth S-Curve is a critical point in time for the maturity of Six Sigma. It's during this time when several elements of the maturity journey set up the organization for future success.

The most significant thing that happens during this period of time is the consultant, who originally helped with training and Belt support for projects, begins the handoff to the organization of responsibility and accountability for the delivery of Six Sigma capability. This is one of those points in time that is a make or break for the success of the Six Sigma efforts.

One the big advantage that comes from having internal Master Black Belts and owning the delivery of the training is that they are more

TABLE 17.1

S-Curve 4—Self-Supporting Actions

- Become self-sufficient—the consultant leaves
- MBB team structure – distributed leadership of the key elements of the Six Sigma effort (depends on size and scope of Corp leadership group)
- Integration into the Business Operating System (*Do you have one?*)
- Supplier Sessions
  - o How will you work with suppliers?
  - o How will it affect the commercial relationship?
  - o What are your expectations of them?
  - o Who will own supplier involvement?
- Investigate improvement opportunities
  - o Does Tracker match reality of the projects?
  - o What isn't working well based on expectations/needs?
- More MBBs identified and prepared based on business requirements
- Customer projects? (When? How? Six Sigma project)
- Does the training match the business need? Does it need to be modified? How? (Six Sigma project)
- Begin training/applying DFSS processes and tools as the "how" of new product introduction

connected to what the organization is really all about. Master Black Belts are one of the key linchpins in the success of the Six Sigma effort. Internal Master Black Belts strengthen this relationship to success because it's now their organization.

When Master Black Belts come from the consultant, no matter how hard they try, they never really become a part of your organization. They know that their time with the company is limited. Also, they have other customers at the same time they are working with your company. They don't really know your company organization at a deeper level—the culture, how things work here, the products and so forth. So, they tend to present a more generic approach to how Six Sigma is used.

When Master Black Belts come from inside the organization, they have a vested interest in not only the organization's success but also the success of the projects that they support, because as Master Black Belts they are being evaluated by the organization and their future is tied to that evaluation. It's often during this time that the Six Sigma effort will accelerate because of this vested interest of the Master Black Belts. Ours did, and it's visible in the results.

Of course, this means that Master Black Belts must be prepared for this new role. About six months prior to the consultants leaving, the Master Black Belts were selected and trained in their new roles and responsibilities. This meant spending a lot of time practicing the delivery of training material both with the consultant and by themselves. It meant studying to understand the use of the statistical tools in enough depth that they can understand the basic questions that will be asked during the training and the support of projects. Cummins established a principle that the individual Master Black Belt wasn't expected to be expert in all tools, rather as a community the Master Black Belt network would have a high level of capability in all tools, so that if any one Master Black Belt needed help, he or she could go to others in the network for that help. During the preparation period, each Master Black Belt takes a skills diagnostic to help them understand their personal technical gaps providing direction for their preparation and study.

Another thing done was assignment of a career sponsor to the Master Black Belts. This sponsor helps to prepare them for what comes after their Master Black Belt assignment, which typically will be two to three years.

Another key to success is a strategy that delegates execution to local organizations. The Corporate organization owns the rules, the training, the collection of measures, the governing policies and procedures for how

Six Sigma will work in the organization, and it is the arbiter in disputes. All execution is local. This means the Belts and Master Black Belts report to the local organization. Project selection is a local responsibility. Review of project progress and project closure all belong to the local leadership. Following this strategy requires the Master Black Belts to play a key role in the development of the Six Sigma system that will be used to drive Six Sigma through its phases of organizational maturity.

The reason that the Master Black Belt becomes important in this role is that the corporate organization is kept intentionally small. At Cummins, the staff supporting the global Six Sigma effort never rose above two people, and most of the time it was only one person. To enable the development of the Six Sigma system, one approach that can be used is to organize the Master Black Belts in a team-based structure.

In the team-based structure, Master Black Belts work collaboratively in a distributed model to develop the different elements that will support a Six Sigma effort over time. These elements include, but are not limited to:

- Training improvement
- Master Black Belt preparation processes
- Improving the project tracker/project management tool
- Developing project selection processes
- Defining and improving the data collection mechanism
- Developing Six Sigma communication for the organization.

At this point, it is appropriate to include Six Sigma in the defined business operating system. At Cummins this was the Cummins Operating System (COS). Six Sigma became Practice 10 of the COS Ten Practices. This action formalizes the relationship between the operating system and Six Sigma as the mechanism for continuous improvement. This action formalizes the relationship between the business operating system and Six Sigma. The operating system serves as the source of potential improvements that are actioned using Six Sigma.

During this fourth S-Curve, enough is known about how Six Sigma works. *It is time to consider engaging the supply base in the process.* I have found it to be generally true that the quality of an organization's products and services is held hostage to the quality of its supply base. This is especially true in manufacturing and assembly companies who buy parts and pieces from suppliers. This can be equally true in the manufacturer's service and administration areas that send information to the part supplier.

In this situation, poor data and information to the part supplier will result in poor delivery of service to the manufacturer. In all cases of supplier-to-customer interactions, a supplier has a critical impact on the quality of the organization's products and services.

A focus on problems created by the supplier results in projects that can have a supplier focus. Engaging with the organization's suppliers means helping them to understand what the problems are and inviting them to participate in Six Sigma training for joint continuous improvement work. This also means developing strategies for how to work with those suppliers.

I found it to be a mistake to try to engage in financial give-and-take as part of the Six Sigma process. Trying to extract from the supplier some percentage of the savings generated from the project's improvements often does nothing but create animosity and a lack of trust between the supplier and the customer organization. If the projects selected are the right ones, positive impact on the organization's customers and ultimately revenue and profit far outstrip any savings that come from project execution. That's why it's important to focus more on the problems and any solutions for those problems than on commercial negotiations.

It's also important to provide Master Black Belt access and support for the supplier Belt. Access and support are important because the supplier will generally not have Master Black Belts of their own, so this can be a barrier to success. Using the organization's Master Black Belts to support supplier projects takes that barrier away and gives the organization some ownership and control over the eventual result of the projects.

Cummins also made it a practice to use co-Belts from Cummins to work with the supplier Belt in partnership on the project. Using the co-Belt model and the Master Black Belt supported the projects at a consistent, high-quality level.

One of the keys to success was picking the right projects so that the supplier understood clearly the value and the meaning of completing the work. A supplier training session would consist of Cummins Master Black Belts leading the training and two Belts for each project doing the work together. Project reviews are typically held online. It's important to keep the process as simple as possible so that the projects produce a result as quickly as possible. Selecting the right high-impact projects and achieving a good result quickly has a big impact on the organization's customers and creates a sense of partnership with the supplier.

This is also a time when the organization can begin thinking about continuous improvement of its Six Sigma processes. Enough work is done in Six

Sigma and enough history created that it's possible to do projects on the management of Six Sigma and on the conduct of Six Sigma projects. The purpose of these projects would be an improvement of the management of the Six Sigma system. Improvements would include:

- Developing project selection processes that closely align the projects with the organization's goals and initiatives.
- Updating the project management tracker to be consistent with how individual projects are managed.
- Addressing any areas of the Six Sigma management machine which are not performing as expected or needed.

The Six Sigma management machine (see Figure 17.1) itself requires some explanation. As you can see from the Figure 17.1, the Six Sigma system consists of eight elements. It's important to see the management of Six Sigma as a set of system elements that work together for successful Six Sigma project results. If in your organization Six Sigma is training and projects only, it has projects and Belts that are disconnected from the most important

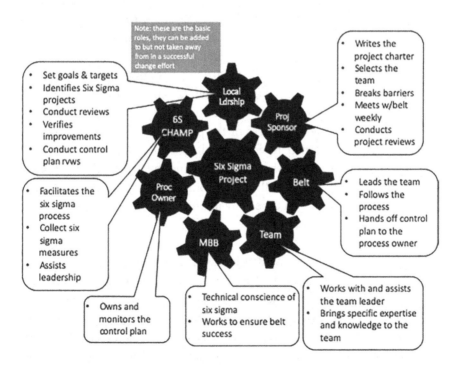

FIGURE 17.1 Six Sigma management machine.

work of the company. Ultimately, connection to the organization's goals, the organization's customers and the capability to systematically continuously improve isn't really changed. This makes it necessary to include all of the Six Sigma Management Machine elements for long-term successful deployment that weaves Six Sigma into the critical areas of the company.

The Six Sigma projects. The projects are the focus of the work and are linked to the goals and objectives of the business.

The local leadership teams. The local leadership team is accountable and responsible for selecting projects that are important to their part of the business. They're responsible for establishing priorities on those projects. They select the Belts who will lead projects. They are responsible for conducting project reviews, verifying project savings and auditing control plans post–project completion.

The Six Sigma Sponsor. The Sponsor has a key role to play supporting the Belt during the project. This role requires some personal time to be spent. The Sponsor is accountable for completing the project charter. This is important because effective Sponsors care about the project being completed. They have a vested interest in the project's success because the problem is in their area of responsibility. It's a mistake to select Sponsors who do not have a stake in the success of the project because they will tend to lose interest over the course of the project's progress. The Sponsor is responsible for selecting the team because most of the team members will be in the Sponsor's area of responsibility. A key role for the Sponsor is to break barriers when they arise during the course of the project. The Sponsor meets with the Belt on a regular basis, especially new Belts. Finally, a Sponsor conducts project reviews with the Belt and the team while the project is in progress. Additionally, I have found it helpful as the Sponsor to be a team member on especially important projects. Active Sponsors play a critical role in project success especially during the early phases of deployment.

The Belt and the Team. The Belt is responsible for leading the team and the project. The Belt establishes the project plan for both the time it will take to do the project, and the tools that will likely be used in each phase. The Belt is also responsible for developing team meeting agendas and frequency, ensuring project data is up to date, reviewing project progress during project reviews, and developing the project value at project close with the support of a finance person. The last responsibility of the Belt is to hand off the control plan to the process owner. The team comes to the project with knowledge and skills concerning the problem or improvement needed for successful project execution and delivery. The team is key to successful projects because no Belt is capable of completing projects alone.

The Master Black Belt. The Master Black Belt is the technical conscience of Six Sigma. The main purpose of the Master Black Belt is to ensure Belts complete projects successfully. They do this by training and coaching the appropriate use of tools and processes. The Master Black Belt also has a role to play with the leadership, helping them to identify important projects and scope them properly for Belt project execution. The Master Black Belt supports the Sponsor writing the project charter. The Master Black Belts are critical to the proper use and growth of Six Sigma over time in the organization.

The Six Sigma Champ. Six Sigma Champions are usually found at business unit level and higher. Their role is to facilitate the Six Sigma process for the organization. They collect and present Six Sigma progress measures and they assist leadership to carry out their Six Sigma responsibilities.

The Process Owner. The process owner should, whenever possible, be a team member. This is important because the process owner is ultimately responsible for the control plan and ongoing implementation of the project solution. If they're not engaged with and participate in the project itself, they can become barriers to solution implementation if they don't agree with the definition of the problem and the solution.

It's not necessary that different individuals fill each of the roles. For example, the Sponsor often sits on the leadership team. The process owner and the Sponsor could be the same person. In the end, each of the roles need to be filled if Six Sigma is to be approached systematically and ultimately impact the continuous improvement culture of the organization.

Typically, in S-Curve four the organization is beginning to do more and more projects. *As projects increase, it's important to assess the appropriate number of Master Black Belts needed to support projects and training.* A general rule of thumb is that, in addition to conducting training launches, working with leadership and participating on MBB Star Point teams, a Master Black Belt project load is 40 to 50 projects at a time. More than that and the Master Black Belt is overloaded. Less than that and the Master Black

Belt can find it difficult to stay busy. Using a trend chart for both training and project launches over time, the organization can determine in a timely fashion how many Master Black Belts they will need to support the organization's deployment. If the organization has defined Master Black Belt duration as two to three years, and if preparation to become a Master Black Belt requires six months in training time, the pipeline of new Master Black Belts has to be established well in advance to the actual need. This will require well-thought-out planning and support from the HR function.

During S-Curve 4, customer projects can begin. Your organization needs to assess its Six Sigma capability because doing projects with customers before the organization is ready can have negative consequences. GE was one of the first companies to publicize its use of Six Sigma with customers. They called it "at the customer for the customer." Cummins developed a similar idea. The goal was to help customers solve their problems using Six Sigma because we wanted our customers to know that we cared more about their success than anyone else. In essence, Six Sigma became part of the product offering to the customer for purchasing Cummins products. Before starting customer Six Sigma projects, it is important to decide and plan for the following:

- Which customer groups will be included?
- Who will be responsible for engaging with the customer and gaining agreement to let their supplier help them with one of their problems using Six Sigma?
- Will you include the customer in Six Sigma training?
- How will the organization address commercial issues in working directly with customers?
- Who will be the Belts for the projects?
- How will savings be counted?
- Will the customer have access to your Six Sigma System?
- How will you track and review customer projects?
- Will the process be owned by the corporate group, or will it be delegated to the business units?
- Given your organization's products and services, what kind of customer projects do you anticipate?
- Who will be responsible for developing common project templates, where will they be stored and who will own them?
- Will you benchmark another organization to understand how they do customer projects before beginning?

Another project that can be done during S-Curve 4 is one that investigates the match of Six Sigma tools to the real projects conducted. This project seeks to understand how to improve Six Sigma training to match the business's need for projects. Included in this analysis can be information about tool use during the phases of the Six Sigma project. This information can be collected as part of the Six Sigma tracking system entered by the Belts during the course of projects. Analysis of this information will yield what tools are used most frequently during the conduct of projects. An option then is to reduce the amount of training time and/or eliminate training on tools that are not widely used in the projects. Assessing the value of the training to the business creates an opportunity to reduce the time spent in training. What also makes this possible is the significant expansion of the infrastructure supporting Six Sigma during the fourth S-Curve.

Following the planning for how to use DFSS and the integration of DFSS into the new product design process, training can begin. The focus of training is on how to use the new product introduction process. Included is application of Six Sigma tools which build concepts of variation into product design. This takes the focus of training off Six Sigma putting it on the company's new products where the focus belongs.

The Self-Supporting S-Curve is one of the most significant transitions. For the first time, the consultant is no longer around on a regular basis. All training, Belt coaching, project selection and chartering, Sponsor training and program administration become the responsibility of the people of the organization. This is the point at Cummins when Six Sigma really began to take off. Some of the reasons for this transition include:

- The Master Black Belts had a personal stake in success. The CEO and his leadership team had engaged in, supported and continually reinforced Six Sigma's importance to the health of the company. Now it was up to Cummins people to make it work.
- The Master Black Belts worked directly with the Belts. The success of the Belts and their projects was a direct reflection of the quality of Master Black Belt coaching. Reputations and careers were on the line.
- Training examples became Cummins examples. This helped the Belts to see themselves in the projects and realize that Six Sigma applied to them.
- The various levels of leadership had no one else to blame if Six Sigma stalled.

This transition can also fail for some very practical reasons.

First, Master Black Belts are selected because of their technical capability only. This can lead to a fixation on the tools and traditional Six Sigma. This ultimately leads to the diminished value of Six Sigma because it is not used to work on the organization's most important issues. Leadership tends to lose interest and Six Sigma does not reach its full potential.

Next, leadership engagement is reduced. Now that the consultants are gone and "our" people are in control, leadership delegates the responsibility. Momentum slows and the organization moves on the next set of priorities.

Those members of senior leadership who didn't really want to make the change in the first place withdraw support from their Six Sigma leaders, Master Black Belts and Black Belts for Six Sigma work, moving them into other important areas.

Corporate Six Sigma leadership lacks an S-Curve mentality and approach. They continue to harvest results based on Six Sigma basics, not pushing the boundaries of Six Sigma application leading to stagnation.

Finally, all the Corporate Six Sigma leaders are promoted and moved to new jobs because of the success of the early deployment. The new Six Sigma leaders implement their ideas, which may or may not be connected to what has come before. This can create confusion and cause progress to stall.

A key event occurred shortly after Cummins entered the Self-Supporting S-Curve. Frank McDonald, who had been the original Quality Vice President reporting to Tim Solso, the CEO, was reassigned to lead one of the major product businesses. His charter was to improve profitability of this business. His first actions were to conduct assessments to understand what was working well and what was not. He assigned his Finance leader to do a complete audit of the finances and produce a feedback report. This report pointed out where the business had cost-effectiveness and reduction opportunities.

At the same time, Frank sponsored a Baldrige assessment using the criteria. This assessment was not intended to produce an application for the award. This was a mechanism for understanding where the leadership and management gaps were in the business. The feedback report was used to set improvement priorities and make assignments to his leadership team.

By combining the two feedback reports, the direction for Six Sigma application was set. Since profitability was Frank's main focus, improving spending effectiveness and eliminating unnecessary costs was a priority.

Frank had seen the effectiveness of Six Sigma improve as projects were tied to priorities as the leader of Quality for Cummins. He applied that lesson learned to his business improvement plan. There were three priorities for Six Sigma focus:

1. Reduce the cost of materials
2. Reduce the cost of warranty
3. Reduce the cost of conversion (manufacturing).

The primary focus of Six Sigma projects in the business would be connected to one of these priorities. Following a relentless drive to reduce waste and variation in the processes of the business, the business went from being a profitability laggard to the most profitable business in the company. Six Sigma worked, and they did it on their own.

This focus by Frank McDonald to dramatically improve his business's results positively confirmed that Six Sigma was a transformational change tool.

S-CURVE 4 PROJECT EXAMPLES

Recalling the discussion about how the S-Curves and the Kano Model are connected, the basic bucket of requirements grows as the organization progresses in maturity. This is also true of project types. The basic "scrap on line 5" projects continue as part of the overall portfolio of projects, and this will be true of all new project types as they come along. Thinking in terms of maturity gives Six Sigma space to grow into more and more important business areas while still encouraging continuing improvement of the basics when needed.

The projects in S-Curve 4 tend to be extensions into other parts of the business. Some examples follow:

Reduce the number of customs brokers supporting the business in the region. Each business managed customs brokers independently of each other, resulting in different service agreements and rates. The project resulted in selection of a single broker, negotiated standard rates and definition of a standard importation process that became a company best practice.

Reduce tooling write-offs. This project improved tooling data collection and customer invoicing timeliness needed to more closely connect these two activities for fewer write-offs due to inaccurate record-keeping.

Recommend product technology options that meet both customer and compliance requirements. This project used a more rigorous, cross-functional, customer-led process to develop technically evaluated and narrowed set of product options.

18

Interview With Ginger Lirette — Black Belt

HOW DID YOU GET STARTED WITH SIX SIGMA AT CUMMINS?

I graduated from Virginia Tech as an industrial engineer. After college I went into the US Air Force, which used its own version of process improvement. I was in the air force's engineering group and was involved in continuous improvement, including helping our unit prepare a Malcolm Baldrige Award submission. I then joined Alcoa as an industrial engineer for five years where I used statistical tools. I was also in the US Air National Guard during that time. I joined Cummins in 1998 as a Quality Engineer in Fuel Systems business.

I was in the first wave of Green Belt trainees in April 2000. My business Quality Champion asked in early 2000 if I would be interested in this new program at Cummins called Six Sigma. After he explained it, I said "Absolutely! Sign me up." I was excited to be in on the front end of something pretty cool.

Most Six Sigma tools have been around a long time. I had already studied and used many of them in school. In fact, I still have some of my college statistics books at my desk at work. We used the tools in the Air Force and we were already using many of tools at Cummins. Six Sigma was attractive to me because it just put the tools into a more logical order to achieve increased project success. I was excited to see them used, for the first time, as a continuous process tool kit where the tools all tie together with one tool leading to the next one.

In the earliest days of the Six Sigma deployment, there was talk that it might be a "flash in the pan" or the "new flavor of the month." Many thought Six Sigma risky, fearing if they got involved and it wasn't successful that it would hurt their career. There were fears you could get stranded doing a Black Belt rotation, getting too deeply involved, and pulled away from your work. That's why some people chose to not sign up to be a Green or a Black Belt.

But I didn't see it that way. I saw Six Sigma as very low risk because its tools were tried and true. Also, there was so much energy and resources being poured into Six Sigma. CEO Tim Solso talked about Six Sigma everywhere. The strong leadership of the company CEO, President and Six Sigma program leader, combined with the tried-and-true tools, made me feel getting involved with Six Sigma was an opportunity with a lot of upside.

I tell those I mentor to look for "springboards of opportunity" to grow, change or move upward on their career path. I see Six Sigma as being similar to a MBA. It is a springboard of opportunity by giving you a platform to show what you can do and save the company money while doing it. This is a factor in making you eligible for new jobs. I think you cannot build to something greater without trying something different. You've got to assess the risk, but if you never do something different, things aren't going to get better. You can't improve without trying new ways.

YOU LED THE FIRST CUSTOMER-FOCUSED SIX SIGMA (CFSS) PROJECT. HOW DID YOU GET INVOLVED?

I completed Green Belt training in 2000, earned my Green Belt certification in 2002, and shortly after became a Black Belt. I had completed 13 projects, all in manufacturing and engineering, and was coming to the end of my two-year Black Belt appointment when my boss asked, "Why not try something different with your last project?" A customer-side executive was looking to try Six Sigma projects with customers. I thought applying Six Sigma to the customer side was exciting and gave me another opportunity to springboard because it gave me the opportunity to try something new.

The leader of the customer-facing group, a Vice President of Sales, had identified three possible projects. One project, involving a large leasing customer, sounded the most interesting to me and most likely to be successful. The Vice President and I decided my final Black Belt project would be with that customer. He planned to stay very engaged to ensure a successful first customer project.

This was early in my Cummins career. At the time I didn't know Cummins was exploring getting into to extensive Six Sigma activity with customers. I also didn't realize how monumental a step this would be for the company. In hindsight, I now realize this was a big deal. A Vice President of Sales had reached out to me, and I was just a Black Belt who was very junior in the hierarchy and from a completely different part of the company. I just thought this was an interesting new realm, it was achievable, and it was something the Sales group supported.

Something that gave me confidence for success: the leasing customer also had a strong Six Sigma culture with deep appreciation for the system, processes and tools. Since this customer was well experienced with Six Sigma, I thought they would get on board quickly, be highly engaged and wouldn't need us to walk them through extensive Six Sigma training. This was very important since this was our first-time trying Customer Focused Six Sigma (CFSS). We wanted to make sure to get that first win. This would enable the company to build off the success, generate momentum and win others over internally so we could do more CFSS projects.

From discussions with the Sales Vice President, I felt this particular project was a real opportunity for building momentum because the customer had a well-defined, quantifiable problem to improve vehicle service times. The project idea had originated with the customer, which was even better. I knew they would engage because it was important to them. The original project idea scope was too large, but I knew we could get it down to something more focused and workable.

HOW DO CFSS PROJECTS DIFFER
FROM INTERNAL DMAIC PROJECTS?

For a CFSS project, the "customer" is someone who pays Cummins for products and services. CFSS project team members come from both the customer and Cummins. CFSS projects have two Belts and two Project Sponsors, one each from the customer and Cummins. Because CFSS projects tend to improve a work process, the overall DMAIC approach fits very nicely.

Customer input and participation is especially important for CFSS projects. The customer's investment in time and energy varies depending on project, but there has to be up-front customer commitment and investment to get the basics right.

A customer-focused project may deviate from the normal straight-line path. They are our customer; we take their input and needs into account. For example, although the data may lead in one direction, the customer might push us to do something else. We might go a little off course to do things the customer pushes for, while also using the data to direct them back to a more straight-line path. We're asking the customer to trust that we will help them get better. But they don't necessarily believe that until we actually produce a result. Since we may only get one chance to do a Six Sigma project with this customer, we want it to be a result that builds customer loyalty.

They are the customer, paying us for products and services we provide, and now we come along with a whole new thing not necessarily directly related to those products and services. We often ask for internal company data as part of the project. We also ask to take their people's time from other important things. We found that customers will sometimes place a Vice President on the project team to make sure we aren't ripping them off. It's all that stuff, having nothing to do with Six Sigma but everything to do with relationships, that can impact the CFSS project. We need to do whatever is necessary to build trust. For this reason, we have to be a lot more flexible in the way we apply Six Sigma, so they'll continue to engage.

Traditional manufacturing and engineering internal projects often have a clear end result. The result of those projects—creating a process, improving a process or reducing defects—all have tangible dollar savings for Cummins attached to the project. In contrast, a customer's objective might be increased revenue or growth, not savings. We figured this out quickly.

CFSS project "savings" come in two types. The customer benefits or saves from the improvement. Cummins benefit is increased customer loyalty generated or sales built. Our first CFSS project shortened technician service times. The customer could attach money to this improvement outcome. But the "money" for Cummins was the customer seeking more business with us—which they did!

HOW DID SALES PERSONNEL REACT TO SIX SIGMA?

At the time, although Six Sigma was becoming ingrained in some parts of the company, it was still new to the customer side. The sales group had mostly laid low, thinking Six Sigma was a passing fad and was generally untouched by Six Sigma. We started up a new Six Sigma wave with this group.

A common discussion among sales people, including some middle and senior personnel, was that "this Six Sigma stuff doesn't apply to us in the customer world, because it's really a manufacturing tool. We're sales guys. We're support folks. We're customer people. Six Sigma is black and white. We live in the gray zone. Six Sigma isn't going to work here."

Sales folks told us they were extremely busy. For them, it was go-go-go all the time. They were often entertaining after hours and coming in early to respond to customer emails from the night before. They said, "C'mon, how can we fit this in, we're already bending over backwards taking care of customers day to day and minute to minute." Additionally, Sales said they couldn't quantify dollar savings or benefits the same way manufacturing could.

A unique concern was that Sales people feared non-commercial people getting involved in commercial questions. They also wondered how Six Sigma might affect the commercial relationship with customers. A Belt without Sales experience might not be well versed in what to say, or not to say, to a customer. These concerns were really different from others we had confronted earlier inside the company.

Customer-facing people approach their work differently and have different skill sets compared to manufacturing and engineering people. Manufacturing and engineering folks follow established processes as a natural part of their work. They want to be methodical and process oriented, doing things the same way every time in a logical series of steps. Customer-facing people tend to be more free-flowing. They're good working with customers, reading situations, nuancing, changing and adjusting to customer needs.

We made adjustments as we did more CFSS projects. I found bringing Six Sigma to the sales force required allowing a more subjective feel to things, accommodating the adaptability part of their work, and adding the inspirational element. Another key was getting people to see that our customers, like us, run businesses and have processes. Our customer's processes are just processes of a different sort. The first CFSS project focused on a process the customer was trying to improve. We also selected a Black Belt from Sales, a person who had lived in the world of sales, to lead CFSS projects, giving Sales leadership someone they trusted to understand the environment.

WHAT IS DIFFERENT ABOUT WORKING WITH EXTERNAL CUSTOMERS?

A big difference is the time dimension. In a manufacturing plant we control the timing and sequence of Six Sigma projects. Say there are 25 projects in the hopper. Plant leadership chooses which projects to do, who to do them and when. But with CFSS, a customer might say a project idea sounds good and they want to start immediately. We can't put them on hold, waiting three months for an available Belt. The customer sets the priority.

Not all customers have Six Sigma experience. We have to be a lot more nuanced working with them on a CFSS project. For customers lacking Six Sigma experience, we train their designated Belt alongside our Belt. In cases where a smaller customer can't offer a Belt, a Cummins Belt leads the entire project.

We learned not to ask the customer for a part of the project savings. We wanted our customers to know we do these projects to make them more successful, without expectation of anything coming back our way, showing them we care more about their business than any other supplier.

WERE OTHER ADAPTATIONS MADE AS CUMMINS GAINED CFSS EXPERIENCE?

To build momentum for future projects, we purposefully had a lot of advertising and recognition at the completion of the first CFSS project. The project team was heavily recognized. Customer testimonials were a significant influencing factor helping us gain support.

We learned it was important to Cummins Belts and team members to know they were making a meaningful difference, not just for the customer but also for Cummins. They wanted to be able to say they moved the dial for Cummins.

We became more flexible and adaptable regarding tools, not requiring use of specific tools on every project but rather only using the tools that made sense for getting to the result.

In time we introduced formal "requirements projects" with customers. These projects were really important to sales and marketing. These projects produced the results we wanted, with discipline and structure, and used customer interviews, customer interview sheets, Cause and Effect matrices and KJ analyses as primary tools.

The phrase "voice of the customer" started showing up more in company language. This spoke to sales people about how Six Sigma helps us listen and extract understanding of what's important to the customer for the organization.

We looked for projects that were repeatable with many customers. Different customers have different fleet sizes and use vehicles in different ways, but they all want better fuel economy. Customer fuel economy improvement projects have definitely quantifiable value, are very data based and have general logical steps. We created a template for a fuel economy CFSS project. As time went along, we continued looking for CFSS projects replicable to many customers and, over time, created additional, specific project templates for these project types.

Now our sales force identifies new internal projects. Sales people see and hear customer pain points every day. There is huge value in translating customer needs into Cummins internal projects. And an internal project may require little or no customer help at all, so they tend to be more straightforward DMAIC projects.

After completing a few customer projects, a group of Belts created a CFSS guidebook listing critical questions. Some questions were commercial, for example, helping screen customers where a project could negatively affect the commercial relationship. Getting those Belts together was important to the ultimate success of doing Six Sigma with customers.

We use a Cause and Effects Matrix analysis to prioritize CFSS projects. Typical prioritization criteria include customer needs, internal and customer resource availability, likelihood of customer engagement and our growth opportunity with that customer. Some prioritization criteria change year to year given the latest business factors.

DO YOU USE SIX SIGMA TOOLS OUTSIDE OF THE SIX SIGMA PROJECTS?

I use Six Sigma tools frequently in day-to-day work and personal life. Many tools are really logical and apply many different ways, even in isolation, outside of projects. For example, the Cause and Effect Matrix is a wonderful decision-making tool I use whenever considering a career move. I prioritize elements important to my next move, list all the options or opportunities, and use the scores to help me make a good decision. When a customer has a problem, I make a Failure Modes and Effects Analysis table, asking what could be causing this to go wrong and prioritizing what to focus on to improve the outcome.

Most projects, professional or personal, end up having one or two tools key to cracking the problem. These tools illuminate the issue in a way that makes me say, "Oh my gosh, no wonder we're having a problem here." For example, I led a project to improve material flows in the plant. When we created the process map, it became obvious the process was really broken. The process flows were crazy! Why were we doing it this way? We then focused on the process map to unbend flows and fix crisscrosses in the flow. It was the process map that cracked the nut.

Another project involved improving accounts receivable with a customer. We conducted a Failure Modes & Effects Analysis, finding lots of failure modes. No wonder we were having so many problems! We then approached the problem from a whole different level, rather than fix individual failure modes, to do something more systemic to fix what was going wrong. The Failure Modes and Effects Analysis was the "Aha!" in that project.

HOW HAS SIX SIGMA INFLUENCED YOUR CAREER AND LEADERSHIP STYLE?

Six Sigma has definitely impacted my career, making it possible to do things I might not otherwise have had the opportunity to do. Here I am, an industrial engineer working in sales. Six Sigma had a huge effect as a springboard moment. If it wasn't for Six Sigma, and my leadership putting me in touch with the Vice President of Sales, I might never have made that transition onto the Sales side. My Six Sigma work experience also led to leadership opportunities in Sales. It probably helped me, a few years later, get into the Kelley School of Business MBA program because company leadership had a lasting memory of our Six Sigma work to make the company better.

Six Sigma definitely influences how I lead. First, Six Sigma teaches you discipline, a process orientation and making decisions based on data. This is very beneficial to figuring out problems in customer-facing roles. Every day we take care of customer problems. Second, using actual tools to solve specific problems was a really helpful tactical learning I gained from Six Sigma. Third, being able to see and experience in detail how the Six Sigma program was implemented was important strategic learning for me.

In general management roles with big customers, a lot of the job is more strategic. Our strategic approach to implementing Six Sigma is a good model for strategic thinking in other areas. An important thing we did as a company was not trying to "swallow the elephant whole." If we had tried to jump to the end, right from the beginning, it would have failed. There's just no way it would have worked. Taking Six Sigma in phases, and clearly defining those phases, is a huge piece of Six Sigma's success at Cummins. Thinking through the S-Curves of improvement for Six Sigma for the company and applying the same logic on the customer-facing side, helps me think through implementing strategies for my big customers.

19

Moving From the Self-Supporting to the Business Integration S-Curve

During the transition from the Self-Supporting to the Business Integration S-Curve, scope and scale begin to separate more rapidly. The main reason is that during the early phases of deployment, everything is new. Following the first four S-Curves, the pace of new additions to the system slows down as most of those new things have now become part of the basic bucket of requirements (see Kano discussion). Figure 19.1 shows many elements of the Six Sigma system that have now become basic quality expectations to be met on an ongoing basis.

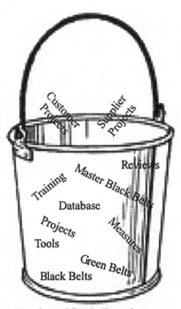

Bucket of Basic Requirements

FIGURE 19.1 Bucket of basic requirements.

These basic requirements must be maintained and managed over time. This means documentation and ownership of processes, training developed and deployed, measures maintained, and continuous improvement actions taken. This also means allocation of resources to the work. Remember, these basic requirements are *expected and unspoken*. A huge amount of effort is needed to sustain and maintain the basic quality requirements of the Six Sigma system. This maintenance work is critical to ongoing success of the change, but it is not glamorous. It is the work of people who are dedicated to the value of staff work and its ultimate value to the business and its customers. It is also staff work that is not seen by the business leadership as value adding to the enterprise because it is not work that can be directly measurable in monetary return on investment (ROI). However, if they aren't done well, because they are the basic requirements of the system, it causes internal turmoil because they are essential to the other aspects of the Six Sigma deployment and the expansion into new and more complicated areas of improvement. Some of the key responsibilities include:

- Deciding how the Master Black Belt pipeline will be maintained
- Maintaining and upgrading training material
- Connecting projects to business goals and objectives
- Maintaining and improving the data collection mechanism
- Managing the return of Black Belts and Master Black Belts to the business following their Belt assignments
- Maintaining and improving the measurement system
- Building and maintaining the Master Black Belt communication network
- Developing a mechanism for knowledge hand-off from legacy to new Master Black Belts
- Maintaining ongoing engagement of leadership at all levels.

Further, the new areas of improvement tend to be more complex, affecting larger and larger parts of the organization in new ways. These new applications are tried, improved, documented, trained and improved some more. Additionally, these new applications tend to be unique to the company where they are being tried. It is hard to find others who are doing the same thing exactly. This is the process of adapting Six Sigma to the business and its customers. Therefore, fewer changes can be done at one time and the change reflected in each S-Curve slows down.

Moving from the Self Supporting to the Business Integration S-Curve prepares the organization for new applications of Six Sigma in ways not previously anticipated. This means the broadening of Six Sigma into other areas of the business that require improvement.

At Cummins, the first of these areas was standardizing Supplier Focused Six Sigma (SFSS). Moving into the supply base with Six Sigma was based on the reality that the quality of our products was held hostage to the quality of the parts and pieces acquired from the supply base. Cummins had been and continued to address the improvements needed inside the company. If those improvements were to succeed, however, improvement in the supply base was critical because most of the parts and pieces that were assembled into a power system were purchased from other companies. Therefore, the logic and necessity of expansion into the supply base was non-controversial and began during S-Curve 4.

Supplier Focused Six Sigma was introduced at a supplier conference. It began based on some key characteristics (mistakes in **BOLD**):

- If the problem or improvement is one that affects Cummins customers the training is free. **If the problem or improvement is internal to the supplier, the supplier is charged for the training**.
- **The supplier Belt will attend training with other Belts from other suppliers in a suppliers-only training launch.**
- The supplier Sponsor attends Cummins Sponsor training.
- Cummins provides Master Black Belt support.
- Cummins will not act as a Six Sigma deployment consultant. If the supplier desires a broad company deployment of Six Sigma, the deployment will be independent of Cummins. This stipulation was an element of the contract with the consultant, SBTI, so that we didn't compete with SBTI using their intellectual property, which had been licensed by Cummins.

The mistakes impacted the use of Six Sigma with suppliers differently. Charging the suppliers for training distracted us from the goal of working on projects making a difference for Cummins customers. There was no process to invoice or collect the money leaving Corporate Quality to try to do this with a very poor result.

Holding supplier-only launches didn't work because it minimized support for the project. Most supplier Belts had little or no support in their businesses for Six Sigma, therefore project completion was very difficult. Additionally, competing suppliers were sometimes in class together, making it difficult to openly review project progress.

These problems led to two changes as part of the maturity process. First, supplier Belt charters focus on a problem affecting Cummins customers approved by the Cummins Master Black Belt.

Next, Cummins no longer tried to charge for training.

Finally, supplier Belts and Sponsors formed a team with a Cummins Belt and Sponsor, the Belts attending training together. This arrangement gave the Belt and Sponsor support for improvements that crossed the supplier/Cummins boundary and served as a form of project support infrastructure that was typically missing back at the supplier location.

The company ultimately defined Six Sigma for suppliers in the Critical Supplier Six Sigma Reference Guide shown in Figure 19.2.

The Reference Guide provided the suppliers with details of the Cummins Six Sigma process and included the following sections:

- Six Sigma at Cummins
- Critical Supplier Expectations of the Program
- Six Sigma Training for Cummins Critical Suppliers
- Roles and Expectations of Participants
- Project Selection
- Critical Supplier Six Sigma—Miscellaneous
- Design for Six Sigma.

FIGURE 19.2 Critical supplier reference guide.

The Reference Guide codified how Cummins and its suppliers would work together on Six Sigma projects improving products and services for Cummins customers.

It was during the transition to the Business Integration S-Curve that the deployment of the Cummins Business Model and Operating System (COS) accelerated. The Cummins Operating System has its roots in the Cummins Production System (CPS), discussed earlier in the pre-history section. The purpose of COS is to continuously improve products and services for customers by reducing waste and variation in the company's processes.

The COS Model is bounded by Customer and Business Requirements on the left and Customer and Business Results on the right. This reinforces a central tenet that the customer defines quality. Customer experienced quality is more than the physical product. It includes how the product is serviced, accuracy of billing, availability of parts, accuracy and readability of service literature, and on and on and on. The customer's perception of the company's product and service quality is impacted by hundreds of things, both big and small. The implication is that quality is the outcome of the integration of the company's processes. This goes well beyond manufacturing and assembly work. All of the company's functions have a role to play in making the company's processes work well for the customer so that they experience the quality that they expect and pay for.

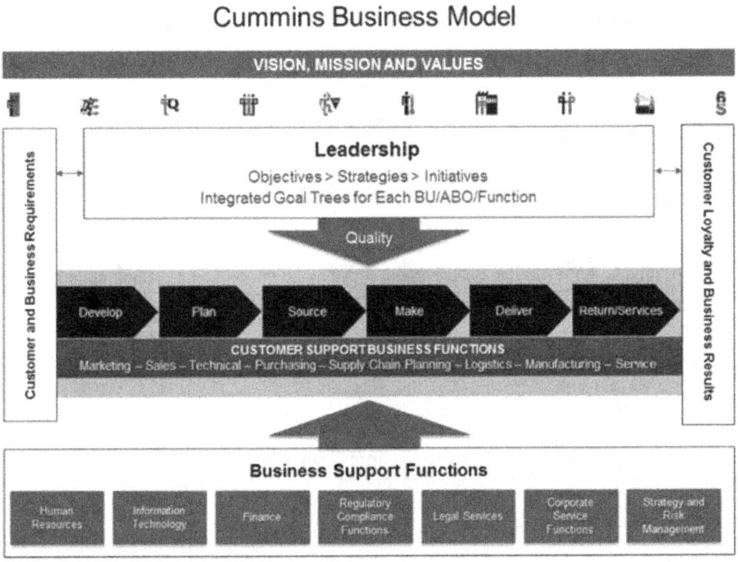

FIGURE 19.3 Cummins business model and operating system.

A simple way to think about this is to answer the basic question, "Where is it OK to have bad quality?" Look at the Cummins Business Model asking that question at different points. Can you see that bad quality in any part of the model ultimately affects the customer and the business results? This is a way to begin driving Six Sigma into all parts of the business. Also, thinking about it in this way gives purpose and meaning to the deployment of a business operating system (BOS) as a driver of continuous improvement for customers.

The work of the Cummins Operating System (COS) links the company's critical processes together by continuously assessing how those processes are working for the customer, identifying problems and opportunities for improvement which become Six Sigma projects and other improvements. Effective deployment of the BOS became possible as the company developed a critical mass of common Six Sigma language so that people could work together solving the company's biggest problems and improving critical processes and process linkages.

A key to successful application of the COS is the role of the functions in the business. The functions are made up of people doing similar type work. The people who perform accounting, budgeting and invoicing tasks

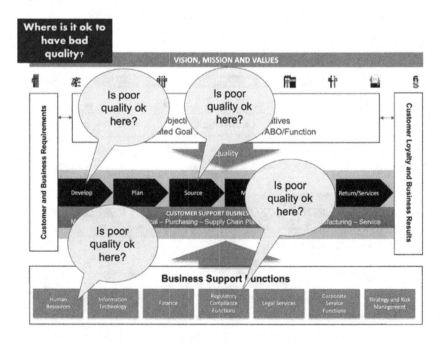

FIGURE 19.4 When is poor quality OK?

are part of the Finance function. The people who work on the line building machines in the plants are in the Manufacturing function. The people who support the work of the company with electronic information systems are in the IT function. The functions of the company are accountable for the processes, tools/methods and skills/capabilities used by that function to do work. All the work of the company falls into one of those three categories. Continuously improving the processes, tools/methods and skills/capabilities is creating Functional Excellence. Since almost all processes in the company require cross-functional involvement, the importance of a common language of improvement cannot be overstated.

The ongoing improvement of COS required leadership and broad participation of the functions across the regions. As with the deployment of Six Sigma, the CEO actively engaged with COS in 2011. He met with Business Unit (BU) and Function leaders once a year to review progress using COS to drive improvement and set direction for the next 12 months. The review focused on critical processes using a common set of questions that served as the format for the review. All BU and Function leaders were invited to all the reviews so that they heard firsthand how others were driving improvement and the CEO's priorities. Additionally, the company published and widely distributed a Cummins Business Model and Operating System Reference Guide with an introduction by the CEO. Corporate Quality scheduled quarterly calls with BU and Functional leadership to discuss progress and help where needed. Each function and BU presented once each year but were invited to listen in on all of the reviews.

All of this effort focused on impacting customer experienced quality and business performance by driving improvements in the company's critical processes.

The preparation for this S-Curve transition also saw the first experimentation with Customer Focused Six Sigma (CFSS). An early example of Six Sigma with customers was GE's "at the customer for the customer" effort discussed earlier.

By the time we decided to begin working projects with customers, the company had completed several hundred projects. This was important because we wanted to make sure the process was well understood before extending it into the customer base where the consequences of failures are more far reaching. Cummins began by experimenting with a couple of projects with customers that had launched their own Six Sigma efforts. Following these early experiments, we developed templates and checklists to be used in the conduct of CFSS projects.

20

Interview With Tom Linebarger— Cummins CEO (2012+)

WHY DID CUMMINS DECIDE TO PURSUE SIX SIGMA?

Tim Solso was moving from President to CEO of Cummins in 1998. As he prepared for the new role, he developed and launched a strategy to help the company improve financially, meet customer expectations, and improve quality. Quality at the time generally meant product quality or how our products performed in the field. He laid out a multi-part plan to achieve his strategy objectives, and launching Six Sigma was one of them.

In preparing for the CEO job, Tim talked with the CEOs of an OEM customer and a supplier, both of whom he had known well. They talked to Tim about Six Sigma and convinced him it was worth a try.

He was going to have a platform to address quality; he just had to figure out which one. Six Sigma looked like it was worth trying to address the quality aspects of his plan.

This is a very common move for a new CEO. I did the same thing when I became CEO. I wanted to have a platform that built on things from before while introducing some new things that have some runway in front of them. It is important to do this while not departing too radically from the past unless it is really necessary to take the company forward. Tim launched Six Sigma as his platform to address quality with relatively limited knowledge of how it was going to evolve. But he had a very clear view from 30 years with the company that we had to get better at quality and waste reduction.

When Tim launched Six Sigma, how we would deploy it wasn't clear in his mind. But Tim had a company leadership partner in Joe Loughrey, the leader of the Engine Business at that time, who was a fantastic implementer.

Tim turned to Joe and told him what he wanted to do. The challenge was Joe wasn't sure that Six Sigma was the right method because he hadn't been on the visits and done the benchmarking himself. It took a while to get alignment with Joe that this was the way to go. We had to go from Tim saying we were going to do it to Joe, once he agreed, figuring out how we were going to do it.

WHAT WERE SOME OF THE OTHER THINGS INCLUDED AS PART OF THE SIX SIGMA DEPLOYMENT?

Two things that were very important to the success of Tim's strategy were sustainable financial performance and performance for customers. This was a company that missed its Return On Equity (ROE) targets seven out of the previous eight years. We had a very poor track record. We had much higher financial aspirations than we were achieving.

For perspective, during the '90s we were trying to go from 5% average Earnings Before Interest and Tax (EBIT) to an average of 6%. We called it the "6 to 9" initiative, which we did not make, by the way. During that period of the '90s we were averaging close to 5% EBIT. Today, by comparison, we are close to 12%. The difference between 5% and 12% is comparing a not very good company to a very good company.

We were in a very difficult situation because even in years when we had good performance, it was not sustainable. This was Tim's context as he was becoming the leader of the company. Tim is a no-nonsense execution person. He was convinced that we were in this situation because we didn't set priorities, put good people in charge, and do what we said we were going to do. He was convinced that we were not living up to our commitments.

One of Tim's strategies was to establish a performance culture. This meant doing what you said you would do, meeting your financial commitments and not making excuses for why you didn't do it. It was all about, to put it simply, doing what you said you were going to do. If you made a commitment, live up to your commitment.

We had engaged a set of consultants in the '90s to help us create our strategies. We had a growth analysis and an organization study done. We also had a purchasing operations assessment completed. The consultants offered to do a quality study too. But Tim didn't think their quality proposal was as well thought through as the others. We didn't use them for quality.

Tim was thinking about starting initiatives related to the high-level strategic goals. He saw Six Sigma helping us reach our quality goals but also having other impacts. One of those impacts was using Six Sigma to help with the performance culture issue. He came to this conclusion after his benchmarking work. He knew that Six Sigma was very rigorous. There were clear goals and people were assigned to achieve those goals. This fit Tim's assessment of the company and the need to create a performance culture. Tim saw that Six Sigma helped him with a couple of his big goals helping improve product quality.

He wrote a memo, which I remember very well, that laid out his strategy and drove us for five to seven years.

WHAT WAS JOE LOUGHREY'S ROLE IN THE DEPLOYMENT OF SIX SIGMA?

Cummins Engine Business President Joe Loughrey, as a strong implementer, was never a guy who liked bluster. He didn't want to make promises without knowing where the improvement was coming from. His approach was to build the plan from the bottom up.

Tim wanted to tell investors what the impact of his strategy was going to be in real terms because we were in the middle of some tough times. Tim was asking where the improvement was going to take place and what's the improvement on gross margin going to be and by when. But Joe was saying we don't even know what Six Sigma is, and so he had no idea where the money was coming from.

Also, since Joe had not been on the benchmarking visits and didn't really see it, it was something he had to get comfortable with.

We had done some projects and training with SBTI, but we weren't getting good traction all across the company at that point. We were seeing some great individual projects and results but not broadly. But the idea was to do x number of projects to meet our results target. The intention had been to run it across the company, but it wasn't really happening. For example, one of the business leaders didn't think his business could start Six Sigma because of some issues they were having. All of their best people were already working on those issues.

One of the key problems we were having deploying Six Sigma across the company was that there were three big challenges that we had to meet to make it work. But we didn't have alignment in the staff that Six Sigma was what we should be doing. Nobody had proven to them that it was going to work for achieving Tim's strategies.

The first challenge was that we had to have a project hopper. The project hopper is a set of projects that are important to do and will yield good results. The projects also had to fit the parameters of a good Six Sigma project. This meant the project could be done in a determined amount of time, you could apply the tools to it, it would be worth so much in savings and so forth.

Second, we had to have a leader who would assign good people dedicated to work on the projects. These were our Black Belts. These were people that the company was willing to assign full time to improvement work. The challenge is that these good people were already busy. The question was, how in the world do we move them to work on something that was unproven with an unclear result?

Third, how do you count the savings? There is project accounting and real accounting. Anytime you are trying to count cost reduction, there is a difficult translation to real reduction. Whenever you count savings at a point in time, there is a problem because the baselines are changing as the periods change. People struggle to figure out how to account for project savings.

Those were the three big challenges and they remained challenges throughout. But at the start, they were in the way of us making much progress. And we didn't have complete alignment among the staff that this was a good thing to do. Were we really going to save money? Were we really going to improve the quality of our products dramatically? Tim said we were going to do it, but the operating staff was not converted yet.

We did a couple of things.

First, Tim picked a leader, Frank McDonald, and convinced Frank to lead the Six Sigma effort. Frank was an implementer, someone who had run operations for years and was currently leading the Mid-range Engine Business. He was a no-nonsense guy who didn't mince words. He was somebody who liked to hit his targets. Frank wouldn't promise big numbers and then not deliver them. Frank was going to want to succeed. So he was a key leader for Six Sigma. Frank was a guy who was leading a big part of the Engine Business and Joe was willing to give him up to lead Six Sigma. Giving up Frank was a big statement by Joe that told the company he was on board.

The next thing that happened, Joe chartered a couple of Six Sigma projects to improve Six Sigma implementation in the Engine Business. He did this because after one and a half years, we still weren't getting the traction that we wanted. Joe ran two projects—one led by Dana Vogt and the other by Mark Kelly—to answer the question of why Six Sigma wasn't working as well as it should. They identified the things that we weren't doing well and came back to the leadership team with the reasons. It wasn't because the process wasn't good; it was because it wasn't led in the right way.

Clearly, we weren't going to generate the improvement that we needed from the beginning if we didn't change. We had done some great projects and saw some results. But we were not going to generate improvement as rapidly or as broadly with the impact that we wanted.

Joe was working on Six Sigma prior to the outcome of these projects, but he wasn't being as forceful as he could have been because he wasn't sure about it. He wasn't asking for results or to see projects. He wasn't creating pointed accountability for results, and he wasn't calling people out who were not meeting their commitments for Six Sigma in the same way he was doing in other things. He didn't have the detailed understanding of how it was going to work. After Joe had the projects done, he understood what was happening. These were his results. Now, Joe knew what to do to make Six Sigma work the way it should. This is when it moved from Tim's program only to Joe's program in the Engine Business.

Once Joe started to drive Six Sigma in the Engine Business in 2001, all the other businesses got their Six Sigma programs going. It didn't happen all at once. But from that moment forward, we saw steady progress toward a full enterprise implementation. Businesses started getting with the program because they felt there were consequences to not getting on board.

The two projects helped a lot because it defined what to do to be successful and it was very compelling. The projects delivered results that made a lot of sense and made it easy to understand what we needed to do.

From the projects, we began to understand the three elements that were the key X's to the success of the Six Sigma program and projects. Those three elements never went away. We had to continue to revisit them during each of the S-Curves during the life of Six Sigma. At some level, because they are the key X's, they never stop being the key elements of success. The three elements are:

1. Pick projects that are important to the business and fit the Six Sigma criteria.

2. Pick good people to work on the important projects and manage them through the process.
3. Develop a good accounting process. Set up the infrastructure on how to do it: project tracking databases, how to count and so forth. Then do it the way it is set up.

In each of our S-Curves, I remember, we had done a really good job of continually improving the hoppers and finding good projects. But we were scoping and sizing them down to meet the definition of good projects. The result was that we were slowly chipping away at their strategic importance. This created a problem. When a project is strategically important, the leader cares about it. He or she doesn't want to give it away to somebody else to solve unless they understand how the charter's going to work. But the strategic projects are difficult to do as traditional Six Sigma projects.

Let me describe an example from my business. I was in PowerGen. I had a couple of big problems to solve and decided to do them as Six Sigma projects. I tried to write a charter for it. The issue was that the problem was huge. I needed to figure out how to reduce the price of small generators to win in the European generator market against all the European competitors. It's a big job because you have to change the competitive situation by changing market share in one of the biggest, most competitive markets in the world. When I talked to a Black Belt about taking that project, it was difficult for them to agree to do it. First, they weren't clear what the project was. Second, it wasn't something that could be done in 180 days. Since we were paying Black Belt bonuses for completed projects, their project bonus would be jeopardized. I couldn't find anybody to do it! Black Belts wanted to work on more focused projects that they could complete quickly. If we gave them a project that changed the output on a line from 183 units to 189.5 units, they would do that one. And, by the way, all the training people were telling them to do the smaller project because it's definable, it's clear, and you know how to do it. It's really the sensible thing to do.

The problem was that we had done so many of the simpler projects that business leaders were wondering if we were beginning to run out of things to do. The big, complicated, strategic projects were being left on the table, and they were the ones that mattered most. The other thing that was happening affected the perceived value of project savings. If we had added to the gross margin all the savings that had been generated by the projects, we would be more profitable than Google. But we weren't. So, where did the money go? It wasn't that the projects weren't generating real savings, because they were. It turns out that the competitive environment was really difficult. It's real improvement, but when you add up all the savings it's hard to see it because, as I said earlier, the baseline is not the same. It's changing over time.

We wanted to start working given the reality of this environment. We asked ourselves how we could get more work done on our strategies by turning them into Six Sigma projects. We began doing something called umbrella projects. These are projects that have a strategic "umbrella" with projects underneath that are cut into definable problems. That's an obvious point in retrospect, but we had never done that before. That means that the leader of the umbrella needs different skills than the traditional Black Belt. The traditional Black Belt that takes on a more narrowly focused, traditional Six Sigma project. Going all the way back to the early days of Six Sigma at Cummins, the Belts could not work on a project that asked, "how can we double our market share in the European GenSet market?" This gives you an example that shows how Six Sigma evolved at Cummins.

This is an S-Curve point. We had taken it across the whole business. We were doing projects in all the regions. There was a lot of attention paid to projects. We had run the course on traditional Six Sigma projects. Now, we needed to take on bigger, more strategic projects. Strategic projects would give us better traction tor improving our overall financial performance. This would take us beyond the incremental improvement we saw from doing many smaller projects. We kept doing the smaller projects because there is always improvement that is needed. But shifting to do strategic projects was a pivot point toward a different kind of thinking about how to use Six Sigma.

This pivot meant that we needed to assign a different kind of person to the projects. It meant we assigned more senior, broader-thinking people to lead these umbrella projects. It also meant that we needed bigger teams of people working together because the projects became so much larger in scope. Leadership involvement from BU presidents and staffs increased because now the projects were so much more important.

We also decided during this time that a key improvement area was how we developed our product designs and not just the production of our products. We wanted to do more on the new product development side to improve the quality of the resulting products. This change was important because while we had done a good job of making operational improvements and getting overall costs down, we weren't driving our new product launch costs down. So, we expanded the program into the development arena.

These were new S-Curves in the Six Sigma program. A simple way to think about it is that we continued to ask and answer several new questions over time. How are you going to decide which key projects to run? How are the projects structured so they can be done? How do we select the right people to run the projects given that the right people are never easy to find and they're always busy? Finally, how do we ensure that we are getting the results that we want? That's why I think that with each S-Curve, those same three X's I talked about earlier were key.

The S-Curves were several years apart. Deciding to apply Six Sigma in design, applying it to strategy, and others were each several years apart. And they were planned by the company.

For example, I remember when the leadership team began the discussion to improve the execution of DFSS. George presented us with a proposal to improve new product quality by folding DFSS tools into our stage gate process. There was significant debate within the leadership team about whether this was the right thing to do. We asked several questions. Do we have time to do it? What resources we wanted to put to it? And there were other questions that were important to the decision.

We had learned from the early deployment of Six Sigma the value of alignment among the company's leadership. We did a lot of work as a team to get alignment and agreement. When we decided to do other new things, we started by gaining alignment first before proceeding.

When we decided to change new product development, we had lots of debate to figure it out on the front end. When we made the final decision, the team was aligned and supportive. Six Sigma helped us learn the value of alignment. This became a big improvement for the company on issues that went beyond Six Sigma. The company of 1998 had many more problems with alignment and agreement than the company of 2008 and beyond.

The effort to get alignment is harder because of the time it takes to gain agreement. It's no longer possible to just get one leader to approve or support it. It's a lot of work to get everyone's support for things we want to do. But once agreement is reached, it has become much easier to move forward.

Leadership alignment plays a very critical role in any large-scale change, whether it's Six Sigma or something else. The time it takes to gain alignment is often underestimated by vendors who are trying to sell something to you. But if you can't achieve leadership alignment, you probably shouldn't do it. Lacking alignment, you are going to waste a lot of money and time. Leadership alignment is a whole different process than improvement. So, you need to think about how you are going to get both of those.

I hear a lot of talk about benchmarking. The second-best quality of benchmarking is that you get new ideas. The best quality of benchmarking is that you get everybody to go to the mountain together to see the thing you are trying to do. If you want to do good benchmarking, you should think about the people you need to help you drive the change and take them to see it. Get a vision by seeing what it looks like when it is done well. When they come back it is much easier for them to agree with your challenge. When they don't see it, they often will not agree because it wasn't their idea.

ARE THERE A COUPLE OF OTHER S-CURVES OF MATURITY THAT YOU THINK ABOUT?

Another development in the maturity of Six Sigma was that we began to see it as an employee development program.

The company has a strong focus on diversity. We want to find and develop talent from different regions, backgrounds and experiences all around the company. We wanted to make sure we weren't only focusing on MBAs from Harvard. We had a suspicion that there were good people around the company, but we weren't having much success finding them. Getting people into leadership roles often means doing some accelerated development. But what is your source? Where are the feeders to that development? We wanted to find good people from everywhere to feed into the leadership pipeline.

We discovered that we were running into some very good people by seeing them on Six Sigma projects. We were exposing the leadership team to a new group of people as the Belts completed and presented their projects. We were meeting people from all over the company.

We met new people in a couple of different ways. For example, the corporate Six Sigma office would create visibility to Six Sigma results and leaders of projects through our award ceremonies and other recognition processes. Leaders got a chance to meet people from all over the business by running hopper sessions and reviewing projects in the businesses. We learned about both the projects and the people in this way. We would discover not only talented people but people who had different talents and skills that now we could see.

We started to think about Six Sigma as a way to develop and get access to talent. This new capability added to the staying power of Six Sigma as an initiative. By participating in the Chairman's Award and reviewing projects, I had a chance to see who was doing interesting things across the company. It gave me a forum that introduced me to people who I would rarely run into. This gave it another breath of life in the company.

Another change I want to highlight is our understanding of "quality." Using Six Sigma expanded the definition of quality in the company for good.

Up until that point, we had two definitions of quality in the company. One was warranty. When the customer has a problem, we have to pay him for it. The other was manufacturing quality, or product defects. What we didn't have was an understanding of process quality. We didn't think about whether this activity we were doing was producing the results that we wanted. The concept is not a new one in business. But we didn't have a focus on making process quality improvement a real and meaningful activity.

We had a good functional excellence program. We were able to say this is what excellent performance looks like in a function. Joe Loughrey had driven functional excellence in the business. But we didn't have good process metrics that linked functional processes across the functions. While Six Sigma projects didn't solve that exact problem, the Six Sigma initiative evolved. We began to conduct process analysis to understand if a process was yielding the results that we wanted. If we weren't getting the results, we used Six Sigma on the process to improve it. It didn't matter if it was in the payments area or the insurance area. Six Sigma wasn't used only in the plants.

As company leadership was presented with a new idea for how we could use Six Sigma. We would think about it and debate it. This would begin another wave that gave Six Sigma another breath of life. These waves of new ideas repeatedly gave Six Sigma a new breath of life that kept it going. Many companies don't keep Six Sigma going as long as we have at Cummins. This continuing wave of new applications as Six Sigma matured is the reason that we were able to do it.

Each one of these waves gave it a new breath of life so it didn't become tired. We weren't able to say, "We've already done this, this is boring." Six Sigma was solving incrementally more important problems each time which gave it another breath. The other types of projects that we had done before kept going. For example, we are still doing line improvements. But you just don't get CEO attention for ten years if that's all you do because they begin to think that the change is now part of the DNA of the company. The CEO is interested by the change aspect, because that's what is difficult to do. With each one of these changes, we kept it visible at the top of the company because these new projects were going to be difficult to do.

The person who runs the initiative has to work with company leadership to understand what the biggest problems in the company are and think about how to apply Six Sigma to these business problems. From an improvement initiative point of view, that's the way you get and keep the attention of senior leadership. Sometimes it's a push saying this is something that the CEO should care about and I, as the CEO, have to decide if I do care about it. Other times, it is at the top of my list and I am asking how can Six Sigma help. The leader of the initiative is trying to figure out organizational challenges. Then the leader defines how the initiative is relevant to the challenges of the day. From an improvement initiative standpoint, the leader of the initiative is in the guts of the organization. He or she might see problems that senior leadership is not seeing. The leader has the opportunity to bring attention to problems that senior leadership is not observing helping to create more relevance.

There were several of these breaths of life over the years of Six Sigma that kept the initiative relevant at Cummins.

WHAT IS THE NEXT S-CURVE FOR CUMMINS?

We want to keep and enhance the strategic focus. We are starting to build hoppers from the leadership down. It doesn't mean that the plant level can't have hoppers and they do. But we are going to build key hoppers and crowd out a lot of the day-to-day hoppers. We have moved Belts and resources to the leadership team hopper. This is a pretty big shift. When we started all the resources and work were distributed all the way down to plant and function level.

Now, we have gathered 30% of the resources at the leadership level. They are going to work on three or four most important strategic areas. It is another evolution to make sure that the most critical things in the company have the most capable people working on them.

The second thing we did was expand the tool set. We started with the Six Sigma tools. We gathered the other tools that we were using around the company and brought them in. We said, "Here is the portfolio of tools that you can use to work on improvements and solve problems." We have started training the tools and making them available. People can get certified in all the different areas. We want people to use what works best given the problem that is being addressed. We are sending the message that you don't have to shoehorn everything into a Six Sigma framework. We worried that if we made this shift people would think that Six Sigma was being devalued, that it wasn't important any more. We didn't want that. We wanted them to see this is an extension of what we have been doing. This is our next generation that keeps it from getting old and less interesting so that leadership doesn't care about it. We have to keep it changing to the next level to keep it interesting. So, we are taking it one more step forward.

21

S-Curve 5—Business Integration

The fifth S-Curve is a time of significant growth and maturity. At this point in the maturity of Six Sigma, it is being used in all aspects of the organization. Six Sigma is helping with the creation of new products and services. It does this by focusing on and designing for variation in all facets of product and service application. Six Sigma has become the primary improvement and problem-solving approach.

If a business operating system does not exist, this is a good time to create one. The business operating system (BOS) is a high-level description. It shows how the organization converts customer and business requirements into customer and business results. This description connects the organization's processes with their functional owners.

Variation and waste appear in even the best processes. Thus, continuous improvement is a business imperative. Six Sigma is the language of continuous improvement that undergirds the operating system. It is the common continuous improvement approach used to address cross-organization problems.

TABLE 21.1

S-Curve 5—Business Integration Actions

- MBBs add business improvement initiatives to their portfolio
- Six Sigma is focused on continuous improvement of the business
  - Invention
  - New products
  - Process improvement and problem-solving
- Changing the culture—certification for promotion and moves for key positions
  - Leadership only?
  - Everyone?
  - What are the certification criteria?
    - o Projects?
    - o Training?
    - o Testing?

During this time, the Master Black Belts become more connected to the organizational leadership teams. Using the Kano Model, Six Sigma basic quality includes training, using the tools and coaching Belts. Since basic quality is an expectation that is unspoken, it is taken for granted that this is what Master Black Belts do.

This is also the time when most of the Six Sigma supporting elements have been created, used and improved. The Master Black Belts have spent a lot of time and energy on the supporting infrastructure of Six Sigma. At this phase, Master Black Belts are included in leadership meetings so they can understand the organization's problems and issues. The Master Black Belt's role is to think about how to frame these issues as Six Sigma projects. They can facilitate planning sessions connecting continuous improvement work to goals and objectives. Master Black Belts, at this point, lead focused hopper creation exercises.

An opportunity also exists for the Master Black Belts to begin working in Master Black Belt teams (example shown in Figure 21.1). The purpose of these teams is to tackle large, organization-wide problems. They lead improvements that are difficult for anybody else in the organization to address. Each of the focus areas have a senior organizational Sponsor. The Master Black Belts work with the Sponsor to identify and launch projects critical to the customer and the business in the focus area.

This approach accomplishes a couple of things. It helps the organization attack some important but difficult issues. Leading these projects introduces the Master Black Belts to senior leadership. Meeting senior

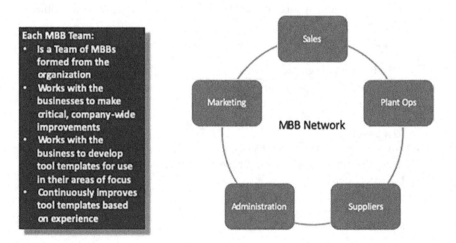

FIGURE 21.1 Master Black Belt Star Point example.

leaders helps to support their move back into the organization at the end of the Master Black Belt assignment. The Master Black Belt teams have a unique ability to see the problems of the organization. They represent different organizational elements. They think in a common way about continuous improvement. Together, they enable the Master Black Belts to lead improvement across the organization. These improvements drive solutions that have enormous payback.

During the maturity journey, it is important to remember the reason for deploying Six Sigma. The main reason is improving customer and business results. The goal is not becoming a great Six Sigma company. Reinforcing that Six Sigma is a business-focused activity and not a "Six Sigma for the sake of Six Sigma" activity requires continuous communication and discipline. Focusing the project selection process on customer needs and business objectives is critical. Leaders will increasingly see Six Sigma as a business-focused improvement approach.

A subtle decision impacting Six Sigma's business focus is how long Master Black Belts stay in the role. At Cummins, we decided to move Master Black Belts back into the business after two to three years in the role. This prevented the company from having professional Master Black Belts. In my experience, professional Master Black Belts tend to see their role in Six Sigma terms instead of business terms. Their focus becomes statistics and the fitness of projects for Six Sigma. They tend to do this instead of seeing the business issues first and Six Sigma as a way of addressing them. It is important to avoid this outcome because it tends to stunt the maturity of Six Sigma as a business improvement tool.

This S-Curve is an appropriate time to consider Six Sigma certification. Certification can support expanding and maintaining the culture by involving all leaders. There are different approaches to and definitions for certification. I prefer an approach that requires certification for all leaders above a defined level (for example, plant and function leaders up to and including the CEO). Certification is based on completion of a set number of projects. The goal of certification for leaders is to ensure that they personally understand Six Sigma's value. This is accomplished when they spend focused time on Six Sigma projects. Requiring certification for all leaders of the organization tends to pull high potential people into the process. These key people often want to be leaders. Making certification a priority for leadership reinforces the importance of Six Sigma.

The goal of the Business Integration S-Curve is to move Six Sigma deeper into the operations of the business. All parts of the business can be improved.

S-CURVE 5 PROJECT EXAMPLES

Projects continue to expand into new parts of the business during S-Curve 5. Supplier and customer projects become more common in the total portfolio of projects. Some project examples are as follows:

Improve the process to accurately value excess and obsolete inventory in the business. This project developed a repeatable and controllable valuation methodology. It was deployed across the company.

Reduce the gross margin impact of special metals used in certain production parts. This project implemented a regular process for pricing, purchasing and accounting for special metals used in some products.

Reduce the impact of vibration on key product components. This project identified and controlled the most critical characteristics for reducing vibration affecting key product components.

Improve customer fuel economy by 33%. This project teamed with the customer to improve fuel economy which is a large expense experienced by the company's customers.

Improve customer experienced freight damage by 75%. This project partnered with a key customer to improve packaging and freight handling operations. The project result reduced damage experienced during freight movement.

Joint projects with a key customer. Over a four-year period, Cummins conducted joint project work with a key OEM customer. Projects focused on problems or improvements impossible for either company to solve alone. A monthly online meeting was held. The Quality leaders from both companies, the project Belts and Sponsors attended. Project progress was discussed, assignments made, and help defined when needed. New projects were also identified during these monthly reviews.

22

Moving From Business Integration to Continued Growth and Expansion and Business System Improvement S-Curves

At this point in the Six Sigma maturity journey, many if not all of the basics are established. Leaders are assigned. Procedures and processes are documented. Targets and measures are defined and collected. Maintenance of the basics requires the company to devote significant effort and resources. This is because people have come to expect high-quality performance from the process.

The transition between S-Curves has become a repeating pattern:

- Select a new area of improvement for use of Six Sigma.
- Select a Belt to conduct an experiment to validate its use.
- Review, improve and publicize the application to the new area.
- Work with business leaders to charter potential projects in the new area.
- Collect data and improve the application.

This approach is described using two example applications of Six Sigma. The examples are community improvement projects and investigating enterprise risks.

One of Cummins core values is to serve and improve the communities in which the company lives and works. The company began by working with a couple of community partners to test the value of conducting Six Sigma projects with them. One project was with Boys and Girls Clubs, and another was with Earth University in Costa Rica.

The success of these first projects led to the conduct of projects in communities all over the world. Eventually, community projects were included as a specific category in the Annual Chairman's Quality Award.

Enterprise risk projects resulted from the Board of Directors asking the company's leadership a question. How were large, potentially company-damaging risks identified and addressed? These risks were things like pandemics, acts of God and major product safety recalls.

We began developing the process. First, we studied the literature describing how other companies were addressing risk. We conducted a few benchmarking visits. The purpose of the visits was understanding how risk was addressed by companies known to have a risk approach.

We adopted the Committee of Sponsoring Organizations of the Treadway Commission (COSO) Framework for Enterprise Risk. The framework was the industry best practice. Using the COSO Framework, we developed a plan and a process for identifying potential risks. We set priorities on those risks. The last step was gaining approval and launching projects to address the risks.

This approach was presented to and accepted by Cummins leadership. This led to adoption of a new category of Six Sigma projects: Enterprise Risk Management (ERM).

23

S-Curve 6—Continued
Growth and Expansion

S-Curve 6, Continued Growth and Expansion, is when Six Sigma truly became a full part of the company. Projects had been done in many different areas so that the use of Six Sigma in all company activities became common practice. The company developed documented processes and procedures supporting different project types during this S-Curve.

Supplier Focused Six Sigma (SFSS)—The company began including a requirement for Six Sigma projects in critical suppliers. Supplier-focused projects are intended to make improvements to products and services that the company provides its customers. As is the case with many problems, supplier problems often require participation with the company to solve them. When an improvement or problem has been identified, typically a

TABLE 23.1

S-Curve 6—Continued Growth and Expansion Actions

- Evaluate MBB requirements based on future intent
- Supplier
- Customer
- Revenue generation
- Strategy
- Enterprise risk
- Community involvement
- Project goals (for example)
  - o 1/3 customer
  - o 1/3 supplier
  - o 1/3 internal
- Evolve training strategy
  - o Online
  - o Distance learning

Belt will be nominated from both the company and the supplier. These Belts co-lead the project to ensure that all possible causes of the problem are identified. The goal is to make the most important improvements regardless of which organization owns them. This also means co-Sponsorship with a Sponsor in the company and the supplier. The company's Master Black Belt provides project support and coaching. If necessary, the Belts will attend training together but, most importantly, they work on the project together.

A key to SFSS project success is to separate commercial considerations from process improvement work. This means the improvement teams work on the problem. Discussions of "who pays" takes place outside of the problem resolution work. This eliminates a distraction for the project team. This also helps to build trust among the people leading the improvement work that the goal is improving products for customers. We learned from benchmarking and experience that trust breaks down when the improvement team discusses who owes money to whom. When the teams begin discussing "who pays" as part of the project conversation, it becomes very difficult for them to focus on a problem or the improvement. Typically, the purchasing or pricing functions are responsible for commercial negotiations.

Customer Focused Six Sigma (CFSS)—By the time of S-Curve 6, several customer-focused projects had been done. Rules and guidelines for working with customers were established and documented. By this time common approaches and templates were being used for common customer problems. Six Sigma and the company's problem-solving capability emerged as a competitive advantage with customers. Some of the company's customers became partners working together to make improvements for their customers. Customer-focused projects became a powerful tool for building customer relationships. These relationships became a factor when customers were choosing which products to buy. This is especially true during trade-off times when the customer is deciding about which suppliers to work with. During negative economic cycles the customer is often forced to go with the most economic option if all other variables are equal. Customer Focused Six Sigma added an element that competitors couldn't match.

Revenue-generating projects—Six Sigma was increasingly used to address company growth during S-Curve 6. Using the process and tools of Six Sigma to understand issues like profitability, market penetration, share, margin protection and strategic decision-making became increasingly natural. These are projects chartered by company leadership. Members of company leadership are often on the project team. Sometimes, given the scope and importance of the project, a company leader is the Belt on the project. This is the kind of project that catches the imagination of the leadership of the company reinforcing the value of their involvement. These projects further solidify the role that Six Sigma plays in company success. This type of project also gives high potential employees an opportunity to show what they can do. The Belts work for members of the leadership team on problems and issues that have a big payback for the company helping to highlight their potential.

Strategy and enterprise risk projects (ERM)—Enterprise risk and strategy projects are often sponsored by the highest levels of company leadership. Strategy projects address issues of company health and long-term success. For example, strategy projects answer questions about long-term goals and objectives for the business. These projects have implications for the application of significant company resources.

Enterprise risk projects address risks to the overall health of the company. These projects include many points of view including, but not limited to, environmental issues, competitive issues and governmental compliance issues. These tend to be projects for Belts with high potential because of the significance of the issues addressed and the opportunity to work for the highest levels of company leadership.

Community projects—Improving communities where we live and work is a Cummins core value. Working on Six Sigma projects in the communities where the company is based had a significant impact on both the community and the company. These projects have little direct bottom-line savings for the company. The projects reflect the stewardship responsibility the company has for its employees and the surrounding environment in which they live and work. These projects can also extend beyond the local community, having a broader global impact.

Project targeting—During the sixth S-Curve, targets move beyond cost reduction to bottom-line impact. For example, we set a long-term target for expanding the scope of projects. The goal was one-third of the Six Sigma projects to be done with customers, one third with suppliers, and one third focused on internal issues. Expanding the targets reinforces the need to think holistically about improvement across the company's supply chains. When looking for projects from raw materials through to customer use and retirement of products, Six Sigma processes and tools are more deeply in the company's culture.

The sixth S-Curve is also a time to think more broadly about how training is delivered within the company. By this point, Six Sigma projects had been done on how Six Sigma works. We had also used Six Sigma to improve the training. Because the company was spread out around the globe, we began thinking about ensuring that all employees in the company had access to the training which helps them use the tools and processes of Six Sigma. This was especially important for employees in many small sub-organizations. It was at this point that we began exploring how to use modern technology to provide online access to Six Sigma education. This was an increasingly important consideration.

24

Interview With Julie Liu—Black Belt,
Quality Champion, Six Sigma Leader

PLEASE DESCRIBE YOUR BACKGROUND
AND SIX SIGMA EXPERIENCE?

I was born and grew up in China. I earned a Bachelor's degree in Economics from Nankai University in China and a Master's degree of Professional Accountancy from the Indiana University Kelley School of Business.

My first job was as an auditor for the Chinese government. I joined Cummins in 1999 as a project analyst and accounts payable manager. My first Six Sigma experience was as a Green Belt. I became a Six Sigma Black Belt in 2003, completing 16 projects as a Belt and winning the Cummins Chairman's Quality Award in 2015.

After completing my Black Belt assignment, I became the Enterprise Risk Management director, supporting the implementation of shared service platforms. It was during this time that we transformed Cummins into a true globally integrated operation.

In 2006, I relocated to Beijing as the Quality Director for the China business. I led the continued deployment of Six Sigma in China. In 2009, I changed jobs again becoming the Engine Business Customer Service Director, overseeing IT, HR and Finance operations for China, Mongolia, Japan, Korea, Singapore and the Philippines. I returned to the US in 2012 to lead Cummins Supply Chain Quality.

In 2014, I led the first end-to-end-process umbrella project focusing on improvement of parts availability for customers.

I currently lead the Cummins Six Sigma and Continuous Improvement program.

One of my passions is a commitment to community development. I chaired the Cummins China Corporate Responsibility Committee from

2007 to 2010. This group cultivated 30 Community Involvement Teams and executed more than 250 community involvement projects. Cummins China won the Best Corporate Citizen Award in those years. Additionally, I have led the Cummins Chinese Affinity Group since 2013.

WHAT IS AN UMBRELLA PROJECT? HOW DO THEY WORK?

Umbrella projects are the latest Six Sigma frontier at Cummins. You can think of them as the newest S-Curve. An umbrella project is a big, complex, important improvement to make for the customer and the business. It is made up of many parts or individual projects.

Most Six Sigma projects are well defined with clear project criteria. A project typically uses clear measures like savings and key performance indicators (KPI). We don't have too many rules governing umbrella projects. In fact, umbrella projects violate some of the original rules of Six Sigma. For example, one of the original rules was to avoid a project that was "boiling the ocean." The intent was to avoid projects that were too big. But the purpose of an umbrella project is to take on a really big improvement. We want to boil the ocean! The challenge we are trying to meet is to execute a complex change effectively.

The project goal itself will be very complex. The complex goal is the focus of the umbrella. The umbrella is broken into multiple projects underneath it. These projects are typically defined in a traditional Six Sigma way. What ties them together is a "shared vision" of a common improvement goal. The name "umbrella" comes from grouping the projects under a common goal.

Our first true umbrella project, which we have been working on for two years, was to tackle the number one complaint of our customers in the service business. We have recently audited our progress and found that this area has fallen to number nine out of ten with our customers, and we are not done making improvements.

The common goal is the most important thing because it drives the selection of projects that we will do. But we found that it is not very clear-cut what the projects should be in the beginning. You learn so much by doing the work. What we originally thought would be an important improvement turned out to be not as important as other lower priorities. This learning reinforces the need to think in terms of phases of improvement.

One project that made a big impact created a mechanism to access the right information in real time measuring our performance. This improvement gave us the capability to address issues more quickly. The old system only measured once each month, so we were always playing catch-up.

The umbrella is flexible. Initially there is a sequencing of projects that occurs under the umbrella based on how the projects are related to one another. But the sequencing can change. As the team learns more and more about the systems and processes affecting the goal flexibility allows for adding or deleting projects.

Another question we are facing now is, "When is the umbrella project complete?" There is still work going on, but the original intent has been achieved. This is something we are discussing and still learning about.

ARE PROJECTS ADDED TO AN UMBRELLA THAT DON'T FIT NEATLY UNDER THE ORIGINAL UMBRELLA QUESTION?

Yes, they are. For example, we have added projects that caused us to think very differently about how we were managing our inventory and where that inventory was housed. It resulted in a rebalancing effort and caused some parts of the business to increase inventory and others to decrease it. This is controversial because of our internal metrics but critical to the umbrella's success. However, inventory was never in scope for the original umbrella goal. When we recognized that inventory was part of the system that directly impacted the customer's need for parts, it quickly became a project under the umbrella.

A critical benefit of the umbrella project is that it reveals interdependencies between projects. These interdependencies aren't apparent in the early phases of an umbrella or when doing projects independently of one another. Understanding project interconnectedness often results in adding projects to the umbrella charter. This is how an umbrella matures and evolves. You find that there are a set of S-Curves under an umbrella that describes that maturity.

HOW DO YOU DECIDE WHAT'S OK
TO ADD TO THE UMBRELLA?

One of the things we are wrestling with now is the question of how to determine if a project should be under the umbrella. How do we measure and think about it? There are projects that are spawned by the umbrella. Some of these are stand-alone projects. We are just now beginning to understand when and when not to include individual projects under the umbrella. We want to avoid the umbrella taking on a life of its own by continuing to add projects that don't necessarily fit underneath it.

The shared vision is the key. Approving new projects requires that connection to the shared vision or goal is clear. An example of a project that we didn't include had to do with changing to an automated system. It was important, but it was clear that it wasn't related to the shared vision. The solution was simply a financial decision to add money to the budget for IT support.

Any big umbrella project can include many different projects. And it will, if the leadership of the umbrella is not clear about what the shared vision is.

The difficult part of deciding which projects should be included under the umbrella has less to do with quantifiable results. It is more about addressing unquantifiable system requirements. These decisions can have a direct impact on different parts of the organization. That makes them hard.

DOES AN UMBRELLA PROJECT
HAVE ITS OWN CHARTER?

Yes, but the charter for the umbrella project is unique. We started our first umbrella by pulling together a large hopper or project selection meeting with about 50 people. The meeting used customer feedback we had been collecting but was difficult to action. We developed a list of priorities and organized the umbrella to address the top priority from the data. The very first umbrella charter "Y," or goal, was to clearly define the big problem that would become the umbrella goal.

The normal Six Sigma process is to focus at a relatively low level looking for projects that will fit the Six Sigma project paradigm. Let me give you a simple, real example. We may have a customer that is very important to the business. They are unhappy about some service that we are delivering to them. We will launch a Six Sigma project to figure out the best solution. The project might result in deciding to create a "special" inventory for that customer. In reality, inventory is a symptom of a system that cannot reliably deliver to the customer what they want when they want it. It's a failure of the delivery system.

Approaching the failure of a system by attacking problems one at a time produces results that are, often, too narrowly focused. This approach cannot see the problem as part of a much bigger system that needs improvement. This is what umbrella projects can do. The umbrella allows the company to see the interconnectedness of systems, processes and functions. Seeing the interconnectedness enables us to solve problems in a way that will have the most positive effect on the output of the whole for the customer.

There is no additional benefit to creating the umbrella if it is just a collection of problems that we already understand. The umbrella allows the team to dig much deeper to find the systemic causes of the big issues. Ultimately, it means doing more work with fewer resources better than we could do the work before.

WHAT IS THE UMBRELLA LEADER'S ROLE?

A main responsibility of the person leading the umbrella is to lead the search for the connections between the projects. It is easy to get people to work on the symptoms because they are generally easy to see. It is harder to get people to understand and value addressing problems three levels down.

Most people have a hard time seeing the total system. They only see what they are personally responsible for. A big "Aha!" for our first umbrella team was the construction of the system-level value stream map and the should-be map. It was the first time that we could see that the customer complaints were coming from problems that were caused by our system. This was a major breakthrough! It played a huge role in how we were able to make so much progress. We worked on projects that really fixed the umbrella problem not just a small part of it.

We were using a "war room" to meet and organize our work. Following the "Aha!" discovery, we held a management review in the war room. The story was on the walls of the war room. We did the review with everybody standing up at the boards walking around the room as we told the story and showed them what we needed to work on and why. It was a very exciting moment for me! I remember the Sponsor of the umbrella saying at one point, "Even a blind squirrel can understand what the problems are!" This was a very big moment for us.

The war room was a critical element in the overall process. Everything was there for anybody to see instead of hidden in separate files in the computer. Being able to see the system is very important.

WHAT ARE THE LESSONS LEARNED FROM THIS FIRST UMBRELLA PROJECT?

The most important lesson we learned was the criticality of the shared vision. The shared vision of solving a big problem for our customers empowered the team to work across the boundaries of the business. It involved multiple businesses and functions. It is a business problem coming from the customer that requires cross-business collaboration to fix it.

This first project didn't come from any specific business or leader's work plan. The driver of the project was the customer. The problem required several different businesses and functions to come together to solve it. No one person owns the whole system. Different people own pieces of the system. Nobody owns the whole thing. If the umbrella project comes from one person's work plan or business, it is almost guaranteed to be limited in scope. The project will be limited to that person's span of accountability. It's the big cross-cutting problems that are the most difficult to work on. But they have a huge payback.

The company has problems that no one function or business can do anything about. Traditional Six Sigma almost always pushes you to look for problems that can be solved using the tools and processes in a given time frame. The cross-boundary work requires a different way to think about the definition of problems. They require a different approach to tackling them.

DO THE BENEFITS OF AN UMBRELLA PROJECT ACCRUE TO A SINGLE FUNCTION OR GROUP?

Credit for an umbrella project is spread around. The team leading the umbrella receives credit for leading improvement of a big, macro problem. The different parts of the business receive credit for the individual projects under the umbrella that they complete. I think this is a more mature way to think about how project benefits are realized and credited. In the end, the customer is the real beneficiary.

This is a new way for Cummins to apply Six Sigma. As an umbrella project starts, I have observed that it is difficult for many people to see and understand how using Six Sigma in this way will work. They can only see it from their own point of view. In our first project, people couldn't see it until we put together the end-to-end flow in a high-level value stream map. Then, they could clearly see how the end result was affected by actions they took during the hand-off between processes. They could clearly see we were creating unintentional barriers to the smooth flow of information and material through the system.

WHO APPROVES AN UMBRELLA PROJECT?

There is a Sponsor who has accountability for the end product or service that the customer experiences. The person who is accountable for this end product should be the Sponsor. Other functions and businesses will be involved but the Sponsor should be the person most accountable for the result.

For large cross-organization problems, the only person or group who can champion or approve the work is the CEO and staff. At the business unit level, it is the business leader and staff who has the authority to champion an umbrella project.

The umbrella project can be an expensive thing. Typically, no single group has the resources to support it. This is why the senior leadership of the organization has to agree that this is an important thing to do.

This first project was a big experiment to see if it would work. We had a lot of information coming from the customer that we weren't sure how to handle. There were a lot of problems that were too big for any one group to solve. We conducted a big hopper process with a group of about 50 people and came up with a "top ten" list of projects. We ultimately narrowed that list down to a top three. This first project was a learning effort as much as an improvement effort.

The previous umbrella projects were collections of projects or focused on a small part of the company. This was a first time that we intentionally looked for an umbrella that had multi-project interdependencies. The problem came from a system not a single process.

The workshop was in July 2014. The project started in October 2014. It is important to look at a project of this size as a series of phases or S-Curves. There will be projects launched continuously over a longer period of time than a typical, single Six Sigma project. The Define phase is the work done to decide what the problem is. The Improve phase of DMAIC in our umbrella project became a series of projects under the umbrella. We saw the first phase of the project, the Define and the Measure phases, as a single project. We closed this project in April 2015. The Improve phase is ongoing.

HOW DO YOU DETERMINE PROJECT DEPENDENCIES?

We used a relationship matrix to look at the dependencies between projects. This helped us see what the project relationships were and what the order of the projects needed to be. The relationship matrix showed us that some projects were dependent on other projects. Some projects had to come first to enable the other projects. Failure to understand the relationships leads to sub-optimization of the whole system. Each project could be done independently. However, the result of individual projects is much less than doing them in the most effective sequence.

Understanding the relationships is important. Many processes are not designed to work with other processes. They are created in response to some need or problem. Over time they become part of running the business. An organization rarely looks at the complete set of its processes for interdependencies so that information and material will flow seamlessly through them. This is a way to start seeing the process linkages and making improvements that impact the output of the company not just some small part of it.

Many companies are deploying information systems to enable the processes of the business. Cummins is too. However, unless the work is done to fix the flow first, the information systems will not make things better. We have learned that the umbrella project is a great way to address the flow across the boundaries of the company. You have to do this kind of work on the front end. This is a new way of integrated thinking that is necessary if information system deployment is to work as intended.

We are now seeing the leadership of the company using umbrella project thinking to address the company's biggest problems. It is likely that these big umbrellas will spawn smaller umbrellas underneath them. A big change, one that brings real value, is seeing that there is a relationship between projects leading to a company-wide result. This is why this kind of work is a later S-Curve in a company's Six Sigma journey.

One thing that we have to be very conscious about is not allowing the umbrella to become something permanent. It can't take on a life of its own. We are seeing right now the need to define when one phase is complete and a new one started. This is important to keep progress moving. This is S-Curve thinking applied at the problem level.

This is a shift to a new S-Curve for the company. The normal rules of Six Sigma don't always work for umbrella projects. What's most important is understanding that it's not always necessary to meet the rules of Six Sigma. It's much more important to do what is necessary to meet the needs of both the customer and the business by improving products and services. This is the priority. A goal is to transform the behavior of people in the company to one of consciously pursuing continuous improvement for the customer. And we use Six Sigma to do that.

This is also a way to leverage the Cummins Operating System (COS), because it requires the functions of the business to engage and improve processes that have an impact on the shared goals of the company.

ARE TARGET COMPLETION DATES FOR UMBRELLA PROJECTS DEFINED?

A date can be set for the first project to define the umbrella. But as the second and following phases are launched, it is more difficult because of unknowns and complexity. A total umbrella project end date is unknowable.

HOW IS THE SET OF PROJECTS MANAGED?

We review progress with a Management Review Group (MRG) and the umbrella project Sponsor. We do these reviews at least monthly.

I also hold monthly meetings with the business Quality Champions to review progress of the projects. We also continue to have the regular Master Black Belt project reviews. The leadership team reviews look at how the projects are linked and address coordination and other issues that come up.

Success in these kinds of projects is not dependent on any one person. It requires a lot of people coming together to accomplish the shared vision.

DO YOU HAVE ANY FINAL THOUGHTS ABOUT UMBRELLA PROJECTS?

The key enabler of umbrella projects is the way people think about it. I am sometimes asked for a template or a guideline for how to do an umbrella project. I am asked to show a Belt a work instruction for how to do it. The moment I'm asked for this, I think we are really off-track. When they ask this, I know that they don't really understand. I can do presentations and training, but people will still ask for how to do a project. This means to me that they are only seeing a piece of the elephant and not the whole thing. They don't really understand what we are trying to do when they ask this.

The people working on umbrella projects need to think about the whole umbrella and not just their small part of it. The question for me is how to help them learn and understand the interconnectedness of the projects. It's systems thinking. We need to learn how to prepare people to think this way. Systems thinking is foundational to success. This also reinforces that the selection of the right people is really important to the success of umbrella projects.

25

S-Curve 7—Business System Improvement

Curve 7, Business Systems Improvement, expands the use of Six Sigma processes and tools into broad, integrated, systemic umbrella-type problem areas. An example is shown in Table 25.1.

Projects in S-Curve 7 focus on disruptions in the flow of information and material in the end-to-end supply chain. This chain begins with raw materials delivered to suppliers, through the company's processes and on to the company's customers. This is the main characteristic of projects in S-Curve 7. This approach addresses problems and improvements that exist in the boundaries between organizations.

Boundaries between organizations exist for many reasons, including:

- Internal measures of performance against which subunits are evaluated.
- Internal management competition.

TABLE 25.1

Example—Integrated Supply Chain Improvement Actions

o What is the product path to market?
- Single
- Multiple
- Mixed

o Pick a path
- What is the flow?
- What are the problems in the flow?
- What function "owns" the problems? (all are cross-functional)
- Define priorities
- Run projects linked together under the umbrella

o Project maturity
- Company supply chains
- Supply chain including suppliers
- Supply chain including customers

- Commercial relationships between the company and its suppliers and the company and its customers.
- The natural inclination of people to control the resources that have been assigned to them.
- The need for each part of the organization to satisfy its customers.

The starting point for these projects is a significant customer need or problem. It could also be poor company performance in a specific area. The common characteristic is that these problems or improvements are not solvable by any one part of the organization.

The first step is to identify a cross-company problem for the umbrella. Next, a detailed description of the high-level flow is created to identify where waste and disruption is occurring. This is performed using one or a combination of tools. Examples of these tools include but are not limited to value stream mapping, process mapping and voice of the customer interviews.

Following the identification of wastes and disruptions, a validation process occurs to ensure that the team got it right.

Next, priorities are set based on importance to the customer and business. This importance ranking is combined with an analysis of systemic impact which can be determined using tools like relationship diagrams.

Following establishment of priorities, an overall project plan is developed. Key to the project plan is clear identification of project dependencies. This ensures projects are implemented in the correct order. This means some projects will have to wait until other projects are completed. Waiting is necessary because outputs from the earlier projects are needed by the follow-on projects.

Project reviews for umbrella projects are open to the whole team. They are open so that all the Belts can see the work of others and understand the impacts projects have on each other. The objective is to highlight and encourage project-to-project connections. These connections are necessary to ensure that the original big issue is improved. More importantly, the customer experiences a real change in the performance of the company's products.

S-CURVE 6 AND 7 PROJECT EXAMPLES

The projects found during S-Curves 6 and 7 reflect a high level of Six Sigma maturity. One will find all project types during this phase. The projects listed below are illustrative of the project diversity seen at this level of maturity.

Reduce total product lead time from 18 weeks to 10 weeks. This project was an umbrella project requiring the participation of multiple businesses and functions to reduce total lead time. The result was increased competitiveness and sales and a reduction of total system inventory by 20%.

Improve competitiveness and market penetration in a rapidly growing market segment. This project focused on understanding the market, the customers and the competition. The result was a data-based, redesigned product and sales strategy with an execution plan that improved Cummins performance.

Develop and implement a STEM-based mentorship program in collaboration with local community youth organizations. This project used DFSS tools and processes to develop a STEM-based mentorship program that improved the visibility of STEM educational options.

Reduce the recordable incident rate in a facility by 90% while not compromising safety or quality. This project addressed systemic and cultural issues impacting a safe work environment. A cross-functional team delivered four key improvements positively affecting the incident rate.

Improve repair part availability for customers. This was an umbrella project that started with customer feedback to identify a critical improvement need. The umbrella consisted of several coordinated projects involving multiple global entities.

26

Interview With Holly Duarte—Black Belt

WHAT IS YOUR BACKGROUND?

I started at Cummins right out of college. I graduated from Tennessee Tech in 2002 with a degree in international business and Spanish. I started with Cummins right out of school and only planned to be here for three months. The long-term plan was for my husband and I to move to Brazil and live on the beach. That was the grand plan at 21. Here I am almost 15 years later. There was something about Cummins that really resonated with me and has worked really well in my life.

My first role was in customer service. I worked there for about two and a half years and had a really interesting view of different aspects of our supply chain as well as our customers. Then, I was moved into marketing. I worked in marketing communications for about eight years or so. After having been in marketing communications for a long time, I really felt like I wanted to learn more. I had learned a lot and wanted to expand my understanding in the field of marketing. So, I accepted a Black Belt role.

Like a lot of people, I had been involved in Six Sigma at that time. I was on several projects related to marketing and communication as part of my marketing and communication role. I sought out the Black Belt role for personal development. I wanted to expand my capability in marketing so that I could go and do other things. I enjoyed marketing, so that's why I was focused on it. I saw the Black Belt role as a development option.

Being a Black Belt was a very interesting role. It would allow you to show your capabilities while at the same time learning a lot. It was a unique development role, so I took it. My goal was tackling a couple of different projects in marketing to learn about other aspects outside of communication. I was in the Black Belt role for a little over two years.

Following my Black Belt role, I joined the customer support excellence group leading the Net Promoter Score work for about two years. Now, I'm doing something similar to the Black Belt role, but with a different slant. I'm leading a customer-focused project using new tools that we're bringing into Cummins. We will probably bring them into Six Sigma as well. We call it Human Centered Design at Cummins. It's really exciting! After nearly 15 years in Cummins, I am doing something completely new and learning a whole lot. I hope we're making a difference for our company too. That's a bit of my journey.

DID THE BLACK BELT ROLE MEET YOUR EXPECTATIONS FOR DEVELOPMENT?

Yes, it did meet my expectations for development. I was involved in the selection of a lot of my projects. It was always a collaborative effort. I didn't just pick projects out of the air and say, "Hey, I want to go do this." I discussed projects with the executive director of Marketing and the leader of Quality for the business I was working at the time. I would say, "This project looks very interesting to me. I want to go tackle this." It gave me exposure to several different aspects of the business.

One of the unique challenges of my Black Belt role was that the function I supported had a lot of people changes. My project Sponsors changed a lot.

WHAT WERE SOME OF THE PROJECTS THAT YOU WORKED ON?

One very interesting project that I did was with our group in Brazil. I had thought that I would like to go work at our Brazil facility, but it didn't work out for a number of reasons. But I was able to lead a great channel development project for the Brazil market supporting the launch of a new emissions product there.

I led another interesting project to improve the marketing communications organization structure. This was an important project. The president of the business unit wanted to centralize the functions for the components businesses. The charter was to figure out how to centralize marketing communications function for the business unit. That's not the typical charter for a Six Sigma project. We had to do a little work to reframe the Y statement, but it was good to know what my Sponsor was looking for from the project. I think this was an especially challenging project because it affected people's jobs. I had to involve people from multiple functions. But I couldn't involve too many because it was a confidential project focused on restructuring that group. The outcome of this project was disappointing because it wasn't implemented. It was overcome by events shortly after the project closed. The company had already planned on centralizing several functions. However, they did dig up and use my project to help with how to go about it, which I was happy about.

Another great project that I led focused on developing the company's plan for implementing our environmental sustainability practices. The project developed the company's strategy for environmental sustainability. It defined the different short- and long-term elements. At the end of the project, my Sponsor was reassigned to corporate strategy. Sponsors are so important. I can only do so much as a Black Belt to try to push a major strategy change. The project needs support at the leadership level to see the improvements through. Leadership changes make it difficult. Implementation was a struggle. This was exactly the same thing that happened with the marketing project.

A reality in corporate America is that leadership changes every couple of years. That can have a big impact when the project improvements are at the big system level. That's part of the risk when identifying a Sponsor.

I learned something during my time in marketing. When I'm leading a system-level change, I need a Management Review Group (MRG) that involves multiple leaders affected by the project. I think that is a best practice. An MRG has become a common practice for Belts leading big projects. It eliminates relying on one leader for everything when change at that level happens.

One of the great things about the Black Belt role is you learn so much about the business because of the different projects that you lead. You actually learn new things whether you want to or not. For example, I learned that marketing techniques can apply to a lot of different situations.

From a personal standpoint, the Black Belt role was great for me. I was able to manage my time a little bit better than if I was leading these projects in addition to a day-to-day role. As an example, I was going to school for my MBA at the same time. In fact, I was pursuing an MBA with a concentration in environmental sustainability. I was doing this at the same time I led a project on environmental sustainability.

Using full time Black Belts means having people dedicated to the biggest, most complicated problems. This is an important benefit gained by the company.

FROM YOUR PERSPECTIVE, HOW HAS SIX SIGMA AT CUMMINS CHANGED OVER TIME?

Six Sigma has changed quite a bit over time. In the early days of Six Sigma, some people may have seen it as more of an operational/technical tool. They saw it as a tool that drives day-to-day improvements using lots of data and Minitab. They saw Six Sigma depending on statistics because there was a lot of numbers and data. Six Sigma wasn't seen as something that applied to marketing, even though there are numbers involved with that work. Marketing is much more process-oriented, so people didn't see how Six Sigma fit.

I came into the Sigma world around the time that the Six Sigma organization was working to expand their training. They wanted it to apply easily to office employees working in administrative processes. It was great to see that, because it was very empowering for people around Cummins outside of manufacturing and engineering. In general, I believe people like to help. People want to fix things. There are those people who check in and check out, who go home day to day and don't worry about things. But most people, particularly the type of people that come to work for Cummins, want to make improvements. They see a problem and they want to fix it. Having a common tool set and a common language like Six Sigma was extraordinarily powerful. Understanding Six Sigma empowered them to say, "I want to lead this project to make this improvement." I think that from a grassroots sort of perspective, it really helped to empower employees to drive improvements that they saw were needed. Involving them in Six Sigma was asking them to help improve things.

Expanding beyond what one would think of as the traditional Six Sigma applications in operations was earlier in the deployment. As time has passed, there have been more changes. The company recognized that we weren't driving our projects with common vision and common goals. We have all these different individuals driving their individual improvements, which could be good or could be bad. It just depends on the outcome of the project. It's good to empower people, but at the same time, if you have thousands of people running off to fix little things, you could easily miss the big picture.

If you're not tracking the effect of projects on a common goal, you're not leveraging the true power of Six Sigma to drive improvement for the business. The company has made that change in just the past couple of years. The best Black Belts are working on the biggest problems overseen by a Management Review Group (MRG). The MRGs are tracking progress toward very specific project goals linked directly to company goals. I think that's been a significant improvement. However, if we are not careful, the pendulum could swing a little bit too far. We can't afford to leave out those grassroots improvements that come from employees who feel empowered.

Another thing that comes immediately to mind is the creation of a common language. We are an enormous company. It is very powerful to pick up the phone and talk with someone in India or in Europe or in Africa and say, "We've got all these opportunities, we're going to evaluate them using a C&E matrix." Everybody understands what you mean. You can pull out a C&E matrix at any meeting and everybody in the room knows how to use it. That's a very common occurrence. Having a common improvement language that we all speak has been extremely powerful.

Having common skills and capabilities, and all of these tools that we have given to the people, is very empowering. We learned many things at different schools, but we don't bring a lot of those to our work. One of the great things about Six Sigma at Cummins is that people are empowered to use the tools to make improvements in their day-to-day work. This is a huge benefit for driving a culture of continuous improvement for the business.

The last thing is hard to put your finger on, but it concerns the company's culture. I would say that Six Sigma has built this culture of never being satisfied. We're never perfectly satisfied with everything that we've done, because there is always something more we can improve. I think this is a good thing. Hey, I come from strong Protestant stock. I had a grandmother who worked in the garden until she was 90 years old, making it better because it was never good enough. I totally get it. It resonates with me that you're never good enough. You always having to do things to make it better. There's this culture at Cummins that pushes constant business improvement. I believe that is a good thing. This culture helps to drive the business to continuously get better. We have to do it to survive and thrive.

HOW DID SIX SIGMA INFLUENCE THE COMPANY'S RELATIONSHIPS WITH CUSTOMERS?

I'll speak to my direct experience and what I have seen. There has been an enormous number of great projects that were Customer Focused Six Sigma (CFSS) projects. I have been involved in a couple of CFSS projects. I believe that the Cummins people participating would say that it was a very positive experience. The projects improved not only their relationship with the customer but helped the customer's operations.

Another place where Six Sigma has been used to improve with customers is in support of the company's Net Promoter Score (NPS) work. We collect feedback, analyze it and identify improvement opportunities. We then assign Belts to lead the improvements.

Right from the beginning of our launch of NPS, as we analyzed the data brought into the business, we used Six Sigma as a platform to do the improvement work. We assigned Belts to tackle the issues that came from the NPS system. I've seen lots of really great projects that helped make improvements for the customer. One of the things that we noticed though, as we were going through the process, is that we were looking at different pockets of the business. We were driving improvement with Belts for a location but not for the company as a whole. People were doing good work, but we were missing the big picture.

For example, I would go to a workshop where we're analyzing the data and identifying opportunities for one OEM. Then, I would go to another workshop for a different OEM, and I heard the exact same thing discussed. This is when I first joined the NPS group. I thought we needed to begin looking at the issues coming from our customers in an aggregate form. We needed to do this because we were asking two different account teams to fix the same problem individually. This was duplicating work. For some problems, it's not even fair to ask them to do it, because the problem is something that is bigger than one group could possibly address.

Eventually, we began bringing the data together and asking, "'What's something that is common across our customer base that can become a bigger improvement impacting all of them?" Julie Liu's project is a great example of that. George helped sponsor that project. They continue having progress update meetings. Improvements continue from Julie's original project charter.

We have a significant challenge when aggregating data from multiple customers. We are identifying really big, complicated issues. These things are not easy to fix. They require a different approach than the traditional Six Sigma project framework.

To do these big, complex projects well requires very experienced Belts. Julie Liu is fantastic. This was her 16th Belt project. I have enormous respect for Julie. She came in to lead this big project on improving a critical process for our customers in one of our major North American markets. The scope was just huge. It has been a very successful project. We identified on her project roadmap a series of projects that we needed to do to really move the needle on improvement. I think the beauty of the approach is that required a combination of bottom-up and top-down efforts to make it work.

First, we received feedback from the customer. We looked at it and identified possible improvements. As we developed the roadmap and strategy for improvement, we found that a lot of the directions coming from the top down regarding Cummins supply chain strategy were closely linked to the bottom-up message from the customer telling us what is wrong. I think there were some real synergies. But there were some additional projects that we identified that weren't part of the original supply chain strategy. The synergy with the supply chain strategy enhanced the improvements we were driving for customers from the NPS feedback. It's been a successful effort that has lasted almost three years.

We did the same thing not long ago with our new NPS data. We identified a project to improve our responsiveness to customer requested product changes. I have been leading that project. We used a lot of the lessons learned from Julie's project. We began by identifying a roadmap. We are already showing significant improvements from that work. It's been an interesting journey. We leveraged Six Sigma, but then we also brought in some human-centered design tools, which has been very interesting. It's the first time we've married those tool sets together. Ultimately, some of these human-centered design tools will be added to the existing tool box, which I think is really good.

One of the things that is really important for Sigma evolution is to avoid saying that only this one set of tools can be used. It is very important to continuously evolve and grow. We may need different types of tools as the challenges of the company change. I think this is a really good thing. There's a lot of interest in learning how to apply human-centered design methods within the Six Sigma framework.

WHAT HAVE YOU LEARNED BY LEADING THESE BIG, COMPLEX PROJECTS?

The big projects tend to be very cross-functional. For example, a project I am leading now includes the technical, purchasing, manufacturing and marketing functions. One of the things that I have learned is that it's been beneficial to take the big, umbrella approach. The umbrella brings the perspective of the customer into strategy development and execution. Often the strategies that are developed to drive some big changes for the business are not connected to the problems that our customers are experiencing. Making that connection is very beneficial.

When we do these big projects, we don't always uncover new actions to take. Too many times we create a brand-new roadmap that we never envisioned before. That's not how it works. That's not how it worked for Julie, and that's not how it worked in my current project. In fact, a lot of what we identified reinforced the need to continue to improve product quality because it's very important to our customers. I think we have been doing a lot of the right things to drive improved product quality in the business.

In my current project, there are several things it reinforced. One is that we need to better enable our people to do good work. The project reinforced that we need to have the right systems, the right tools and the right oversight of the ongoing work. The improvement must be connected to the problems customers are facing. Our strategy decisions are negatively affected when the connection isn't made between the pain that the customer is feeling, the pain that the customer-facing account team is feeling, and the pain of the customer support people. When those connection haven't been made to the big things that we're trying to drive, it leaves people feeling that we might not be doing the right things. Or worse, the customer tells us, "I keep telling you about this problem and you're not doing anything." Frequently, the customer's message isn't getting to the right people. In this current project we identified how it all really works. We identified new work in addition to reinforcing the need to improve work we are already doing.

We are driving some things that we weren't already doing. One of the challenges with any of this work to make it happen successfully is engaging leadership. You absolutely have to have leadership buy-in and support for the long haul because it requires a multi-year endeavor. I've led the project. The team has identified all the improvements that are needed. But it's got this big long tail of actions to be taken over time. Typically, I would close the project and move on. But fortunately, my leadership has said, "Okay Holly, you need to keep a finger on the pulse of this project and stay engaged." I have the latitude to continue to meet with key stakeholders. I continue to hold MRG meetings and meetings with leadership teams. I also meet with project leaders to make sure that they're making progress on the improvements. All of that work is critically important to make sure that we keep the improvement momentum created by the project.

Another success factor is making sure you've identified short-, medium- and long-term goals. You can't only have all big strategy statements like "live the brand" as the only improvements. That's important, but you need to answer the question, "What can I do right now to improve our experience with the customer?"

As part of the project, we work very, very hard to identify short-, medium- and long-term improvements. This is important because if my MRG disbands after a year, I've at least been able to drive some immediate improvements to the customer. Often those big strategies are moving along anyway. They're being managed by other teams.

It's also important not to add a lot of bureaucracy. That's the other important lesson learned that's top of mind for me. I don't want to add a whole bunch of bureaucracy on top of initiatives and work that is already underway, either. I think striking the right balance, making sure the right work is happening, but not adding a lot of additional meetings and reports for people. That's very tactical but it's something that's been on my mind while we're into implementation mode for my most recent project.

HOW HAS SIX SIGMA HELPED BREAK DOWN THE BARRIERS BETWEEN THE FUNCTIONS?

That's a good question, because traditional Six Sigma always starts by trying to narrow the scope. Six Sigma traditionally pushes you to do the opposite of what we're doing right now. But over time as we have evolved, there's emerged a common understanding that we're hearing the same issues across the businesses. As much as we tried to tackle the issues as one-off Belt projects, it hasn't eliminated the common problems. We continue to hear the same themes in different parts of the company.

Six Sigma has enabled us to tackle the big issues, but I also think it's a sort of a circular relationship. Because Six Sigma was requiring us to tackle projects of smaller scope, we have recognized that we weren't tackling the big darn deals. Now we have recognized that we need to do that. I think that because of Six Sigma, we have developed a culture that drives us to work together no matter the size of the issue.

I think this goes back to the cross-functional nature of it. Right from the beginning of our Six Sigma deployment, working cross-functionally was encouraged. We were encouraged to know not just how your process impacts you, but how your process affects the next person in the chain. By encouraging everyone to understand the handoffs between functions working in a flow of processes, an understanding was built over time that we don't work in a vacuum. We all impact each other, which impacts the customer, so we have to work together. This has enabled us to tackle the big issues. It's been part of the evolution of Six Sigma more than anything.

The common language has become very important for making cross-functional improvements. The common language and a continuous improvement culture enabled us to have really tough discussions between functions. Often these tough discussions can turn into functions blaming each other. If you let it get down to argument and blame, you really don't get anywhere. Having this common tool set and these common processes helps to break down barriers. People may come into it not agreeing on anything except that they are going to tackle an issue using these tools. They agree that they are going to go through this process. People agree that they will go through the process together in good faith. At the end of it they will use the data and the results from the process to come to the solution. We do this so that we can come to a common solution. This happens ever when people may have been in two completely different places before the project started.

One of my Black Belt projects was a great example of this phenomenon. It was a supply chain project involving the functions in supply chain. The disagreement that I just described was exactly what was happening. One group was saying we just need to fix forecasting and another group was saying we just need to put more inventory in our warehouse.

By going through the process, we were able to say, here are the actual factors that are affecting this problem. Here are the things that we need to work on together. We clarified the actions that we needed to take. It really helped to bring people together to help solve the problems.

For the big system issues, we may very well not agree on what the issue is. By using these common tools and processes, we're able to work together to an agreed-upon solution. It enables consensus and that is really important, particularly when you're trying to tackle these great big darn deals. When you have consensus on a roadmap, that's a powerful thing. It drives everybody to agree that we're going to work toward this common goal and here's how we're going to do it: step one, two, three. It is very helpful in that sense, particularly for these complex system projects.

One thing that I would like for you to notice, we have been talking for over an hour and haven't talked about capability studies. We haven't talked about t-tests, or any statistics. What we have talked a lot about is how people work together. We've talked about how Six Sigma connects to different strategic elements of business. We've discussed the importance of culture, and the importance of leadership. In the end, it has less to do with statistics and much more to do with all the softer things that people tend to downplay.

Tackling the big issues with Six Sigma like we are, is the right way to go about it if you have the right support. The way we've structured the big projects using an MRG, team metrics, regular reviews, and keeping the project linked to the company's goals and objectives is something you have to do. But at the same time, you can't dismiss the power that Six Sigma can provide at a grassroots level to really drive change.

HOW HAS YOUR SIX SIGMA EXPERIENCE INFLUENCED YOUR PERSONAL DEVELOPMENT?

First, there's definitely learning how to lead projects in general. Next, one of the prerequisites is to have a Sponsor for your project. So, you have to have conversations with leaders in the business. It's definitely been an element of my career development to be able to lead, converse with, and learn from leaders across the business.

I don't know if there's any better way to say, "Yes, it's a great way to learn professionally, but also to develop your own career." It has been a great opportunity throughout. I would say as a Green Belt, to a lesser degree, but definitely as a Black Belt because you're leading projects primarily for executives. Even now, as I'm leading projects for big system improvements, I'm meeting with my MRG and Sponsors on a regular basis.

HAS SIX SIGMA HAD AN IMPACT ON DIVERSITY AT CUMMINS?

Yes, I believe it has. For example, let's say a company wants to develop women in the organization. Six Sigma is an opportunity to do that. I think it absolutely has at Cummins. Some of our strongest women leaders at Cummins have come through the quality organization and through Six Sigma. Absolutely, I think it's an excellent opportunity to develop groups that may need more development to make it.

For me, Six Sigma has always been about development. Driving the big improvement projects is something that I constantly learn from because driving big change in a company like Cummins is so complicated. So, Six Sigma has always been a development journey for me. My growth began with learning the tools initially as a Green Belt and then as a Black Belt. I was able to develop my skills in different functional areas. It was a big help in other areas of marketing as we drove change for customers through Net Promoter Score driven projects. It's been great learning how to get a handle on a complex subject and drive it as a cultural change.

So, it's always been a development journey for me, and it continues to be. As I continue to lead, I benefit from all of the learning that I had as a Belt in project management and the tool set that we've used, implementing without power. All of those things. It's a journey that continues for sure.

27

The Effect of Maturity on Organizational Communication

The purpose of this chapter is to show, in a practical way how internal communication between leadership of the organization and the Six Sigma office changes through the S-Curves.

As the figure below illustrates, the communication is not one-way. The leadership tends to communicate directions, requests individually and in reviews. This communication creates a response from the Six Sigma office in the form of updates, resource needs and improvement recommendations.

The communication that takes place during maturity, as represented by the S-Curves, changes in a way similar to the activity itself. Communication begins as basic information about the program; for example, number of people in training, number of projects launched and closed, cost of the training and so forth. By the seventh S-Curve, the communication has become more strategic, focused on how the Six Sigma program is delivering cross boundary improvements and where the next big opportunities lie. Tables 27.1 through 27.7 offer a brief description of the communication that occurs during each S-Curve.

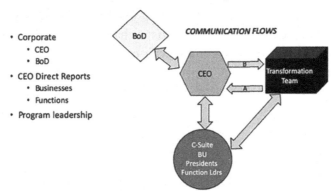

FIGURE 27.1 Communication flows.

TABLE 27.1

S-Curve 1—Preparation and Pre-launch

Leadership to the Transformation Team	Transformation Team to Leadership
• *Direction*	• *Updates*
o CEO role and actions	o Launch readiness
o Senior leadership role and actions	o Emerging risks
o Funding (one-time and annual)	o Spending to plan
o Support consultant selection	o Knowledge capture plan and progress
o Corporate staffing and strategy	o Consultant effectiveness
o Targets	o Belt selections
o Expectations and responsibilities	o Delivery of requested drafts
▪ Consultant	o Plans and schedules
▪ Corporate staff	• *Resource needs*
▪ Businesses	o A project tracking system and cost
• *Requests*	o Additional staffing
o Plan and schedule update	o Master Black Belt requirements
o Draft future state	o BB/GB required to support targets
o Draft strategy and criteria	• *Improvement recommendations*
o Draft project selection process	o Any changes to original planning
o Draft measures and reports	o Changes to the consultant curriculum
o Draft project list and timetable	
• *Reviews*	
o Progress to plan and schedule—monthly	
o Consultant review—monthly	

During Pre-launch, S-Curve 1, the leadership is focused on understanding what is required to begin the process of introducing something new to the organization, setting direction based on that understanding, and requesting drafts of plans for review.

Of special importance from leadership during this phase is an understanding of the resources committed to the change, the role that leadership will play, performance targets and specific expectations.

Critical communication from the transformation team includes emerging risks, the spending plan and any issues concerning the consultant.

TABLE 27.2

S-Curve 2—Launch and First Projects

Leadership to the Transformation Team	Transformation Team to Leadership
• *Direction*	• *Updates (in addition to requests)*
o CEO visit agenda to include Belts	o Facilitate project selection processes
o Communication plan strategy and requirements	o Lead assessments
o CEO and senior leadership scheduled for training	o Feedback to senior leadership teams
o Any plan changes	o Early warnings on potential
• *Requests*	o Projects that aren't connected to business goals
o Project updates	o Budget risks?
o Emerging opportunities and risks	o Assessment of senior leadership support of continuous improvement transformation
o Variances to plans	
o Consultant assessment of organization performance	o Assessment of business continuous improvement leaders
o Corporate staff assessment of consultant performance	• *Resource needs*
o Upcoming projects from the hoppers	o Based on speed of progress
• *Reviews*	• *Improvement recommendations*
o Progress to plans and schedules— monthly	o Slow down/speed up
	o More or fewer launches
o First completed projects—on call	o Finding from assessments
o Measures—monthly	o Strengths and weaknesses
o Consultant performance to contract— monthly	o Problems/risks/weaknesses avoidance recommendations
o Upcoming projects connection to business priorities—quarterly	
o Business leader reviews with senior staff—monthly/2x yearly	

During S-Curve 2, the communication changes to focus on the initial execution of the organization's plans.

Critical elements of communication from the leadership include leadership support activities, reviews of progress, reviews of business unit progress and key projects.

Critical information from the transformation team include assessments of performance, recommended improvements, assessment of project quality and any budget risks.

TABLE 27.3

S-Curve 3—Building a Foundation

Leadership to the Transformation Team	Transformation Team to Leadership
• *Direction*	• *Updates (in addition to requests and reviews)*
o Six Sigma projects on the Six Sigma processes	o Facilitate project selection processes
o Standard common critical measures	o Lead organizational assessments
• *Requests*	o Feedback to senior leadership teams
o Develop a schedule of ongoing regular reviews with leadership	o Early warnings on potential problems
o Select first group of company Master Black Belts	o Projects that aren't connected to business goals
o Develop a recognition award and process	o Budget risks?
o Develop a plan for DFSS deployment	o Assessment of senior leadership support of continuous improvement transformation
• *Reviews (includes carryover from SC 2)*	o Assessment of business continuous improvement leaders
o Progress to plans and schedules— monthly	• *Resource needs*
o Select completed projects—monthly	o Additional Master Black Belt and Black Belt needs
o Measures—monthly	o Additional budget needs?
o Consultant performance to contract— monthly	o Support for DFSS planning and deployment
o Upcoming projects connection to business priorities—quarterly	o Requirements to support reward and recognition
o Business leader reviews with senior staff—monthly/2x yearly	• *Improvement recommendations*
	o Master Black Belt development process
	o Black Belt leadership development processes
	o Succession planning requirements and processes for Black Belt, Master Black Belt and Quality leaders
	o Reenergize leadership with focused training and discussion

The most significant change in S-Curve 3 communication is the development of an internal Master Black Belt cadre. This includes recommendation of candidates, development plans and progress reports.

Communication from S-Curve 4 on is very similar. The main change is related to new project types tried, lessons learned and recommendations for adoption.

TABLE 27.4

S-Curve 4—Self-Supporting

Leadership to the Transformation Team	Transformation Team to Leadership
• *Direction*	• *Updates*
o Targets	o Facilitate project selection processes
■ Master Black Belts and Belts	ensuring connection to key business
■ Projects	goal and initiatives
■ Savings	o Lead organizational assessments
o Develop plans for the next S-Curve:	o Feedback to senior leadership teams
how will we expand C.I.	o Early warnings on potential
• *Requests*	problems
o Assess impacts of self-support	o Projects that aren't connected to
o Develop templates for bringing on	business goals
new businesses	o Budget risks?
o Process for new employees	o Assessment of senior leadership
• *Reviews (includes carryover from SC 3)*	support of continuous improvement
o Progress to plans and schedules—	transformation
monthly	o Assessment of business continuous
o Select completed projects—monthly	improvement leaders
o Measures—monthly	o Effectiveness of strategy
o Profitability impacts—quarterly	o DFSS progress
o Upcoming projects connection to	• *Resource needs*
business priorities—quarterly	o Additional Master Black Belt and
o Business leader reviews with senior	Black Belt needs
staff—monthly/2x yearly	o Additional budget needs?
	o Risks to additional requirements if
	not properly resourced
	• *Improvement recommendations*
	o Define how to work with suppliers
	and customers
	o New project categories
	o Where and how to use Six Sigma tools
	to manage the business
	o Changes to training?
	o Changes to roles and responsibilities?
	o Best practices to replicate and where
	o Develop libraries of tools (FMEA,
	FTA, VSM, etc.)
	o Change project tracker to match real
	process

TABLE 27.5

S-Curve 5—Business Integration

Leadership to the Transformation Team	Transformation Team to Leadership

• *Direction*
   o Define the relationship between C.I. and the operating system
   o Expand the role of Master Black Belt to include C.I. partnership with leadership teams
 • *Requests*
   o Prepare a recommendation on individual C.I. certification
   o Assess current state and make improvement recommendations
   o Develop recommendation for new areas of application
 • *Reviews (includes carryover from SC 3)*
   o Progress to plans and schedules—monthly
   o Select completed projects—monthly
   o Measures—monthly
   o Profitability impacts—quarterly
   o Upcoming projects connection to business priorities—quarterly
   o Business leader reviews with senior staff—monthly/2x yearly
	• *Updates*
	   o Facilitate project selection processes ensuring connection to key business goal and initiatives
	   o Lead organizational assessments
	   o Feedback to senior leadership teams
	   o Early warnings on potential problems
	   o Projects that aren't connected to business goals
	   o Budget risks?
	   o Assessment of senior leadership support of continuous improvement transformation
	   o Assessment of business continuous improvement leaders
	   o Effectiveness of strategy
	   o DFSS progress
	   o Assessment of effectiveness by project category
	 • *Resource needs*
	   o Additional Master Black Belt and Black Belt needs
	   o Additional budget needs or opportunities for reduction
	   o Risks to additional requirements if not properly resourced
	 • *Improvement recommendations*
	   o New project categories
	   o Where and how to use Six Sigma tools to manage the business
	   o Changes to training to meet organization-wide needs
	   o Changes to roles and responsibilities?
	   o Best practices to replicate and where
	   o Develop a library of tool paths for different types of projects

TABLE 27.6

S-Curve 6—Continued Growth and Expansion

Leadership to the Transformation Team	Transformation Team to Leadership
• *Direction*	• *Updates*
o Continue to set targets for savings/ revenue	o Facilitate project selection processes ensuring connection to key business goal and initiatives
o Add targets focused on other customer and business priorities	o Lead organizational assessments
o Ensure Six Sigma use in all areas of the business	o Feedback to senior leadership teams
o Develop a process to find the most important customer issues cutting across the business	o Early warnings on potential problems
	o DFSS progress
• *Requests*	o Assessment of effectiveness by project category
o Develop recommendations for new measures	o Progress against plans and measures
• *Reviews (including carryover from SC 3)*	• *Resource needs*
o Progress to plans and schedules— monthly	• *Improvement recommendations*
o Select completed projects—monthly	o Additional project categories
o Measures—monthly	o Any improvements needed to support the total business
o Profitability impacts—quarterly	o Changes to training and project support approaches?
o Upcoming projects connection to business priorities—quarterly	
o Business leader reviews with senior staff—monthly/2x yearly	

TABLE 27.7

S-Curve 7—Business System Improvement

Leadership to the Transformation Team	Transformation Team to Leadership
• *Direction*	• *Updates*
o Continue to set targets for savings/ revenue	o Facilitate project selection processes ensuring connection to key business goal and initiatives
o Add targets focused on other customer and business priorities	o Lead organizational assessments
o Ensure Six Sigma use in all areas of the business	o Feedback to senior leadership teams
o Develop a process to find the most important customer issues cutting across the business	o Early warnings on potential problems
	o DFSS progress
• *Requests*	o Assessment of effectiveness by project category
o Develop recommendations for new measures	o Progress against plans and measures
	• *Resource needs*

(Continued)

TABLE 27.7

(Continued)

Leadership to the Transformation Team	Transformation Team to Leadership

• *Reviews (including carryover from SC 3)*
  o Progress to plans and schedules—monthly
  o Select completed projects—monthly
  o Measures—monthly
  o Profitability impacts—quarterly
  o Upcoming projects connection to business priorities—quarterly
  o Business leader reviews with senior staff—monthly/2x yearly
	• *Improvement recommendations*
	  o Additional project categories
	  o Any improvements needed to support the total business
	  o Changes to training and project support approaches?

28

How to Use S-Curves

We do want to address a question that has come up frequently. The question goes something like this, "The S-Curves are good for documenting what happened, but can they be used to plan for the future?" Our answer is an unqualified absolutely.

The reason we can say "absolutely" is that we, and others, have done it. Admittedly, the first time one uses S-Curves to plan program maturity, there are many unknowns. These unknowns impact the accuracy of S-Curve to S-Curve prediction and transition further out in time. The reality is, there are always unknowns in any planning process. An expression common among professional boxers is, "Everybody has a plan until they get punched in the face," which is another way of saying it is impossible to plan for unknowns. A deeper understanding of S-Curves helps to address this reality.

The gaps from S-Curve to S-Curve is intentional. The gap is recognition that conditions change over time. What was true a year or two ago isn't necessarily true now. Progress does not happen in a straight, uninterrupted line. The gap prompts several questions to consider given the current maturity of the change effort addressing the conditions that exist now. These questions include:

- What have we learned during implementation/deployment to this point?
- Based on what we have learned from implementation, do the goals of the next couple of S-Curves change? Is it necessary to change the measures of success?
- Which changes require ongoing maintenance and upkeep? Who is accountable for this work?
- What changes made in the past have become obsolete and need to be discontinued?
- Does the future state description change based on what we have learned so far?

- Is the future state still supportive of the organizational goals and objectives?
- How can the organization leverage the maturity already achieved?

Stop and consider your own maturity for a second. When you were a small child, you probably touched something hot at some time and were the unwilling recipient of an "ouchy." It was not a pleasant experience and you probably even cried because it hurt. It is unlikely that each time you came across something hot, you had to touch it to learn that lesson again. Once was quite enough! The same thing happens in organizations. There are many types of organizational ouchies. Some examples include:

- A warranty issue results in a change to the product or process to eliminate the problem.
- A customer uses a product in an unexpected way resulting in a product failure requiring improvement.
- A new material is introduced to the product requiring an improved manufacturing process in one location. This is the only location where the product can be produced until the change is introduced across all the company's plants.
- An unknown change to tax law results in a fine and requires that expenses are recorded in a specific way everywhere the company operates.

The question, then, is how to learn from organizational "ouchies"? How do we communicate or spread the word so that everybody does work the correct way? We suggest that S-Curve to S-Curve maturity is a form of ouchy learning. The organization uses S-Curve maturity as lessons for others to learn. The goal of this learning is to repeat effective behaviors and eliminate ineffective ones.

Different terms have been created through the years to deal with organizational ouchies; best practice sharing, learning organization, process documentation, quality systems and so forth. The individual stores up lessons learned in the brain. He or she uses those lessons to avoid ouchies as they present themselves. (Note: we are not doctors, or psychologists, or psychiatrists . . . we are only making a general observation.) The organization can do the same thing. A key is accessing the lessons learned broadly for organizational growth and improved effectiveness.

In the military, the review of lessons learned is called an after-action review. After an event the unit comes together to review what happened. The good and not-so-good results are reviewed, documented and shared in the unit. The goal of the review is to repeat the good things and avoid the not-so-good ones. This process is replicated up and down the chain of command, up to and including, the highest levels of accountability. One of the main results of this work is the development of standards and processes that describe the "right" way to do certain critical tasks.

We have seen a tremendous amount of current literature that is encouraging independent action to unleash innovation and creativity. This idea seems to argue against standardization of best practices across an organization because it stifles creativity. At the very least, this is an inference that can be drawn by those who don't really like standardization of any sort. We would argue that you need both.

There are certain aspects of work that lend themselves very well to independent action. An example that comes quickly to mind is the service center representative who is creative in taking care of an urgent customer need. But even in this example, there are boundaries or standards. The service representative cannot take an action that will bankrupt the company or cause bodily injury to somebody in the company. Some might call this common sense. Time teaches that us that the only thing common about common sense is how uncommon it really is!

Standards and common approaches are absolutely necessary in all parts of the organization. Let's use the example of a company that makes products that require micron tolerances. It is not ok for each manufacturing person to creatively decide how that product will be made, or the machine that will be used, or how the product will be assembled. If unstructured creativity and innovation were allowed the customer experience would be chaotic. At least for a while, until all the customers started using another product that actually worked!

The point here is that it is important to define boundaries. Where is creativity and innovation allowed and encouraged and where does it need to be controlled? This is the responsibility of the leadership of the function. The function is responsible to own and improve the processes, methods and capabilities needed to make the company run.

What can an organization do to learn from an S-Curve approach and continue that process over time? The following is an approach. It is not the only approach, but one that can work for your organization.

Identify the owner of the S-Curve process for a business or function. A likely owner is the person most accountable for or impacted by the future state. This person is accountable for planning, tracking, documenting and communicating maturity.

Assemble a team of knowledgeable people. Lead the creation of the future state and develop an assessment of the current state.

Develop S-Curve 1. (Note: If there have been other S-Curves used, collect them and use them as reference for creating the current set of S-Curves.)

- Pick a time period for the S-Curve (3 months, 6 months, 1 year)
- What are the goals for that first time period? (select consultant, staff in place, etc.)
- Define the success measures for the top of the S-Curve
- Develop a project plan.

Develop succeeding S-Curves. Repeat the process used for S-Curve 1. Using available information, complete as many S-Curves as possible. Stop when the when clarity diminishes and ideas falter.

At regular intervals, S-Curve owners meet to discuss and share what they have learned. The overall system owner consolidates those lessons and creates a library of S-Curves for others to use.

One of the "Ahas" that takes place with repetition and sharing of lessons learned is that a common foundation for S-Curves is created. The similarities act as a foundation for the creation of other S-Curves created for different future states. There is less variation in the first S-Curve or two and more variation between S-Curves the longer the change effort goes on. See different S-Curve sets in Figures 28.1, 28.2 and 28.3 as examples.

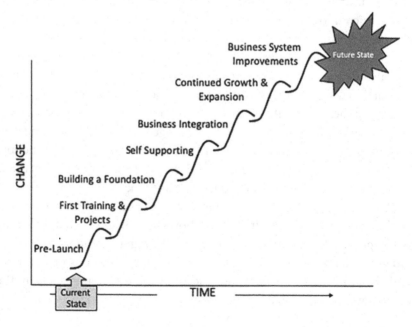

FIGURE 28.1 Six Sigma S-Curves.

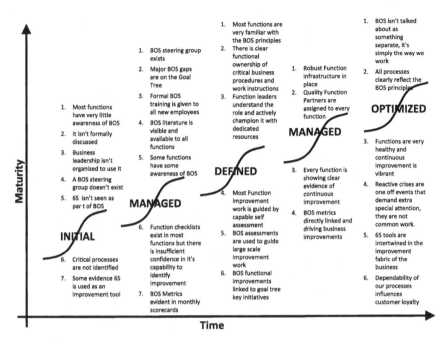

FIGURE 28.2 S-Curve example.

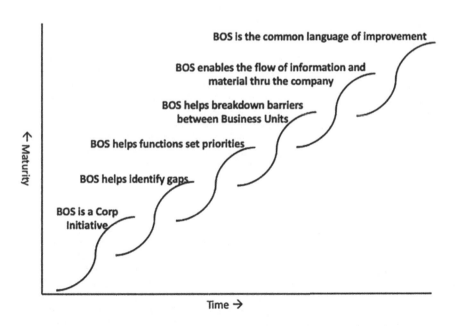

FIGURE 28.3 Business operating system S-Curve example.

29

Important Considerations for a Healthy Long-Term Six Sigma Deployment

MASTER BLACK BELT GROWTH AND ENGAGEMENT

A guiding principle for Cummins Master Black Belts focused them on the business. We wanted MBBs who were business people who brought unique skills and capabilities to the work, not Six Sigma technicians who happened to be working in the company. This distinction was important because we didn't want a cadre of people who saw statistics and adherence to Six Sigma rules as their primary job. We wanted MBBs who understood that Cummins was trying to become a great company that used Six Sigma, not a great Six Sigma company. Cummins products and services made the business go. We wanted Six Sigma to make those products and services better for our customers. This was an important principle that helped Six Sigma thrive.

As discussed earlier, the Master Black Belt is a critical element of the successful maturation of Six Sigma at Cummins. The Master Black Belts tend to come from the Black Belt population and are chosen by local business leadership based on a strong performance track record and promotion potential. They have served as a Black Belt for 18 to 24 months working on projects of various types and complexity. These projects generally have senior leadership Sponsors. There was ongoing upper management visibility during the life of the project. Additionally, the Black Belts received 3% of their salary for each completed project in the year, capped at seven projects. The bonus was eliminated in 2009 during the economic downturn. The Master Black Belt cadre consists of motivated, intelligent, upwardly mobile people. They tend to be highly thought of by senior management. It is very important to give these Master Black Belts opportunities beyond project coaching and Six Sigma training. We accomplished this by doing several things across the S-Curves of Six Sigma maturity.

Master Black Belt in Training—We implemented a six-month preparation and development period. This preparation was called Master Black Belt in Training (MBBiT). During this period the Master Black Belt candidate was assigned a Master Black Belt mentor. They received coaching from the BU Quality Champion. Each candidate took a technical test to identify potential weak areas. The test results combined with a mentor and Quality Champion interview were used to create an individual development plan focused on preparing them for the full-time MBB role. The MBBiT period provided the candidate with an "opt out" if they found that the role really wasn't for them. In practice, candidate Master Black Belts rarely, if ever, opted out of the role. They received a 10% pay increase on completing the MBBiT period as they were entering the full-time phase of the job (18 to 24 months). This recognized both their potential impact on the business and offset the loss of the bonus that they received for project completion as a Black Belt.

Master Black Belt Star Points—In 2002 we began the Master Black Belt Star Point structure with the first cadre of Cummins Master Black Belts. The Star Points were a variant of the Team Based Work System (TBWS) that had been started in the manufacturing plants some years earlier as part of the Cummins Production System (CPS). The TBWS in manufacturing identified different areas of responsibility for the team. A leader was appointed to represent the team for each area. For example, one person was responsible for maintaining the training record for the team, another was responsible for worker safety briefings, etc. We started the Master Black Belt Star Point structure because we had a strategy of keeping the corporate support staff small. This meant that many of the activities needed to keep Six Sigma moving along would have to be performed by somebody other than corporate. The solution was the Master Black Belt cadre. We established a policy requiring 25% to 30% of a Master Black Belt's time to belong to corporate. This gave us the latitude to use Master Black Belts for all the various activities that were needed to drive Six Sigma deployment maturity. Additionally, the MBBs were a company resource to train people outside of their BU and to attend corporate sponsored events. The initial Star Points included:

- Six Sigma database maintenance and change management
- Training material development and upgrade

- Master Black Belt in Training (MBBiT) process development and management
- Communication
- Training schedule
- Master Black Belt pipeline management
- Master Black Belt Symposium planning.

As we moved beyond those areas of basic deployment, the original Star Points were retired and the Master Black Belts moved into new business-related Star Points. Some examples of the new Star Points include:

- Business strategy
- Customer strategy
- HR strategy
- Supply chain improvement
- Manufacturing improvement
- Environmental regulation compliance improvement
- Community involvement improvement.

In each case the Master Black Belt Star Point worked for Cummins senior executive. They focused on developing improvement projects led by Belts in the businesses.

Master Black Belt Networking Calls—We discussed difficult technical issues during monthly MBB calls. An important subject was the best way to conduct the training.

Master Black Belt Symposiums—We started the Master Black Belt Symposium in 2002. A goal of the symposia was to create a Master Black Belts company-wide network of Six Sigma experts. This network was established so that MBBs could call on each other for help and support. Over time and Six Sigma's evolution the purpose of the symposia expanded to include business discussions from senior leaders, technical topic breakouts, "how-to" leadership discussions, Star Point progress, COS and new products among other subjects. The Master Black Belt Symposia were mandatory attendance for the Master Black Belts and held twice annually. By 2009, over 100 Master Black Belts and 150 people in total attended the symposia. This connected Master Black Belts together in a way that online sessions and phone calls could not. When one considers the designed 25% turnover of the Master Black Belt population every six months, the Master Black Belt Symposium was a critical tool for keeping everyone on the same page and moving in a common direction.

Master Black Belt pipeline—Each Master Black Belt had the task of assisting the businesses in the search for their replacement. The specific guidance given to build that pipeline of future Master Black Belts was "find somebody who is better than yourself." This tactic generally helped drive overall Master Black Belt quality to increasingly high levels.

Master Black Belts support to business leadership—Master Black Belts were located in the businesses reporting to local leadership. This made them responsive to the needs of the business first because that's who paid them and gave them direction. During the transition to the Business Integration S-Curve, business leadership teams were encouraged to invite Master Black Belts to sit in on leadership staff meetings. Sitting in on leadership meetings gave the Master Black Belts the opportunity to identify and scope projects in support of the strategies and initiatives of the organizations that they supported. For the Master Black Belt, this was an opportunity to show leadership that they were business people first who brought their unique skills to bear to solve business problems. It also helped pave the way for their next assignment when their Master Black Belt time was up.

CERTIFICATION

During the transition to the Business Integration S-Curve conversations about culture change were taking place. A key question asked was, "How do we make Six Sigma part of the culture of the company?" Over a period of 18 months, we decided to require certification for directors and above. The main goal of the certification requirement was to ensure that leaders of the company had engaged in enough Six Sigma improvement work to understand how it works and its value to Cummins customers and the business. Certification was implemented in two phases:

> *Phase 1—January 1, 2008*: As a minimum requirement, directors and above become certified as Sponsors. A person is certified as a Sponsor following completion of three sponsored BB or GB projects.
>
> *Phase 2—January 1, 2010*: As a minimum requirement, directors and above become certified as Green Belts (GB). A person is certified as a Green Belt following completion of three projects as the Belt.

The policy governing Six Sigma Certification included:

1. Sponsor—Three projects completed as a Sponsor.
2. Green Belt—Three projects completed as a GB.
3. Black Belt—Five projects completed as a GB and/or Black Belt and completion of a two-year assignment as a Black Belt.
4. Master Black Belt—Completion of a two-year assignment as a Master Black Belt.
5. Directors and above who are not certified as a GB will not be moved or promoted absent an exception to policy from the HR Vice President and CEO.
6. New employees who have previous Six Sigma experience can be exempted from training following approval of their local Master Black Belt and Quality Champion. They are still required to complete the Cummins certification requirements. This rule existed because there is no Six Sigma standard, creating significant variation in Belt capability from organization to organization.
7. Human Resources owns the process for ensuring the policy is followed company-wide.

Certification has both positive and negative impacts. Discussions regarding its value continued long after it was implemented. Some of the positives include:

Positives	Negatives
• Creates a pull for Six Sigma knowledge and projects as part of the path to senior leadership positions.	• Creates a "projects for the sake of certification" attitude.
• Requires leaders to set the example for their organizations.	• Senior management pressure on Master Black Belts to allow shortcuts in the process.
• Ensures that the company's leaders have a good understanding of how Six Sigma works and why it is important for the company.	• Some "game playing."
	• Some see Six Sigma as a career tool vs. a process for improvement for the customer.

When all is said and done, I believe that Six Sigma Certification had a generally positive impact on the company because leaders who may never have personally engaged learned the value of the process and the tools giving them an objective reason for supporting the work. It is a decision to consider carefully. A tool for that purpose is the FMEA to help anticipate things that can go wrong and do something about them.

UMBRELLA PROJECTS

To achieve the benefits of the Business System Integration S-Curve, significant preparation is necessary. This preparation takes the form of experiments at various levels linking projects together for the purpose of achieving higher order improvements.

As maturity progresses through the S-Curves people in the company see that Six Sigma is applicable to more than just manufacturing. "Scrap on line five" type projects continue to be done and are important to ongoing operations improvement. As projects are implemented with suppliers, customers, in the functions, with communities, and other non-traditional applications, the company habit becomes one of using Six Sigma any time there is a question with no clear answer. Evidence of this habit is best seen when, during any senior management meeting or discussion, one of the participants asks unprompted, "Wouldn't that be a good Six Sigma project?" When this level of maturity is achieved, using Six Sigma to improve the Business System is achievable.

Some other characteristics of readiness include:

1. Assessments are seen as a tool of leadership. Often "assessment" and "audit" are perceived to be the same thing. They are not. Audit is about compliance to an existing standard. When deviations are discovered, the organization typically has a defined amount of time to correct the problem and prove compliance. Audit is often seen as a threat because finding problems is negative creating more work and people tend to get in trouble because of the negative findings.

   Assessment is about improvement. It supports an attitude that finding problems is good because it helps us to improve for our customers. Only by assessing organizational system performance relative to critical customer needs are integrated sets of problems identified for improvement.

2. A critical mass of common language has been achieved. Business system issues will involve several functions, multiple business units, suppliers and customers in the solution. An umbrella project is intended to improve the flow of information and material from raw materials to customer use of the products and services of the business. As such, many organizational boundaries are crossed. If a broad common language is not practiced, working together is nearly impossible.

3. A senior leader is willing to invest personal management capital seeing the umbrella project through to a conclusion. This means that each umbrella project must be critical to success of the enterprise. It also means that only a few of them can be done at one time because of the amount of change that will be necessary to improve the business system. (See my earlier book *Making Change in Complex Organizations*.)
4. The infrastructure exists to support projects across businesses, functions and regions. This includes Master Black Belts, individual project Sponsors, project management systems and statistical analysis tools that are accessible company-wide, regular senior leader reviews as well as access to team members and data supporting the projects.
5. Overall umbrella project leaders who are chosen because of their ability to see the systemic nature of the umbrella. These leaders value linking individual projects together for success of the umbrella project.

One of the first umbrella experiments performed focused on improving the output of a large assembly plant. The first step was the completion of an assessment. The assessment was a combination of a Baldrige-like Cummins Operating System (COS) set of questions posed to customers, suppliers, line workers and managers of the plant. The framework for these questions is the COS Ten Practices. The second part of the assessment was a value stream map (VSM) of the flow of information and material from suppliers to the customers. The outcome of the assessments was a long list of improvements. The improvements fell into three basic categories:

1. *Just-do-it*: These are well understood simple changes that are easy to do. A just-do-it requires people, time and money to do but often goes undone because it seems so simple.
2. *Programs to manage*: These are well-understood changes. They require a more significant commitment of resources to accomplish. Examples include software deployment, installation of a new machine or implementing a new procedure.
3. *Questions for which we don't know the answer*: These are the types of improvements or problems that lend themselves to the use of Six Sigma.

Each of the three categories requires time, money and people to accomplish. The next step in the process is to set priorities on the list of improvements. For priority setting, a Cause and Effects (C&E) Matrix is used. Finally, the project priorities are planned using standard planning tools.

Unexpected results of this approach were a databased approach to understanding capacity limitations relative to projected volumes. This, in turn, provided evidence and justification for spending capital for the acquisition of new machines. Another result was the analysis of personnel requirements over time. These results were in addition to improvements in the flow of information and material through the plant.

The concept of "flow" is key to moving forward into the realm of umbrella projects. The simple idea is that information and material move from the raw material state through various processes ending with use and disposal by the customer of the products and services offered. Waste or disruption in the movement often negatively impacts customer experienced quality. This movement is flow. Improvement in flow requires cooperation across business and functional boundaries to link processes to eliminate waste and disruption. The umbrella project is a way to improve end-to-end flow for better customer experienced quality.

Waste and disruption can happen anywhere, creating a negative impact on customer experienced quality, which is why improving the flow is so difficult.

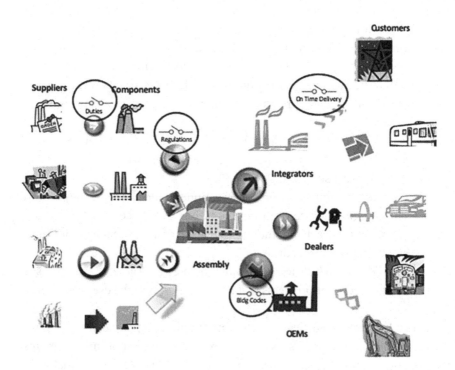

FIGURE 29.1 Supply chain break-down.

In Figure 29.1, each icon represents a place where some type of operation is performed leading to the creation of a product or service. Each arrow represents movement between operations. Waste and disruption can happen anywhere along the path to the customer. Waste and disruption are represented as an open switch which is how it behaves in a flow of information and materials. In a light circuit, when a switch is open, the electricity doesn't flow and the light doesn't come on. Similarly, in a physical flow when there is waste or disruption something unintended happens disrupting the flow impacting the products or services. This causes unplanned activity of some sort to try to close the switch and resume the flow. Many of the problems causing the waste or disruption never make it to the customer because of strong internal mistake correction processes. But unfortunately, some mistakes do make it out and this affects the customer's perception of the company and the quality of their products and services.

The unique role of the umbrella project is to see across the flow, to understand where waste and disruption is occurring, and organize to make improvements that optimize for the customer. This is what is different and why the seventh S-Curve represents the maturity level necessary to pursue improvement of the flow effectively.

What follows is a description of the process of developing and delivering an umbrella project.

Select a Focus Subject

Unless the company offers only a single product, pick one of the company's businesses as a starting point.

- What are the business's offerings?
- How happy are the business's customers with each of the offerings?
- What is the position against the competition?
- How profitable are each of the offerings for the business?
- Where are the offerings created?
- Where are they offered? Countries? Regions? Cities?
- How many entities are involved in the end-to-end (supplier to customer) supply chain of each offering?
- Based on the answers to the questions above, select an offering as the area of focus (a C&E Matrix is a good organizing tool for setting priorities).

What's the BIG "Y" Improvement Focus?

Assemble a cross-functional team representing the end-to-end flow of the offering. Included in this team are representatives of Marketing, Sales, Engineering, Logistics, Manufacturing/Assembly, Service, Quality, Finance, Customer Support and so forth.

Select people who will facilitate the process. Master Black Belts are good candidates for this work since they are used to facilitating groups to accomplish different kinds of work.

Collect data that represents the performance of the offering. This data includes but is not limited to:

- Customer feedback
- Financial results
- Warranty data
- Competitive comparisons
- Internal problem information
- Delivery information.

During a two- or three-day event, conduct an analysis of the information using Six Sigma statistical tools.

Identify the five most important areas for focus.

Select the top most important area for focus and the BIG "Y" that is the umbrella for the project.

Select a person to lead the development and deployment of the umbrella. We recommend a commitment of at least two to three years or longer. A person with a Six Sigma background is preferred.

Identifying the Wastes and Variations in the Flow

Identify the big blocks of activity that are measured by the BIG "Y." Document the high-level flow of material and information starting with suppliers, extending through the company to produce the selected offering, ending with customers who purchase and use the offering.

Tools to use in this to see the wastes and variation include but are not limited to:

- Value stream mapping
- Process mapping
- Flow charting
- Interviews of people who work in or manage the flow.

30

Special Situations

Every organization-wide Six Sigma deployment will have special situations that are unique. This chapter gives examples of some of the unique challenges Cummins faced and how they were addressed. The future state and the goals established are the drivers of potential solutions. It is critical to remember the future state as obstacles of any type become clear. Some examples of obstacles included here are:

- Sub-unit size
- Language barriers
- Education barriers
- Distance from headquarters
- Type of work.

Sub-unit size—Large sub-units of the organization have a couple of different options available during the deployment. They can host their own Six Sigma training launch because they have enough candidate Belts and on-site support to make a local launch feasible. They also tend to have a large enough budget to send people to a central training site. Smaller sub-units create challenges for a traditional deployment.

One of the biggest obstacles faced during deployment for the smaller sub-unit is a lack of available people. It is not unusual for small sub-units to run very lean organizations. This means that there are just enough people to do all of the required work of the business. Often, this means each supervisory person has multiple jobs. This makes it very difficult to release people for multiple weeks of Belt training and the consequent project work.

A second barrier is a lack of local support. Support means local people are knowledgeable about how Six Sigma works and what to expect of the DMAIC phases of a project. Often, the result is a Belt in a small sub-unit is the only person on-site who knows anything about Six Sigma especially in the beginning stages of a deployment. This condition makes it difficult for projects to close successfully.

Another issue faced by the smaller sub-unit is lack of budget allocated for extended travel. The budgets of smaller organizations tend to be fully allocated for the specific work of the organization. There is little left over for special assignment activity. For example, traditional Green Belt training is two weeks separated by a month for project work. This means expenses will be incurred for four travel segments, ten nights in hotels, and all the meals for those days. This is a heavy burden for smaller budgets to bear.

Some potential solutions for the smaller sub-unit include:

- Provide Six Sigma training online either live or recorded, breaking the training down into one- to two-hour segments.
- Provide all support online.
- Assign specific Master Black Belts to provide direct support.
- Assign all budget allocations to the corporate or business headquarters.
- Take extra care to ensure that projects done locally have immediate, real payback to the bottom line of the organization.

Language barriers—Many companies have expanded to include locations outside the home company's base language. Whether the reasons are meant to lower the costs of production, gain closer proximity to target markets, supply chain enhancements, or something else, the lack of a common spoken language makes full system deployment more difficult.

A typical example is that English-speaking ability is a hiring requirement outside the US. However, in practice this generally stops below the senior staff. And even at the senior staff level, proficiency is variable. This variability at the staff level and complete lack at the working level makes a traditional Six Sigma deployment difficult because the technical language of statistics is not easy to translate on the fly and is incomprehensible in English.

As an example, we realized that English language capability was creating a barrier to Six Sigma progress in our China operations. We could have purchased a Chinese version or hired a translator to do the work for us. Both of these solutions came with some significant negatives.

A purchased Chinese version would be out of sync with the evolved Cummins training resulting in two Six Sigma languages in the company. Hiring a translator would not ensure that the technical language would be translated correctly.

We employed a solution that was unique to Cummins. The company's Chinese affinity group volunteered to accept the challenge of translating the Six Sigma training. This group, led by Julie Liu, was made up of Cummins Belts who were committed to helping their compatriots back home join the Six Sigma transformation. This was a critical event in the progress of Cummins Six Sigma effort in China.

For other countries, translations were already available from the consultant and we used those. In one instance, the local organization paid for translation.

Another obstacle faced when multiple spoken languages exist is updating training material when changes are made to the base. This was a significant barrier when the statistical software was updated. We had to decide if the change to the software was significant enough to change the training. Often it was not. Our statistics software was typically a few versions behind.

We also had to decide which languages would be translated. Ultimately, we limited the company-supported translations to the main languages spoken across the company: French, Spanish, Chinese and so forth. This was an imperfect solution.

Finally, often the challenges of small sub-unit and language exist together. Thinking through the options available during the first or second S-Curve is an important planning event and provides space for experimentation early in deployment.

A solution to this issue is to work with a consultant who offers a strategy that separates statistical software from core training material. We did not understand this issue when we started our Six Sigma deployment and would have pushed for alternatives if we had.

As part of the planning for deployment, some of the key questions to answer include:

- How many languages are spoken in the organization?
- Is there a common deployment goal for the whole company, or is there variation?
- Will the company translate training material into all languages spoken? If not, which ones? What are the options for translation? What is the cost of each?
- Who will carry the budget for translation?
- How will the company provide translation updates as training material evolves?
- Which consultant offers a viable alternative separating statistics software use from core Six Sigma training?

Education barriers—Often, when opening operations in emerging econo-mies, the education of lower level employees is not sufficient to handle Six Sigma training, the use of statistical software, or project planning or man-agement. This is not a universal issue, but something to evaluate situation by situation. Solutions will be unique to each organization. Some potential areas to evaluate include:

- Reading level and comprehension
- Basic math skills
- Project management
- Communication skills
- English (or other home language as appropriate) proficiency
- Team leadership skills
- Basic computer use and application proficiency (i.e., Microsoft Office).

Distance from headquarters—"The single biggest problem in communica-tion is the illusion that it has taken place" (George Bernard Shaw).

The greater the distance from headquarters, the more difficult commu-nication of complex messages can be. It is much more than a couple of e-mails, a speech to leadership or a conference. It can be all of these things, but much, much more consistently delivered over time. As discussed ear-lier, developing a communication plan, executing it and assessing effec-tiveness followed by improvement is the only way to address those parts of the organization that are distant from headquarters.

Type of work—Most companies are made up of functional groups that carry out different activities. Marketing, Sales, Finance, Customer Service, Human Resources, Information Technology, Manufacturing and Engineering are all examples of groups of people and processes that do the work of the company. This is not new news to anybody reading this. But it does highlight a potential barrier to fully deploying Six Sigma across the organization. Because the work is different, the expectations and activities of the functional management are different.

A simple example is the difference between Manufacturing and Sales. The Manufacturing organization is heavily dependent on high-quality repetition of its various processes which are visible in operation. A Six Sigma project on scrap reduction or material throughput yields almost "instant" results. The results can be measured and even seen on the shop floor. This reality makes Six Sigma a relatively easy sell; do more Six Sigma projects get better results and the plant runs better.

Sales, on the other hand, depends on the output of manufacturing to create relationships that result in customer purchases. The processes are less obvious. They are not like manufacturing at all. A Sales Six Sigma project to improve advertising material is less obvious to the manager. Results tend to have more of a lag effect that are hard to see and difficult to measure. It's not that Sales doesn't have repeatable processes and manufacturing doesn't have processes with lagging results, but the work is generally different.

In both instances, selecting projects that will have a measurable impact is important to improving results. It also has an important relationship to the buy-in of the leadership of the function.

NOTE, THIS IS IMPORTANT BUT HARD TO DO . . . The remedy for this obstacle is to ensure effective project selection processes are in place prior to launch of Six Sigma training. This means working with the consultant to make sure that the processes for selecting the right projects are introduced to leadership during early leadership and Sponsor training sessions. The expectation is that these processes will be used to pick projects that are meaningful for each of the company's functions.

Launch of effective project selection processes is an easy thing to miss in the early days of deployment. It is also one of the most important things to do well. The lack of effective project selection processes is one of the main failure modes impacting company-wide deployments, often leaving local managers blaming Six Sigma for poor results instead of the selection of poor projects.

31

Conclusions

The secret of change is to focus all of your energy, not on fighting the old, but on building the new.

—Socrates

Apparently making change was as difficult 2,500 years ago as it is today.

It's humbling to know that it only took Socrates 21 words to say what it took me over 100,000! Hopefully, what you understood from reading this book is that successfully changing takes a lot of work by people at all levels of the chain of command.

Was it perfect? No. It was definitely not perfect. There were bumps and missteps along the way. The normal politics of people working together in a large organization sometimes complemented, but more often, impeded progress as personal agendas and egos worked against deployment. However, the focus of this book is how we made it work. I have attempted to describe the journey in a way that makes it possible for others to follow the road map that we created at Cummins. This is, hopefully, what the reader has found here.

As a reinforcement and summary of the various elements described, I want to spend a few minutes reminding the reader what is required to make a successful Six Sigma transformation and, by extension, any system-wide change that is undertaken.

ONE—Leadership alignment and engagement. Leadership alignment and engagement is hard, personal work by the company's leaders over a long period of time. It includes several key activities. For example,

- Selecting the right change for the organization. The right change is based on the goals and objectives of the organization and a clear-eyed assessment of where the greatest improvements are required to achieve it. Further, the new capabilities are most likely something that is lacking in the organization as it exists. Deciding how to acquire the capabilities (i.e., consultant, hire from the outside, internal team) is a responsibility belonging to leadership.

- Leaders learning the change in sufficient detail to talk to people about it and to ask informed questions during reviews. This helps them make course corrections when needed. It also helps them know the right kinds of people to assign key roles in the change deployment. Finally, learning about the change helps them know whether or not it is working to help customers and the business succeed.
- Selecting the right people to perform key change deployment roles. The people selected are trusted by the leadership to not just effectively project manage the change effort but, maybe more importantly, tell leadership the truth about how the change is progressing. These reports include both the good and the bad, but, especially the bad, and recommendations about how to fix it.
- Participate in change progress reviews over a "long" period of time. The length of time required is based on organizational deployment depth and the size of the organization. Has the change taken root? Are critical elements of the change visible in day-to-day work of all sorts? Has the language of the organization changed? Further, what do internal change program assessments say about the effectiveness of change deployment? Taken together, these are indicators the change effort is becoming successful.
- All key leaders in the company are on-board and engaged. Those who cannot, are moved following whatever has been decided an adequate period of time for personal adoption.

If the company leadership does not do these things, your change effort will fail. The company will waste a lot of money, time and energy trying to make something work that the people in the organization know from observation isn't that important. At the earliest practical opportunity people will move on to the next priority.

TWO—Pick the right change to make. First, and most important, an organization cannot make more than two system-wide changes at a time. I would encourage leaders to limit it to one but certainly no more than two. If the most important change is selected other changes can be connected to it as maturity progresses. The example that I gave in this book was connecting the Cummins Operating System (COS) to our Six Sigma deployment.

Picking the right change starts with clearly defining the long-term goals and objectives of the company. Then, assessing current capabilities and their relationship to successful accomplishment of the long term.

THREE—Assign the organization's best people. This is one of the hardest actions to take. The company's best people are already doing important work because leadership trusts them to do it right. However, if the change is critical to organization success who do you want to assign to it? Your average people? The hard question leadership has to ask itself is "Is this change make or break for the company?" If the answer is yes, the company has to find a way to make its best people available for the work.

FOUR—Stick-to-itiveness. Our general observation is that senior leadership has a bias for moving forward to the next product, purchase, plan and so forth. They are comfortable starting an initiative but are, generally, quick to delegate it to a subordinate who has responsibility for moving it forward while they move on to the next thing. Go back to *THREE* above. If the change is make or break for the company leadership must stay with it until there is clear evidence that the change has been made. Even then, don't completely disengage.

FIVE—Resource it. This means fund it. But continuous, adequate funding is only possible if the company is also measuring return. I did not fully understand this in the beginning of our Six Sigma deployment, but Frank McDonald was adamant that we had to measure the dollar value of our projects to prove that we were achieving the main measure of success. This proved to be a critical element of *ONE* to *FOUR* above.

SIX—Review, review, review. Leadership at all levels is responsible to conduct reviews of the deployment. These reviews include:

- Projects selected
- Project progress
- Project completion
- Progress toward targets
- Plans and plan achievement
- Performance of Belts and Sponsors.

SEVEN—Communicate, communicate, communicate. Tim Solso used to say that he discovered that he had to communicate a single message seven times for the company to understand what he wanted people to do. This is true with Six Sigma as well. What is it? Why are we doing it? What is the value of doing it? Who is responsible? What does a good project look like?

What does good Belt/Sponsor performance look like? On and on it goes. Leaders cannot communicate enough during the deployment.

One caveat here is when to start communicating. Frank decided that instead of telling people what we were going to do, we would do it first, tell them what we did and what ongoing expectations were. This proved to be an important decision for getting Six Sigma solidly off the ground at Cummins.

EIGHT—Small experiments. The expansion of Six Sigma into more and more of the areas of the company is not a given. In the early S-Curves of maturity it is not clear how to apply Six Sigma beyond the more traditional "scrap on line five" types of projects. Expansion is preceded by small experiments in new areas.

This means identifying a candidate project, a Belt and an organization that is willing to try the new area, and leadership that creates an environment that encourages experimenting. It includes documenting lessons learned and improving the approach over time.

Maturity up the S-Curves is dependent on experimenting with new ideas and making the ones that work well part of the organization's expectations for application of Six Sigma.

NINE—Don't stop. This is true of Six Sigma and any other change effort that involves difficult skills that are developed over time. The organizational half-life on these skills is very short. This is analogous to the practice of medicine or law. We call it the "practice" of medicine because there is ongoing skill development that is necessary as well as use of the skills in everyday work. If the skills aren't practiced, they are lost. For example, would you want a doctor performing your heart transplant who hadn't done one in 20 years? I wouldn't. The same idea applies to the skills of Six Sigma. They must be continuously practiced by people in the organization on real problems and improvements. If they are not the skills will be lost. The half-life of the skills is very short.

Too often organizations claim victory assuming that the skills are now so deeply embedded in the company that Six Sigma no longer needs the effort that it once had. It doesn't take long for Six Sigma to decay when this happens. Once gone, it is nearly impossible to recapture.

These nine elements of success are woven through the Cummins Six Sigma maturity story described in this book. They are broadly applicable beyond Six Sigma to any broad scale change that an organization is attempting to make. If you are a leader contemplating a change in your organization, don't ignore them.

32

Authors Final Thoughts

This book is about the people at Cummins and the work they did over 16 years using Six Sigma to improve customer and business performance. Our goal in writing it has been to give other companies a template to follow.

Six Sigma is incredibly effective for driving out waste and variation in a company's processes. Eliminating waste and variation improves customer experienced quality in myriad ways. Unfortunately, we have seen companies fail to realize the benefits, not because Six Sigma doesn't work, but because senior leadership is looking for a fast, cheap, and easy approach to improving product quality and driving customer loyalty. If you have made it this far in this book, we hope one of the lessons taken from it is that transformational change, for Six Sigma or any other change, takes a lot of time, planning, and effort to pull off successfully. IT IS HARD WORK!

The first book, *Making Change in Complex Organizations*, discussed that one of the main differences between the military and business was that the military spends a huge amount of time training people to do their jobs effectively while business spends very little. While this approach by business can work if nothing ever changes, the evidence all around us is that change is constant and accelerating. An organization can only deploy very few "transformational" changes at one time. Selection of those changes is the job of senior leadership, but it doesn't end with the announcement of the change as we have written about here. It is the willingness to stick with it until the change is fully ingrained in the behavior and activities of the people of the company. The larger the company, the more time and effort is required.

Finally, George Strodtbeck, cannot fully express the gratitude that I have for the leadership, mentoring and opportunities given me throughout my career that ultimately led to the writing of this book. Tim Solso, Frank McDonald,

Joe Loughrey and Tom Linebarger deserve the lion's share of the credit because they were the leaders that made the hard decisions. All I have done is write it down.

I, Mohan Tatikonda, am very grateful to George Strodtbeck for inviting me to join him in documenting this magnificent journey of organizational transformation at Cummins. I have learned so much from him.

We thank the many Cummins people, from Green Belts to CEOs, who participated enthusiastically in interviews, provided documents, and helped us to even better understand, appreciate, and share with you this story.

A special thanks goes to Professor Carrie C. Queenan of the Darla Moore School of Business at the University of South Carolina for her assistance in portions of the data gathering and analysis.

Finally, the greatest thanks belongs to the people of Cummins who did amazing things with Six Sigma changing the company in ways not dreamt of in 1999 when the whole thing started. Through the interviews we have tried to capture in their own words some of what happened over 16 years.

We hope that what we have written here is broadly applicable beyond Six Sigma. The S-Curves are a mechanism for planning and implementation that can serve any change well, no matter the scale.

Lastly, thanks to you for your willingness to wade through it all to get to here, the final word.

Appendices

TOTAL QUALITY ASSURANCE (TQA)

During the late 1970s, Japanese products began to take an ever-larger share of the American consumer dollar. Much of their success was due to the culture of quality that emerged from World War II, led by Americans like W. Edwards Deming, Joseph Juran, and Japanese like Shigeo Shingo, and others.

Total Quality Assurance (TQA) was begun in the late 1970s. The main purpose of TQA was to train manufacturing shop floor employees to take ownership for the quality of the company's manufactured products. The training focused on different tools, both statistical and non-statistical, that were coming into common use among manufacturers. Examples of tools trained includes:

- Histograms (shown here)
- Brainstorming
- Capability Studies
- Control Charts
- Pareto Charts.

TABLE A.1

1979—Total Quality Assurance Characteristics

- Focused on the factory floor
- Education for individuals
- Followed the general pattern of quality skills coming from Japan
- Introduced different quality tools to the factory floor
  - o Quality Circles
  - o Control Charts
  - o Capability Studies and Cpk
  - o Failure Modes and Effects Analysis (FMEA)

FIGURE A.1 Total quality assurance example.

TQA was primarily a manufacturing shop floor–focused training program. It began a shift away from "inspecting quality in" and gave the people who built the machines the tools to ensure quality as machines were built. People were taught to use control charts for monitoring their processes. Capability studies were introduced to understand whether or not machines could produce to the required specification. These and other tools like Failure Modes and Effects Analysis (FMEA) and Quality Circles were taught to give people the skills to ensure products met quality expectations during the manufacturing and assembly processes.

This early introduction to concepts of variation and how to measure it would later be foundational to Six Sigma's deployment across Cummins.

THE ACHIEVING PAPER AND NEW STANDARDS OF EXCELLENCE

Following a 1983 visit to Japan, the leadership of Cummins saw a different approach to managing for high quality, low cost, and faster delivery through the methods of Total Quality Control. An outcome of this understanding was the launch of a couple of initiatives to help Cummins incorporate continuous improvement techniques in its operation.

The first of these initiatives was the Achieving Paper. The Achieving Paper introduced several concepts to the company. Central to the paper were the concepts of:

- Continuous improvement
- The role of trust across the organization
- Work as a flow across work groups
- Customers both inside and outside of the company.

The paper was widely communicated to leaders in the company with the expectation that they would communicate the concepts within their organizations. While introducing several great ideas to the company, the Achieving Paper did not result in any lasting change by itself.

Next came New Standards of Excellence (NSE) in late 1983. NSE built on the ideas of the Achieving Paper through a standard three-day training

TABLE A.2

1983—The Achieving Paper and New Standards of Excellence

- Enhance quality and reduce costs
- Introduced the concept of continuous improvement
- Introduced the concept of "customer focused" process (from the Achieving Paper)
  - External
  - Internal
- Introduced the concept of "continuous flow"

program. The training pushed managers to start seeing work in flows as a mechanism for improving quality and reducing costs. It also encouraged managers to emphasize the needs of customers to become more customer focused. Like the Achieving Paper before it, NSE led to little significant change (*The Engine That Could*).

In both instances, concepts were introduced to the company that would form part of the foundation for the success of Six Sigma almost 20 years later.

TOTAL QUALITY SYSTEMS (TQS)

While the Achieving Paper and NSE had not led to significant change in the company, leadership believed the concepts were the right ones. Successful application required more clarity about what to do and how to do it. A next step in the journey was hiring the General Systems Company.

TABLE A.3

1985—Total Quality Systems (TQS)

- Hired the General Systems Company led by Armand Feigenbaum, the developer of the Total Quality Management (TQM) approach
- Cummins TQS approach:
  - Showed the flows of the company as a set of connected processes
  - Reinforced the customer concept introduced in NSE
  - Assigned processes to a group of operational functions
    - Marketing
    - Engineering
    - Purchasing
    - Manufacturing
    - Service
  - Focused on the processes that directly result in products for customers
  - Installed design disciplines (New Product Planning, Design and Introduction NPPD&I)
  - Developed "controlled" documents (procedures) describing how the processes worked
  - Established a procedure hierarchy
    - Corporate
    - BU
    - Plant
    - Individual Work Instructions
- Still in use in 2015 supporting the Cummins Operating System (COS)
- From *The Engine That Could* by Jeffrey Cruikshank & David Sicilia 1997

The result of the relationship with General Systems was the development of the Total Quality System (TQS). TQS stressed the interconnectedness of processes as flows across the company. It reinforced the idea that the next station was the customer. The goal was to figure out how to serve each customer whether internal or external more effectively. This reinforced the importance of the customer that was introduced by NSE.

To that time the company generally performed as a collection of functions each tending to operate independently. Each function did its job and then "tossed it over the wall" to the next function that had to fix or modify anything that didn't work right. TQS drove the integration of processes owned by the different functions. Each function was responsible to document its process as a first necessary step for continuous improvement. These documents were owned and controlled by subject matter experts in each of the functions.

One of the key improvements was the development of a new product introduction disciplined approach called New Product, Planning, Design and Introduction (NPPD&I). This was a cross-functional set of activities that required functions to work together to produce the designs that would become marketable products.

The value of TQS is reflected in the fact that it still exists more than 30 years later. It is still owned by the functions of the business and is where processes and process improvements are documented for repeatability across the Cummins landscape.

CUMMINS PRODUCTION SYSTEM (CPS)

During the late 1980s, Cummins suffered from a series of delivery and quality problems. Improvement was essential if the company were to survive. This problem led to the development of "The Cummins Production System for Customer Led Quality".

The purpose of Customer Led Quality focused the company on the needs of the customer and was based on five principles:

1. Comparative advantage
2. Financial performance
3. Profitable growth
4. Responsible citizenship
5. Development of people.

These five principles served as the governing structure under which the Cummins Production System (CPS) was created.

The *Cummins Production System* (CPS) was created to improve performance in the company's manufacturing sites. It was the result of research and benchmarking conducted by the company's leadership to understand and apply industry best manufacturing practices at Cummins. It created a "total systems" approach to work on the manufacturing shop floor based on six interconnected fundamentals:

1. Synchronized material flow to meet customer needs
2. Shortened lead times
3. Product quality
4. A common improvement process

TABLE A.4

1989—Cummins Production System (CPS)

• Delivery and quality problems in the late 1980s
• Launched Customer Led Quality (CLQ)
o Comparative advantage
o Financial performance
o Profitable growth
o Responsible citizenship
o Development of people
• Key focus area: Improve manufacturing operations
o Based on lessons from Japanese companies (Toyota, Komatsu, etc.)
o Assigned a senior executive to lead the effort directly supported by a team of senior leaders
■ Developed the concepts
■ Leaders of functions
■ Coaches for factory leadership teams
o Developed the Cummins Production System (CPS)
o Attacked "inspecting quality in"
o Required training for all people involved in operations (Team Based Work Systems)
o Functions defined
■ Defined the meaning of "excellence" for each function
■ Training
■ Checklists
■ Positions
o Common measures introduced
o 10 Practices introduced (Practice 10—Common Approach to Continuous Improvement)

FIGURE A.2 Cummins production system (CPS).

5. Cross-functional cooperation in all aspects of production
6. People development.

These fundamentals gave birth to several important concepts. The first concept was *Achieving Manufacturing Leadership.* "Manufacturing is a system of material flow and processes to meet customer requirements. As material moves through the plant, each operation adds value to it. It is the job of the manufacturing leader to manage and improve the flow of material and control processes to meet all customer requirements and to eliminate waste."

The second concept, *Functional Excellence,* identified key functional groupings. These functions were responsible for defining what "excellence" meant for the function as it related to delivery of quality products to customers. Each defined function was responsible for:

- Defining excellence for the function
- Developing the appropriate training for functional skill building

- Developing an assessment checklist which defined the basics of the function
- Defining the positions of the functions and skills needed to do the work
- Defining excellence measures for the functions.

Next, the *Ten Practices* provided a framework for how work is done in the well-run manufacturing operation.

Finally, the concept of *Continuous Improvement* established that everyone was responsible for making their work better. CPS Practice Ten (the Common Approach to Continuous Improvement) defined how continuous improvement work would be done around the company.

Training was developed and cascaded starting with plant leadership teams. At the end of the session, new plant measures were introduced, and each team had to review their plans for implementing CPS back home. This training was widely delivered. Ultimately more than 17,000 people were enrolled in the effort to transform manufacturing at Cummins.

Networks of plant managers and functional leaders were created to share best practices and discuss how to address plant-related problems.

All of this was supported by assessment visits by Cummins leadership teams. Prior to the visit the plant staff rated themselves using an assessment created by each function as a definition of what "excellence" meant. During the visit, the Cummins leadership team reviewed the assessment and discussed it with the plant staff. A key goal of the visit was to drive a common understanding of each excellence element so that a common operational language developed across the company. This effort was critical to successful application of the principles and practices of CPS.

In the end, the only way to assess the value of CPS is the results it produced. Over a ten-year period, CPS improvements included:

- Inventory turns increased 101%
- Productivity increased 41%
- Quality defects decreased 86%
- Safety incidents decreased 62%
- Throughput time decreased 48%.

Leadership, training, measures and improved skills all helped pave the way for deployment of Six Sigma in 1999 by serving as an example of success that felt familiar to the people of the company.

COMMON APPROACH TO CONTINUOUS IMPROVEMENT (CACI)

The Cummins Production System (CPS) included Ten Practices that served as a framework for how a manufacturing plant would operate. The Ten Practices were:

- Practice 1—Put the customer first and provide real value
- Practice 2—Synchronize flows
- Practice 3—Design quality in every step of the process
- Practice 4—Involve people and promote teamwork
- Practice 5—Ensure equipment and tools are available and capable
- Practice 6—Create functional excellence
- Practice 7—Establish the right environment
- Practice 8—Treat preferred suppliers as partners
- Practice 9—Follow common problem-solving techniques
- Practice 10—The common approach to continuous improvement.

The Common Approach to Continuous Improvement (CACI) was CPS Practice 10. The purpose was to provide a common set of steps and tools to be used around the company to make necessary improvements.

As with everything else in CPS the Common Approach was initially focused on the manufacturing operations. Its purpose was to reinforce the

TABLE A.5

1992—Common Approach to Continuous Improvement (CACI)

- Practice 10 of the CPS 10 Practices
- 7 Steps of the Common Approach to Continuous Improvement
  - o Define customers and our products and services
  - o Define suppliers and their products and services
  - o Define the internal processes
  - o Establish improvement goals
  - o Implement improvements
  - o Define the improved system
  - o Evaluate and improve
- Focused on training tools
- Define and work on projects
- Replaced by Six Sigma in 2000

need for the plants to work together to solve problems and make improvements and to use a common language to do it.

The 7 Steps of CACI were:

1. Define customers and our products and services—understand who the customers of your process are, what they need from the process and how they use the output. This was another extension of the concept of the customer and the need to work in connected flows introduced in the New Standards of Excellence.
2. Define suppliers and their products and services—for the process to improve, the supplier to the process requires involvement. What does the process need from the supplier?

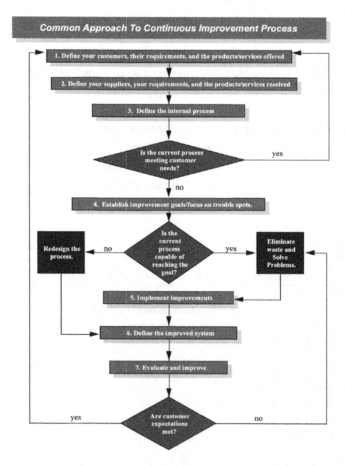

FIGURE A.3 Common approach to continuous improvement (CACI).

3. Define the internal processes—identify the steps of the process and inputs and outputs of each step. Identify where problems exist in the flow.
4. Establish improvement goals—based on the findings of steps 1 through 3, what are the needed improvements?
5. Implement improvements—define the improvements and test them to ensure that they work.
6. Define the improved system—make the appropriate changes to the process and document the new process to ensure that the improvements stick.
7. Evaluate and improve—measure the performance of the new process and continue to improve it over time.

The Common Approach was consistent with much of the continuous improvement work that was practiced in the US at the time. CACI included some statistical tools like SPC and Cpk but depended heavily on the "social" tools of quality. The social tools of quality gather knowledgeable people together for focused discussion using certain tools as a framework for that discussion. Examples of these tools include process mapping, brainstorming, and Failure Modes and Effects Analysis (FMEA) and were included as part of CACI. These tools and others tended not to rely on data for their outcome.

Common Approach training was designed for delivery in modules using a project as the main learning vehicle. "Specialists" across the company were given train-the-trainer preparation making them trainers and coaches for the projects. An online tool was established to record basic information of each project.

From 1992 to 1995, several thousand people were trained in the use of CACI processes and tools. Some projects were completed. However, CACI did not succeed in transforming the company into one that saw continuous improvement as foundational to success.

Many of the traits of CACI would later be seen in the Six Sigma deployment. Some of the carryovers include:

- Project centric training
- Master Black Belt coaches and trainers
- Common language globally
- Use of tools
- Statistical analysis.

These elements helped to give the process of Six Sigma deployment a familiar feel.

7-STEP PROBLEM-SOLVING

CPS Practice 9 is 7-Step Problem-Solving. When the CPS 10 Practices were developed, it was decided that problem-solving was different than process improvement. Additionally, the shop floor needed a simple, direct approach for solving problems as they arose in manufacturing. The 7-Step Problem-Solving Process was the solution in both cases.

The 7-Step flow is not all that different from CACI. The steps are:

1. *Identify the problem*—define the specific problem that needs solving.
2. *Determine possible causes and rank their importance*—a carefully selected team of experts lists all of the possible causes and then determines which are most important to the solution. Often a fishbone diagram is used to aid this process.
3. *Take short-term action if required*—this step was unique 7-Step and to manufacturing. The customer receives the output of production. Therefore, if there was a problem affecting the product it was important to stop shipment to prevent customer issues. One example: If the problem was suspected to be a bad batch of parts, all shipments containing that part are suspended until the issue is resolved.

TABLE A.6

1993–7-Step Problem-Solving

- Practice 9 of the CPS 10 Practices
  - o Identify the problem
  - o Determine possible causes and rank their importance
  - o Tack short term action if required
  - o Gather data and design tests of causes to quantify their contribution
  - o Conduct tests, analyze data and select solution
  - o Plan and implement the permanent solution, failsafe where possible
  - o Measure and evaluate for continuous improvement; recognize the team.
- Training program developed and delivered broadly across the company

---

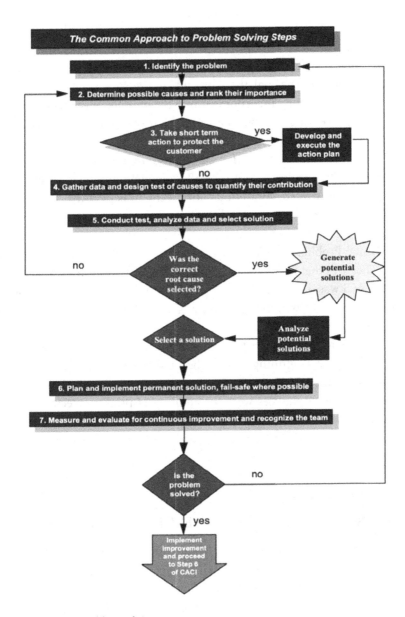

FIGURE A.4 7-Step problem solving.

4. *Gather data and design tests of causes to quantify their contribution*—data would often come from product testing. This data would be collected and analyzed to ensure that the right causes of the problem were identified.
5. *Conduct tests, analyze data and select solution*—the goal of this step was to ensure that the solution selected worked and the problem was solved.

6. *Plan and implement the permanent solution, failsafe where possible—* the permanent solution might include a change to drawings or a change to a supplier process as two examples. These actions take time to complete. The goal, therefore, was to track the solution to ensure it was permanently incorporated into the product or process. Additionally, preventing unconscious error was important to the fix. Therefore, fail-safing was employed wherever possible.

7. *Measure and evaluate for continuous improvement; recognize the team—*the project is not officially complete until it is clear that the solution worked, continuous improvement is planned, and the team is recognized for their hard work.

The 7-Step Problem-Solving process was very similar to CACI. One major difference was that CACI included more statistical tools in its basic design. Also, CACI was deployed differently from 7-Step. CACI was a training cascade while 7-Step was delivered on a "sign-up" basis so that classes were held as the need arose.

It is useful to note here, that 7-Step continued to live on after the introduction of Six Sigma. Beginning in 2008, the focus became solving product issues. Additionally, the DMAIC of Six Sigma was established as the framework for 7-Step. The major changes were the addition of product-specific questions necessary to understanding any product related issue and the relevant tools of Six Sigma were added to those originally defined in CPS Practice 9.

S-PROGRAMS/FUNCTIONAL EXCELLENCE/BALDRIGE

There were several other actions taken during the 1990s which helped prepare the way for the 2000 deployment of Six Sigma across the company.

The *Cummins Technical, Marketing and Distribution Systems* (S Programs) sought to capitalize on the success of CPS for manufacturing by applying the total systems approach to other critical areas of Cummins business. The Cummins House of Quality (shown here) was an attempt to show how all the elements came together in a cohesive whole.

A fuller identification of functions and the meaning of functional excellence was a component part of the S-Programs. The development

TABLE A.7

1994–1997 S-Programs/Functional Excellence/Baldrige

- S-Programs—built on success of CPS
    - ○ Cummins Technical System
    - ○ Cummins Marketing System
    - ○ Cummins Distribution System
- Created Functions and Functional Excellence
    - ○ Defined the meaning of "excellence" for each function
    - ○ Training
    - ○ Checklists
    - ○ Positions
- Submitted Baldrige Application in 1997
    - ○ Documented Cummins Quality Management System
    - ○ Received a site visit
    - ○ Spawned 13 global improvement initiatives
    - ○ This was a one-time event
- ISO/TS 16949 Certifications

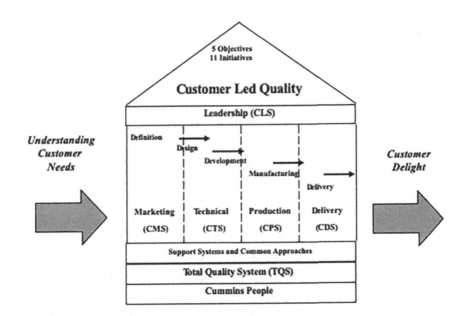

FIGURE A.5 House of quality.

FIGURE A.6 Baldrige application – 1997.

of functional checklists, training, measures and positions was seen as a way to bring best practices and common approaches to an increasingly dispersed, global company. In the end, the S-Programs tended to be less successful than their CPS forerunner but set the stage for applying continuous improvement techniques broadly across the functions of the company.

In 1997, Cummins submitted a *Baldrige Application* to the National Institute of Standards and Technology (NIST). The Baldrige process required the company to document the answers to a comprehensive set of questions across the seven specific categories. The company's application described how Cummins organized to deliver quality products and services to its customers. The company received a site visit, the last step before winning the national award. The company fell just short of winning. However, much was learned and 13 initiatives were launched to address the opportunities for improvement identified in the feedback report.

Also, in the '90s, customers were beginning to request that Cummins show proof of using quality processes by certifying to ISO standards.

FLOWS AND FUNCTIONS AND THE CUMMINS OPERATING SYSTEM (COS)

The next logical step in the evolution of continuous improvement at Cummins was the development of a comprehensive business operating system that connected the company's processes and functions for delivering products and services to customers. The initial attempt created Flows and Functions. Flows and Functions defined that the company's products and services came from five high level flows: Plan, Create, Sell, Deliver, Care. The flows were supported by four major functional groups: Marketing, Technical, Production, Business Support. Each flow had a leader who was accountable to work with the functions to define the processes that when linked together in a flow resulted in products and services for customers.

Over time, Flows and Functions went through an evolution and eventually became the Cummins Operating System (COS) (2014 version shown here) serving as a key source of ongoing Six Sigma projects from 2004.

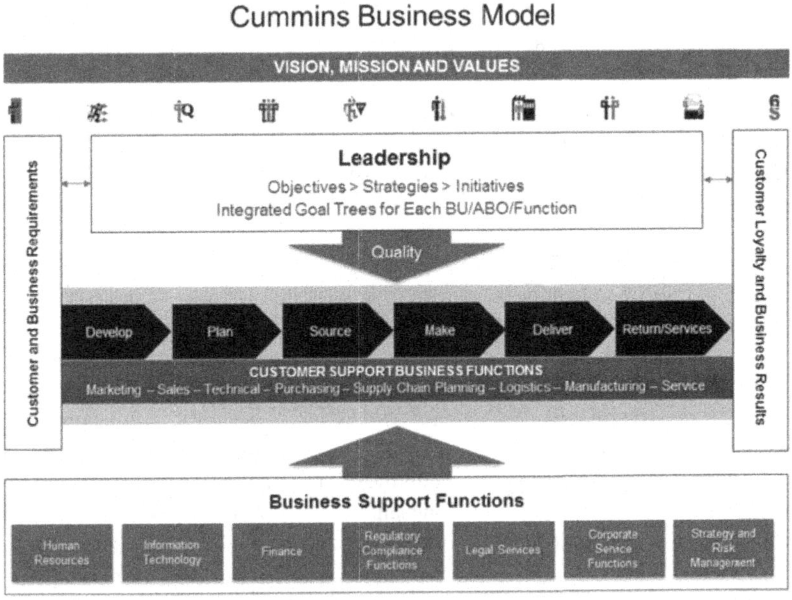

FIGURE A.7 Cummins business model and operating system – 2014.

SUMMARY TABLE OF PRE-HISTORY ELEMENTS AND IMPACTS ON SIX SIGMA DEPLOYMENT

TABLE A.8

Pre-History Elements and Impacts on Six Sigma Deployment

Pre-history Element	What was new?	What change occurred?	What was undone?	How did it help Six Sigma deployment?
Total Quality Assurance— 1979	• Quality to the shop floor • Formal tool training • Quality circles	• Early understanding of statistical concepts	• n/a	• Basic understanding of control charts, capability studies, Cpk in place
Achieving Paper and New Standards of Excellence— 1983	• Enhance quality and reduce costs • Introduced concept of continuous improvement • Introduced concept of continuous flow • Internal and external customers	• Added a leader for Quality • Trained people in the concepts	• n/a	• Continuous improvement • Connected processes • Organized training • External and internal customers
Total Quality System (TQS)—1985	• Letting the consultant lead • Established functions supporting the product flow • Documenting processes and work • New design disciplines	• Functional Excellence • Work as a flow across the functions	• Began to break down functional silos	• Consultant knowledge transfer • Documentation of processes and results of projects • Processes connected between functions
Cummins Production System (CPS)—1989	• Focused on manufacturing improvement • Lead by senior leadership • Internally developed • CPS 10—Practices • TBWS • Build quality in vs. inspect quality in	• Broad improvement in plant metrics • Common language for manufacturing deployed	• Traditional isolated plant approach	• Six Sigma became Practice 10 • Established a pattern of senior leadership ownership • CACI was the original Practice 10, Six Sigma was a dramatic improvement

Pre-history Element	What was new?	What change occurred?	What was undone?	How did it help Six Sigma deployment?
Common Approach to Continuous Improvement (CACI)—1992	• **One standard for continuous improvement** • **Taught Specialists who train and coach locally** • **Project centric** • **Followed a "train and do" approach** • **Made C.I. a team approach**	• **A common language of improvement was deployed company-wide**	• n/a	• **Project centric** • **"Train and do"** • **Specialists were early MASTER BLACK BELTs** • **The value of a single standard**
7-Step Problem-Solving—1993	• Problem-solving is different from C.I.	• n/a	• n/a	• Reinforced the value of a standard approach
S-Programs and Baldrige	• Deployed CPS approach to other key business functions • Made the 10 Practices common • Emphasized standard work for everyone • Required management to assess its effectiveness and make improvements	• Early days of organizing the functions globally • Launched 13 initiatives as a response to the feedback report	• Developed Flows and Functions • Launched first version of Cummins Operating System	• Same as above
Flows and Functions and COS—1997-'99	• Cross-functional cooperation vital to customer experienced quality • Carried the lessons of CPS broadly across the company	• n/a	• n/a	• Same as above

TABLE A.9

Example Projects by S-Curve

S1 (1st Projs)	S2 (1st Projs)	S3 (Foundation)	S4 (Self-Supporting)	S5 (Integration)	S6 (Expansion)	S7 (Business Systems)
—Improve scrap rate from x% to y% on line 5	—Improve material strength from x to y	—Reduce variation in sales reconciliations from x to y	—Develop a labor cost modeling process	—Reduce bank charges from x to y	—Improve accuracy of product costing process	—Reduce revenue leakage in ABC business
—Improve line productivity from x to y	—Reduce the time to generate an invoice from x to y	—Improve the MSA for ABC part characteristic from x to y	—Improve financial data delivery process	—Improve performance experienced by the customer from x to y	—Optimize the product change process with ABC partner	—Develop a competitive price analysis process
—Improve test cell utilization from x to y	—Improve paint process effectiveness from x to y	—Develop a process for increasing diversity representation	—Improve accuracy of material forecast from x to y	—Improve variable pay process	—Improve IT back-up and recovery system	—Develop a process to ensure government grant Compliance
—Reduce material shortage on line A from x to y	—Improve component robustness	—Improve product A margin from x to y	—Reduce assembly time for ABC product	—Develop a global product testing strategy	—Partner with ABC nonprofit to improve donations	—Improve product replacement part availability
—Reduce errors in the product ordering process from x to y	—Improve change request time from x to y		—Increase product ABC sales volume in XYZ region	—Develop a product rationalization strategy	—Determine architecture for ABC component	—Develop robust waste management system

THE INITIAL CUMMINS SIX SIGMA FUTURE STATE (1999)

Master Black Belts (MBB)

- Master Black Belts are selected based on an established set of criteria.
- A certification process is used for Master Black Belts.
- The total number of Master Black Belts is 13.
- Master Black Belts have a development plan.
- Master Black Belt responsibilities include:
  - Leading Black Belt (BB) and Green Belt (GB) training
  - Consulting and mentoring the Belts and Sponsors
  - Certifying the capability of BBs and GBs
  - Serving as a key link to the Quality Champions in the businesses
  - Training future Master Black Belts
  - Most Master Black Belts are internally developed. Some Master Black Belts are hired from the outside based on specific needs and/ or issues.
- Master Black Belts attend the one-year certification program at SBTI.
- Master Black Belts have a separate compensation structure.
- Master Black Belts do not work on projects.
- Master Black Belts participate in DFSS.

Black Belts (BB) and Green Belt (GB) Project

- Projects are not governed by a target dollar value. Projects will be done on the most important business problems.
- A forum is established to communicate potential projects globally.
- Only BB projects are tracked.
- Recognition and reward is defined and practiced.
  - Part of variable compensation for BBs
  - Training and project execution part of promotion path for GBs.
- A best practice and project sharing process is implemented and used.
- Project hoppers are always full.

Design for Six Sigma (DFSS)

- DFSS tools are part of the new product development process.
- DFSS uses a BB process that is separate from DMAIC.
- DFSS evolves as new technology evolves.

People

- All management people are trained as GBs.
- BBs are cross-functionally assigned to any type of project anywhere in the company.
- Training is the same for BBs and GBs.
- Training for leaders is separate from BB/GB training.
- Project reviews are conducted locally and are the responsibility of local leadership and Master Black Belts.
- A recruiting process for BBs and Master Black Belts is in place and includes:
  - A way to volunteer.
  - An identification and selection process.
  - A designed development plan.

SIX SIGMA STANDARDS

Black Belts

1. Follow the Black Belt Selection process.
2. Assigned to project work full time for a minimum of two years but not longer than three years.
3. Receive a 5% increase upon beginning the program.
4. Are eligible to receive 3% variable pay per successful project completion through the year except in those locations where there have been specific policies eliminating this option. This bonus was capped at seven completed projects/year.
5. Are to work on projects which have a minimum annual value defined by the BU.
6. Are to complete each project in less than 180 days.
7. Are to complete a minimum of seven projects during the two-year assignment.
8. Are separately managed in the ODR process for placement into positions of leadership following the Black Belt assignment.
9. Ensure the project database is updated every 30 days.

Green Belts

1. Are assigned projects as part of their yearly work plan.
2. Are to devote a minimum of 30% of their time to the project.

3. Are to work on projects which have a minimum annual value defined by the BU.
4. Are to complete each project in less than 180 days.
5. Are to complete a minimum of one project each year.
6. Ensure the project database is updated every 30 days.

Master Black Belts

1. Assigned to work as a Master Black Belt for a minimum of two years following graduation to the position of Master Black Belt.
2. Receive a 10% increase following graduation to the position of Master Black Belt (TDFSS, DFSS, and DMAIC) (*the appropriate level will be decided based upon how the accountabilities of the position are more fully defined*).
3. On a full-time basis, lead and mentor a group of Belts.
4. Deliver Black Belt and Green Belt training for assigned launches (25%).
5. Conduct and assessment of Charters during M0 training and disinvite Belts whose Charters receive a RED assessment.
6. Participate in potential project selection and analysis; advise BU staff on prioritization of potential projects.
7. Foster sharing of information, best practice sharing, and networking among Black Belts.
8. Administer project closure sign-off.
9. Manage process development and modification while retaining consistency (curriculum, Black Belt and GB project work, etc.).
10. Prepare to assume an advanced leadership position post the Master Black Belt assignment.
11. Report to the BU Quality Champion with a dotted line reporting relationship to the Corporate Vice President Quality.

Sponsors

1. Understand the Six Sigma management basics.
2. Participate in local project selection process.
3. Develop the Project Charter.
4. Communicate with the Belt prior to M0.
5. Understand the basic DMAIC process.
6. Weekly project reviews (minimum).
7. Ensure the project database is up to date.

8. If a project is terminated, follow the Project Termination process.
9. Accountable to ensure connectivity with all impacted areas including cross BUs and North American distributors.
10. For Black Belts, complete a performance review at the end of each project.
11. Performance as a Sponsor is part of the Work Plan and Annual Review Process (CPMS).
12. Participate in Control Plan audits after project closure.

Quality Champions

1. Ensure adherence to the basic rules of Six Sigma within the Performance Cells.
2. Provide communication back to Performance Cell leadership about Six Sigma rules and requirements.
3. Provide guidance to the Performance Cell Leadership regarding the management of Six Sigma.
4. Responsible for BU Six Sigma Strategy.
5. Responsible for approving Belts and Sponsors and registering them in the classes.
6. Communicate payout factor to the Black Belt.
7. Develop and deliver deployment and savings plans in participation with site performance cell leaders.
8. Create an environment where Six Sigma is embraced by the organization as the primary process improvement method.
9. Champion and build Six Sigma capability throughout the organization via:
   - Frequent and targeted communication
   - Recognition and cheerleading
   - Measurement (and corrective action)
   - Six Sigma training
   - "Internal consulting."
10. Drive audits of closed projects to ensure that gains are sustained and corrective actions are implemented as necessary.
11. Lead Master Black Belt and Black Belt selection process and participate in Sponsor and GB selection.
12. Responsible for distribution of shirts and plaques.

Business Leadership Teams (the defined leadership level required to maintain a project hopper)

1. Develop and maintain active project hoppers.
2. Select Belts based on established criteria.
3. Select Sponsors.
4. Establish and conduct project review plans.
5. Monitor key performance measures.
   - Annualized Value of Projects (Black Belt, GB, Total)
   - Current Year Value of Projects (Black Belt, GB, Total)
   - Project Cycle Time (Black Belt, GB, Total)
   - Project Terminations (Black Belt, GB, Total).
6. Audit closed projects months after completion to ensure control plans are actively used, understand if follow-up work needs to be done, and glean any learnings from the project or process where something may have been misjudged.

Corporate Leadership

1. Maintain the training schedule for the company.
2. Provide staff to support the logistics of the training.
3. Training continuity company-wide.
4. Master Black Belt quality and common approach.
5. Reporting key company measures monthly.
6. Six Sigma database maintenance.
7. Provide reward and recognition materials for the Belts and Sponsors.
8. Hold the budget for the training materials.

Bibliography

Cruikshank, Jeffery L. and Sicilia, David B. (1977). *The Engine That Could*. Boston, MA: Harvard Business School Press.

Hanafee, Susan (2011). *Red, Black and Global*. Columbus, IN: Cummins Inc.

Strodtbeck, George (2016). *Making Change in Complex Organizations*. Milwaukee, WI: ASQ Quality Press, 2016.

Zinkgraf, Stephen A. (2006). *Six Sigma – The First 90 Days*. Upper Saddle River, NJ: Pearson Education, Inc.

Anand, Gopesh, Ward, Peter T. and Tatikonda, Mohan V. (2010). "Role of Explicit and Tacit Knowledge in Six Sigma Projects: An Empirical Examination of Differential Project Success," *Journal of Operations Management*, vol. 28, no. 3, pp. 303–315.

Anand, Gopesh, Ward, Peter T., Tatikonda, Mohan V. and Schilling, David A. (2009). "Dynamic Capabilities Through Continuous Improvement Infrastructure," *Journal of Operations Management*, vol. 27, no. 6, pp. 444–461.

Liker, Jeffrey K. (2004). *The Toyota Way: 14 Management Principles from the World's Greatest Manufacturer*. McGraw-Hill.

Shingo, Shigeo (2017). *Fundamental Principles of Lean Manufacturing*. Productivity Press.

Index

Note: Information in figures and tables is indicated by page numbers in **bold** or *italics* respectively.

A

Achieving Paper 16, 278, **278**, 295
ANOVA 122–123
assessments 258

B

Baldrige Application 16, *291–292*, 292–293, 296
Black Belts 12, 14, 27, 30, 34–35, 41, 43–45, 49, 51–52, 56, 58, **64**, 66–72, 76–78, 88, 93, 95, 112–113, 228–229, 298, 300; *see also* Master Black Belts (MBBs)
business integration *183*, 183–189, *186–188*, 203–206, *204*, **244**, *250*
business operating system (BOS) 188, *251*
business system improvement **223**, 223–225, **244–246**, *250*

C

CACI *see* Common Approach to Continuous Improvement (CACI)
certification 113–114, 256–257, **257**
CFSS *see* Customer Focused Six Sigma (CFSS)
Chairman's Quality Award 141
change, organizational 1–2
commitment 64, **64**
Common Approach to Continuous Improvement (CACI) 2, 16, **285**, 285–287, *286*, 296
communication strategy 70
community projects 211
continued growth and expansion 209–212
corporate culture 231–232, 256
COS *see* Cummins Operating System (COS)

CPS *see* Cummins Production System (CPS)
cross-curve analysis 81–82, *82*
CTS *see* Cummins Technical System (CTS)
culture, corporate 231–232, 256
Cummins, Clessie 15
Cummins Inc. 1; financial performance of 2, *2*, 6–7
Cummins Operating System (COS) 16, 97, 111–112, 187, *187*, 188–189, 294, *294*, 296
Cummins Production System (CPS) 2, 7, 16, 18, 40, 44, 53, 84, 91, 94, 187, **281**, 281–294, *282*, 295
Cummins Technical System (CTS) 84
Customer Focused Six Sigma (CFSS) 97, 108, 174–176, 178–179, 189, 210
customer relationships 232–234

D

database system 71–72
deployment challenges 6–7
deployment consultant 65
deployment strategy 65–67
Design for Six Sigma (DFSS) 27, 72, 89, 141–142, 145, 153, 169, 298
DFSS *see* Design for Six Sigma (DFSS)
diversity 238
DMAIC *see* Process Six Sigma (DMAIC)
Duarte, Holly 4, 227–238
Dunlap, Michelle 4, 101, 103–114

E

education barriers 266
electronic database system 71–72
enterprise risk management (ERM) 211
environmental sustainability 229

Printed in the United States
by Baker & Taylor Publisher Services